STATE SALES AN

MW01231910

Number Fifteen:
Texas A&M University Economics Series

State Sales
and Income Taxes

AN ECONOMIC ANALYSIS

George R. Zodrow

Texas A&M University Press
College Station, Texas

The paper used in this book meets the minimum requirements
of the American National Standard for Permanence
of Paper for Printed Library Materials, Z39.48–1984.
Binding materials have been chosen for durability.

Library of Congress Cataloging-in-Publication Data

Zodrow, George R.
    State sales and income taxes : an economic analysis /
George R. Zodrow.
        p.   cm.
    Includes bibliographical references and index.
    ISBN 0-89096-755-5. — ISBN 0-89096-855-1 (pbk.)
        1. Taxation—United States—States.   2. Revenue—
United States—States.   3. Local taxation—United
States.   I. Title.
HJ2053.A1Z63   1998
336.2′01373—dc21   98-8120
                                                        CIP

TO DOREY,

my inspiration . . .

and my favorite (almost) native Texan

CONTENTS

TABLES

PREFACE

The primary sources of tax revenue for state governments in the United States are retail sales taxes and individual and corporate income taxes. Most states use a mix of these two tax instruments, although five states do not have a sales tax, and five other states have neither an individual nor a corporate income tax. In some sense, all states must continually choose between sales and income taxes, as they always have the option of changing the mix of the two taxes utilized (including introducing a new tax for those states that use only one of the two tax options). Moreover, many states face this choice in a very immediate sense, as they are under considerable pressure to find additional tax revenues—either to increase state expenditures in order to meet a wide variety of needs, including those related to declines in federal expenditures, or to reduce the extent of statewide reliance on the increasingly unpopular local property tax.

The purpose of this book is to draw on the academic literature in economics—including some fairly recent studies in the field of public finance that have addressed various issues particularly relevant to the choice of a state tax structure—to provide information that will, I hope, be useful in evaluating the relative desirability of state sales and income taxes. The analysis examines the main arguments typically made both for and against these two approaches to state taxation and evaluates them in the context of this literature. The analysis is thus relevant for any state considering reforms that involve either state sales or income taxes, including the increasingly common need for increased state funding of education coupled with property tax relief.

Policymakers who contemplate the reform of a state tax structure typically face an extremely difficult problem. The pressures for some type of reform are often considerable. In some cases, demands to change the mix of revenue sources used to finance the current level of state expenditures may provide the impetus for reform. In other cases, the need for additional revenues may prompt a re-examination of the state tax structure. In particular, public demands for reductions in property taxes accompanied by greater state financing of local expenditures, especially those for education, are common. In addition, demands for government expenditure increases—either to meet increased service demands, including those attributable to recent reductions in federal expenditures, or to satisfy judicial or federal mandates—are often significant.

Moreover, in many states, the tax structure is such that revenues typically increase less than proportionately with growth in the state economy, resulting in periodic fiscal crises. All of these factors can result in widespread, vociferous calls for the reform of a state tax structure.

However, the direction such reform should take is seldom obvious. Since most states rely on a combination of sales and income taxation for the majority of their own source revenues, they typically choose between increased reliance on one or the other when they wish to increase revenues. A few states currently utilize only one of these revenue sources, and, thus, they must increase reliance on their existing tax system or introduce a new tax to raise revenues. In both cases, states must carefully consider the interactions between their own tax structure and that of the federal government, which (apart from the Social Security system) consists primarily of a personal income tax levied at progressive marginal rates coupled with a tax on corporate income.

The choice between state sales and income taxes is usually a difficult one, and it raises a host of contentious social, political, and economic issues. This book focuses on the last of these factors—the economic issues involved in reforming a typical state tax system. The primary goal of this book is to identify the lessons that can be drawn from the academic literature in economics, especially the field of public finance, regarding the relative desirability of state sales and income taxes in the belief that these lessons can inform debates surrounding state tax reform proposals. The analysis is applicable to any state considering reforms of its tax structure, including (1) financing increased revenue needs or property tax relief with increases in (or the implementation of) either state sales or income taxes, and (2) implementing changes in the mix of sales and income taxation utilized in the state, while holding revenue constant.

Before proceeding with the analysis, it may be useful to provide some personal background in order to clarify the perspective from which I view these issues and to describe in some detail the framework utilized for the analysis in this book. Most importantly, I am not persuaded by conventional arguments that an income tax is inherently superior to a consumption-based tax. In fact, in both my academic research and my more applied policy work, I have argued that, at the national level, a consumption-based approach is for a variety of reasons superior to an income-based tax. In particular, McLure and Zodrow (1996a) offer a proposal for such a consumption-based national tax reform, which is a variant of the "flat tax" proposed by Hall and Rabushka (1985, 1995).[1]

However, I must emphasize that the focus of the analysis in this book is not on the federal tax system, and the book largely ignores the current debate regarding the desirability of replacing the income tax with a consumption-based tax alternative (such as a national retail sales tax). Rather, the book focuses on the tax structure of an individual state, within a framework that assumes that (1) the federal government will continue to utilize its current income tax system, and (2) the state must choose between only two sources of revenue—an income tax system that consists of separate taxes at the corporate and individual levels, and a sales tax, perhaps coupled with some type of business-level tax such as a corporate franchise tax. An important message of the book is that the analysis of the relative advantages and disadvantages of state sales and income taxes—given these two important constraints—is in many cases quite different from that typically made in evaluations of the choice between income-based and consumption-based tax systems at the national level. To cite just one important example of this distinction, individual mobility across states implies that the optimal degree of progressivity of a state income tax will be significantly less than under the federal income tax; this in turn implies that a state income tax should be at most modestly progressive. More generally, however, an implication of the arguments presented in this book is that, given the two initial conditions noted above, the case for a state income tax system is considerably stronger than the case for an income tax system at the federal level.

Two of the main arguments supporting use of a state income tax depend on the fact that the federal government already utilizes an income tax system. The most obvious is the issue of the deductibility of state taxes against individual federal income tax liability. Under current federal law, only state income taxes, not state sales taxes, are deductible. Since deductibility implies a reduction in the effective price paid for government services by state residents, deductibility provides a strong argument favoring state use of a deductible personal income tax over a nondeductible sales tax; that is, with deductibility, the residents of a state that utilizes an income tax can benefit from the fact that the state tax burden is to some extent "exported" to the residents of other states.[2] The second important issue concerns the relative costs of administering and complying with alternative state tax systems. At the federal level, many proponents of consumption-based taxes argue that the measurement of the tax base under consumption-based taxes is inherently simpler than under taxes on income, which results in lower costs of compliance and administration.[3] However, given the existence of a federal income tax, the incremental costs of administering and complying with a state income tax, under which the state tax burden is typically based to a significant extent on federal tax liability, are likely to be relatively small compared with the costs of administering and complying with a state sales tax that is unrelated to the federal tax structure.

The nature of the retail sales taxes currently used in the states also plays a crucial role in the state sales versus income tax debate. If retail sales were the base of a state sales tax, then the tax would be truly consumption-based, and many of the arguments used in support of consumption-based over income-based taxation at the national level would also be relevant at the state level. However, the bases of the sales taxes used by the states are, to varying degrees, in fact not retail sales. The most important reason for this discrepancy is that the sales tax base typically includes a great deal of business purchases; indeed, one often-cited study estimates that roughly 40 percent of the state sales tax base, on average, consists of business purchases that should in principle be exempt under a tax on retail sales.[4] As will be discussed later, the fact that so much of the sales tax is assessed on business rather than consumer purchases means that the state sales tax is more like a haphazard income tax than a broad-based tax on individual consumption. The clear implication is that the advantages that are commonly claimed for a consumption-based tax cannot be claimed for the state sales tax. In addition, for political, historical, and/or administrative reasons, the typical state sales tax base excludes some services (although many states have recently added a variety of consumer services to the tax base). To the extent that exempt services are purchased by consumers, an important component of consumption is excluded from the retail sales tax base. Again, the fact that the base of the sales tax is not a comprehensive measure of consumption implies that the sales tax would not be expected to achieve the advantages of a broad-based consumption tax.

The relevance of at least some of the federal debate regarding the relative merits of income and consumption taxes is limited for yet another reason. Specifically, the most commonly discussed consumption-based federal tax reforms involve direct taxes, that is, taxes that are assessed directly on individuals (and firms) rather than indirect taxes that are assessed on transactions, typically sales or value-added.[5] The important advantage of direct taxes is that they can be "personalized" in the sense of allowing deductions, exemptions, and marginal rates that differ by individual circumstances. This personalization implies that it is relatively easy—through the appropriate choices of deductions, exemptions, rate brackets, and rates—to structure a direct tax system to achieve equity goals regarding the distribution of tax burden among individuals. By comparison, equity concerns under the state sales tax in most states are addressed by allowing exemptions for goods believed to be consumed disproportionately by the poor, including food for home consumption, prescription medicines, and utilities for residential use.[6] The problem with this approach is that exemptions are a poorly targeted means of achieving equity goals, since all consumers would benefit from an exemption for a particular commodity, and the size of the benefit would increase with income (although less than proportionately if the commodity is consumed disproportionately by the poor). Thus, the amount of revenue lost in providing tax relief for the poor is quite high, which in turn implies that the tax system is characterized by relatively high tax rates. As will be discussed at length in this book, such high tax rates are very undesirable, primarily because they create large economic distortions and incentives for tax evasion and avoidance. In addition, the administrative difficulties involved in identifying which goods qualify for exemption can be considerable.

Although all the arguments raised thus far suggest that the case for an income tax, given the constraints noted above, may be stronger at the state level than at the national level, there is a powerful counterargument as well. Specifically, since a state income tax is imposed in addition to the federal income tax, all of the many distortions of economic decision making that characterize the federal income tax are in general worsened by state usage of an income tax. These include distortions of individual savings and labor supply decisions as well as a wide variety of business decisions, including those regarding input use, output mix, level of risk taking, choice of finance, and form of business organization. To some extent, state income taxes simply exacerbate the distortions associated with the federal income tax system. However, in the case of the state corporate income tax, the distortions depend in a complicated way on the characteristics of the business being taxed.

Specifically, for a corporation that has most or all of its operations within a state, a state corporate income tax (that is based on the federal tax) increases the total effective corporate tax rate applied to income generated by the corporation. The distortions of the state corporate tax thus simply compound the distortions of the federal tax. The situation is much more complicated, however, for a large multistate firm that produces or sells its output in many states. This complication is attributable to the fact that in the United States the income of a multistate corporation is allocated for tax purposes among the various states using a "formula apportionment" approach (rather than the highly complex alternative of "separate accounting," which attempts to allocate all of a corporation's revenues and costs and thus profits across jurisdictions). Under the formula apportionment approach, the tax base for a state is determined as a fraction of the firm's total national profits, where that fraction is a weighted average of the fractions of the firm's total national property, payroll, and sales that are located in the state (the weights on one or two of these factors may be zero). For example, suppose that P is the nationwide profits of the firm, "k," "l," and "s" are the firm's property, payroll, and sales located within a state, "K," "L," "S" are its total national property, payroll, and sales, and the state apportionment formula uses the (fairly common) approach of equal weights on the three factors. In this case, the corporate tax base "apportioned" to the state would be $[0.33 \ (k/K) + 0.33 \ (l/L) + 0.33 \ (s/S)]$ P. Tax revenues under the state corporate income tax would be the product of the state corporate tax rate and this apportioned base.

As firms become more national in scope (less of their activities are located in-state), the state corporate tax base becomes more a function of national profitability rather than profits generated within the state. Indeed, for a large national corporation with operations in many states, the state corporate tax is commonly viewed—from the perspective of the taxing state—as a tax on the property, payroll, and sales of the firm that are located within the state (depending on the state apportionment formula), rather than as a tax on the income generated by the firm's operations in the state.[7] As a result, for the operations of such businesses located within the state, the distortions of the state corporate tax are more like those associated with property, wage, and sales taxation than those associated with the federal corporate income tax. In addition, the use of formula apportionment creates its own complex set of distortions of firm behavior.[8] Thus, determining the relative efficiency properties of state sales and income taxes, including the typical state corporate income tax, is a complex matter indeed, and is the focus of a significant portion of this book.

Equity or tax fairness arguments also play a large role in tax reform debates at both the national and the state levels. In particular, an argument that is commonly made against the use of proportional consumption-based taxes, such as a sales tax, at both the national and state levels is that they are highly regressive. However, some recent research, which has played an important role in the debate regarding the use of consumption-based taxes at the national level and is also applicable at the state level, suggests that the regressivity of consumption-based taxes can easily be overstated. In particular, when tax incidence is viewed from a long-term (rather than an annual) perspective, consumption taxes tend to become less regressive while income taxes tend to become less progressive. This argument is developed at length in this book.

To sum up, the choice between state sales and income taxes is a complex one and requires the evaluation of a variety of fairly subtle arguments in the context of a particular state. In particular, one must (1) be aware of the constraints placed on state tax reforms by the nature of the federal income tax structure, (2) take into account the implications for state tax policy of various interactions between the state and national tax systems, and (3) be extremely careful in applying arguments that favor consumption-based over income-based taxation at the national level to the evaluation of state sales and income taxes, both because the arguments may not be directly applicable and because the structures of the various consumption taxes that might be utilized at the state and national levels often differ dramatically.

In addition, as stressed above, the relative desirability of state sales and income taxes depends to a large extent on the two critical assumptions that are made throughout most of the book—that the federal government maintains its current income tax structure and that the only revenue sources available are an income tax or a sales tax. However, these two assumptions are relaxed toward the end of the book. The latter assumption—that income and sales taxation are the sole revenue sources available to a state—is relaxed in chapter 6, which considers the two alternatives of (1) increased state utilization of user fees and (2) state implementation of the rather radical reform of a modestly progressive consumption-based direct (or personalized) tax system. The former assumption—that the federal government maintains its current income tax structure—may be inappropriate given widespread interest in consumption-based reforms at the national level. If any of these reforms were enacted, the analysis in this book would have to be modified considerably. For example, the Armey (1996) "flat tax" proposal recommends elimination of federal deductibility of all state and local taxes. Under such a regime, an important argument for a state income tax over the sales tax option would obviously disappear.[9] Moreover, both the Armey proposal and the Nunn-Domenici USA Tax would result in a consumption-based direct tax at the federal level. As a result, the case for a state consumption-based tax that "piggybacked" on the federal system would be much more compelling, in that the equity advantages of a direct tax would be obtained, as would the advantages of a comprehensive tax on consumption rather than income. Similarly, if the federal income tax were replaced by a national retail sales tax or a value-added tax, the case for a state income tax, which rests largely on the existence of a federal income tax, would be exceedingly weak; this would especially be true if the federal retail sales tax or value-added tax were a well-designed comprehensive tax on consumption, so that it would be desirable for states to "piggyback" their own consumption-based taxes on the federal system. Thus, to the extent that one believes federal tax reform is fairly likely in the near future, the best current prescription for state tax policy may simply be to wait and see what happens in the national arena and then react accordingly.

This book is organized as follows. Chapter 1 provides a summary of the findings of the subsequent chapters. It focuses on a comparison of the relative merits of the sales and income tax options in terms of the main criteria used in this study to evaluate alternative tax systems. These criteria are (1) the extent to which the tax burden can be exported to out-of-state residents, (2) the extent to which the tax system minimizes distortions of business and individual decision making or its relative economic efficiency, (3) the fairness or equity properties of the tax system, and (4) a variety of additional less critical considerations.

The next four chapters present a detailed analysis of the state sales and income tax options. Chapter 2 describes the various criteria, outlined above, that are commonly used in the public finance literature to evaluate alternative tax systems. Chapters 3 and 4, which comprise the bulk of the book, describe in some detail the economic literature on the application of these criteria to the evaluation of alternative tax systems, including the state sales and income tax alternatives; chapter 3 considers issues of tax exportability and economic efficiency, while chapter 4 examines the tax fairness issue and a variety of additional issues. The "bottom line" arising from this lengthy analysis is provided in chapter 5, which describes the relative advantages and disadvantages of the income and sales tax options in terms of these criteria.

The final chapters consider some special issues. Chapter 6 examines two alternatives to the use of state sales and income taxes. First, it considers the case for the increased utilization of user fees at the state level. It argues that such a course of action deserves serious consideration, as user fees, when technically feasible, are an attractive source of revenue on both equity and efficiency grounds. Second, chapter 6 examines a rather radical alternative approach to state taxation—one that is based on the progressive taxation[10] of consumption and thus differs dramatically from either the sales or income tax options. This state-based tax system is a modified version of the "flat tax" reforms that are currently being proposed at the national level.

Finally, chapter 7 provides an application of the analysis in the form of a case study of tax reform options in the state of Texas. The chapter begins with a description of the revenue system in the state, which is relatively unique in that it has no personal income tax and a rather unusual form of corporate taxation. It then draws on the analysis presented in the book to evaluate potential reforms of the state tax system; in particular, the case study discusses the implications of the analysis for the highly contentious issue of whether the state should introduce an income tax system. This chapter concludes the main text of the book by outlining a number of specific areas of future research that would shed additional light on the evaluation of tax reform options for the state of Texas and other states as well. Although this chapter, like the rest of the book, clearly focuses on tax policy, some information on relative state expenditures across the nation may also be useful to those who wish to evaluate arguments that maintain that the tax system in Texas, or in any other state, should be changed because the level of services provided by the state needs to be increased. Accordingly, the appendix provides a brief comparison of combined state and local expenditures, by category and by state.

This book has benefited from the comments and suggestions of many of my friends and colleagues, including especially Charles McLure and Peter Mieszkowski, as well as Walter Hall (who provided the original impetus for the book in the form of an inquiry late in 1992 regarding the academic perspective on the desirability of a state income tax in Texas), Bill Hobby, Helen Ladd, Stephen McDonald, Therese McGuire, Thomas Peel, Michael Palumbo, Gary Price, Robert Stein, Robert Tannenwald, and Michael Wasylenko. The project could not have been completed without the outstanding research assistance of Craig Johnson, who worked diligently on the many incarnations of the manuscript. In addition, I have benefited from the research assistance of Chairat Aemkulwat, John Diamond, Michele Hendrix, Guillermo Rabiela, Loan-Anh Tran, and Zane Williams. Financial support for the project was generously provided by the Center for the Study of Institutions and Values and by the Baker Institute for Public Policy at Rice University. I have also been fortunate to have had the assistance of excellent editors, first Susan Bielstein at the now defunct Rice University Press, and subsequently Tom Saving (whose ideas for thoroughly reorganizing the book greatly improved its presentation). Finally, I want to thank my wife, Dorey, for her never-ending support and my daughters Katherine and Laura for their tolerance of the time I have devoted to yet another "boring" tax project.

STATE SALES AND INCOME TAXES

CHAPTER 1

Overview of Findings

This chapter provides a fairly detailed summary of the main conclusions of this study regarding the relative desirability of state sales and income taxes, focusing on the advantages and disadvantages of these two tax instruments in terms of the criteria that are typically used by public finance economists to evaluate alternative tax systems. These criteria are (1) the extent to which the tax burden can be exported to out-of-state residents, (2) the extent to which the tax system minimizes distortions of business and individual decision making, or its relative economic efficiency, (3) the fairness or equity properties of the tax system, and (4) several additional considerations. The chapter concludes with a brief discussion of two alternative sources of state revenues—expanded utilization of user charges, and an alternative tax regime that provides for progressive direct consumption-based taxation at the state level.

EXPORTING TAX BURDENS TO OUT-OF-STATE RESIDENTS

State tax officials are often very concerned about the extent to which the state tax burden can be exported to out-of-state residents. Although such tax exporting is not particularly desirable from a national perspective, it is consistent with the idea of choosing the tax system to maximize the welfare of state residents. Moreover, any given state is likely to believe that the ability to export its taxes is a reasonable criterion against which to judge its tax system if it perceives that most or all other states are designing their tax systems with tax exporting in mind. Accordingly, exportability will be viewed as a desirable feature of a state tax system in this study.

There are two primary ways that state tax burdens can be exported to out-of-state residents; these are considered in turn in this section. The first is through deductibility against individual federal tax liability, and the second is through higher commodity prices to out-of-state residents or through lower returns to factors of production that are owned by out-of-state residents.

Exporting Tax Burdens through Deductibility

The most unambiguous argument in the state sales versus income tax debate supports use of the personal income tax over the consumer portion of the state sales tax. Under current federal law, only the former is deductible from an individual's federal tax liability. Under these circumstances, the deductible portion of the state tax burden is effectively "exported" to taxpayers in other states. In addition, if the state tax system is characterized by any tax rate progressivity, deductibility implies that the cost of public goods to higher-income taxpayers is reduced more than proportionately, and the differential effects on high income taxpayers of rate progressivity are mitigated, since higher-income taxpayers take their deductions for state and local income taxes at relatively high federal marginal tax rates.

Exporting Tax Burdens through Price Changes

The competition faced by the firms within a state in both national and international capital and export markets severely limits the ability of a state to export taxes through higher commodity prices to out-of-state residents or through lower returns to out-of-state factors of production. Instead, most state business taxes are borne in the long run either by relatively immobile factors—labor and land within the state—or by in-state consumers. In addition, the owners of these factors and/or consumers bear the "excess burden" of the tax—the additional inefficiency cost attributable to the tax-induced outflow of capital that reduces the productivity of a state's labor and land resources.

Thus, the potential for tax exporting through price changes does not provide a compelling argument for either of the two tax reform options (even though both include an important business tax component). Rather, the analysis suggests that—apart from benefit-related user charges on businesses, taxes on externalities such as environmental pollution, and taxes on personal consumption disguised as business purchases—business taxes should either be avoided or limited to specific excise taxes on the outputs of those industries believed to have substantial national or international market power. The clear implication is that direct taxes on a state's residents are generally preferable to business taxes. The rationale is that the direct burden of a tax on residents is roughly similar to that under a business tax, but the excess burden under a direct tax on individuals is lower than under a tax on businesses. Despite these arguments, it is obviously very unlikely that any state will forgo all taxes on business. Accordingly, all of the remaining discussions of business taxes in this book examine the question of whether a system of sales taxation of some business purchases, perhaps supplemented by an additional business-level tax like a corporate franchise tax, is preferable to a corporate income tax.

A final exportability issue is the extent to which the state tax burden can be exported to out-of-state residents, primarily tourists and business visitors. Such tax exportation occurs only with the sales tax. It is difficult, however, to imagine that this is an important source of revenue in most states, and any opportunities for tax exporting in this area can be exploited through the use of special taxes on hotel/motel occupancy, car rentals and, to a much lesser extent, on entertainment and admissions to amusements.

EFFICIENCY CONSIDERATIONS

The relative merits of the two alternative tax systems in terms of the criterion of economic efficiency, which requires that the tax system be designed to minimize tax-induced distortions of individual, firm, and government behavior, are difficult to resolve. The following discussion summarizes the relevant issues.

Business Tax Issues

It is clear that the sales taxation of business purchases under the sales tax as typically administered in the states suffers from many deficiencies. State sales taxes typically impose a significant burden on businesses, and in this sense they are more like income taxes than true taxes on consumption. Moreover, the tax burden varies in a haphazard fashion across industries and thus distorts a variety of business production decisions, including those regarding goods produced, the capital-labor mix, and the extent of vertical integration. As a result, such a tax system lowers the productivity of a state's resources. A comprehensive tax on business income generated in the state would clearly be preferable to this rather capricious and distortionary tax system.

Unfortunately, the federal corporate tax system, and any state tax system that is based on the federal tax structure, is far from a comprehensive tax on business income. Thus, increased reliance on the taxation of corporate income at the state level magnifies the many problems of the federal corporate tax system. The use of formula apportionment in the United States to allocate the national profits of multistate firms among the states for purposes of state corporate taxation mitigates this problem; that is, formula apportionment implies that, from the perspective of a single state, the extent to which a state corporate income tax exacerbates the distortions of the federal corporate tax for the operations of large multistate firms located within the state are reduced significantly. However, the use of a formula-apportioned state corporate income tax creates its own set of economic distortions, which depend in a complex way on the nature of the formula utilized by the state. Accordingly, it is difficult to construct a strong efficiency argument for or against the business component of a state income tax, relative to the typical state sales tax system. Indeed, the most compelling efficiency argument for a state income tax system is probably the simple one that it might result in a lower overall state tax burden on business relative to a sales tax. The previous discussion of the competition faced by state firms in national and international capital and export markets suggests that such a change would be desirable.

Individual Taxes

By comparison, the efficiency case for a personal income tax over the consumer portion of the typical state sales tax is fairly clear. By exempting various items, including necessities and various consumer services, the sales tax distorts consumption choices and encourages out-of-state mail order sales. Such distortions would be largely eliminated under a personal income tax. Both types of taxes distort labor/leisure choices and the savings decision to roughly the same extent, and both taxes distort individual location decisions, although the effect of the income tax on relatively mobile high-income individuals is likely to be larger. On balance, the sales tax is likely to result in greater distortions of consumer choices than is a personal income tax, as long as the rate structure of the income tax is not too progressive.

Government Services

Finally, note that to the extent an income tax results in a smaller tax burden on business than would occur under the typical state sales tax, it may result in improved political decision making regarding the level of resources allocated to the public sector. This result obtains if the "visibility" of the tax burden is relatively high under an income tax because taxes paid are concentrated at the individual level. This effect would be reinforced to the extent that the personal income tax is more visible than the sales tax on consumer purchases. On the other hand, some have argued that income tax adoptions have been associated with increases in state government spending, and that such increases represent excessive allocation of resources to the public sector. A closely related argument is that a progressive income tax is undesirable because it results in an increasing ratio of revenues to income in the presence of economic growth and thus tends to lead to a higher level of services than would occur in the absence of such a relatively easy source of revenue. This reinforces the point that a highly progressive rate structure is generally not desirable under a state income tax.

EQUITY CONSIDERATIONS

Business Taxes

Equity arguments for either of the two approaches to business taxation are inevitably rather murky, since the incidence of such taxes is not entirely clear and the "fairness" of most business taxes is largely in the eye of the beholder. The most compelling argument is that businesses should pay taxes in accordance with benefits received. This provides a weak rationale for the use of a business tax based on wealth or production within the state (as a very rough proxy for services received in excess of other taxes paid) rather than one based on income. As stressed in chapter 6, however, taxation in accordance with benefits received is best achieved with user charges whenever such charges are feasible.

Individual Taxes

The equity arguments in the case of the sales tax and the individual level income tax are more important and more controversial. A common complaint is that the sales tax is regressive and that a progressive income tax is an inherently fairer way to raise revenues to finance government services, both because the latter is progressive with respect to income and because personal exemptions and standard deductions imply that very low-income families are completely exempt from tax. However, a common argument in the literature is that the equity criterion should take into account differences in the relationship between consumption and income over the life cycle (as consumption typically exceeds income during youth and old age and income typically exceeds consumption during the prime earning years), as well as the effects of transitory income fluctuations. The implications of taking these considerations into account are that (1) at least some, and probably a significant portion, of the regressivity of the sales tax as typically measured is due to the use of annual income as a measure of the ability to pay, (2) alternative measures, including simply annual consumption, that attempt to approximate lifetime income (and thus also capture the effects of temporary income fluctuations) are a preferable measure of ability to pay taxes, and (3) most state sales taxes are probably roughly proportional with respect to lifetime income—except for the highest income classes where some regressivity is almost certain to obtain—while most progressive income taxes are less progressive than they appear.

This analysis suggests that the equity issue should be rephrased. Specifically, the primary issue is not so much the regressivity of the sales tax, but the question of whether it is desirable to structure the state tax system in such a way that low-income individuals are entirely exempt from tax, or whether such individuals should bear a tax burden that is roughly proportional to their consumption or lifetime income. If one's views regarding equity are consistent with the former approach, an income tax is the more desirable option since the personal exemptions and standard deductions allowed under the tax provide a simple and effective means of ensuring that families below the poverty level pay little if any tax. In contrast, if the latter view of equity is seen as more reasonable (e.g., because one feels that everyone should make some contribution to the provision of public services), the sales tax is more likely to be viewed as the preferred option. Note, however, that a tax burden could be assessed on very low-income families even under an income tax by disallowing personal exemptions and standard deductions under the state definition of the income tax base. The rate applied to low income levels could be relatively low if deemed desirable.

In addition, it should be emphasized that the achievement of equity goals under the typical sales tax has a rather high cost. Specifically, excluding various items from the tax base on the grounds that they are consumed disproportionately by the poor does reduce the regressivity of the tax, but only at the cost of dramatically reducing the size of the tax base. As a result, the tax rate required to achieve any given level of revenue is relatively high. In contrast, under a personal income tax, a given level of consumption can be excluded through the use of personal exemptions and standard deductions. Such an approach is much more targeted than sales tax exemptions, which apply to all purchases of the exempt items whether they are made by the poor or reflect the relatively high consumption levels of the rich. As a result, the tax rate under an income tax can be lower, which reduces the distortions associated with achieving the equity goal.

However, two other equity arguments favor the use of the sales tax over the income tax. First, the use of an income tax reduces the tax burden borne by the elderly to the extent that they fund consumption with withdrawals of principal from savings and/or tax-exempt forms of income. Since such consumption would generally be included in the sales tax base, a tax reform that involves increased reliance on (or a switch to) an income tax would result in a windfall gain for this group. Similarly, only the sales tax is effective in taxing the elderly who are wealthy but who have relatively little current taxable income, and taxation of this group is likely to be perceived as desirable on equity grounds. Second, only the sales tax is likely to result in at least some tax being paid by tourists and business travelers and perhaps to some extent by individuals in the "underground economy." Such taxation is desirable on equity grounds to the extent that these individuals consume state and local public services.

Finally, an interesting complicating factor is that since the use of an income tax at the state level reduces or eliminates the tax burden on low-income individuals, it simultaneously reduces or eliminates the primary objection to the use of benefit taxes or user charges for public services in those cases in which such taxes are feasible. The discussion in chapter 6 indicates that user charges are highly desirable both because they promote efficiency in resource allocation to the public sector and because they are equitable in the sense of relating taxes paid to benefits received. Increased reliance on an income tax that exempts or greatly reduces taxes on low-income individuals would offset the regressive impact of user charges and make them both fairer and more feasible on political grounds.

ADDITIONAL POINTS

A variety of additional comparisons are drawn in this book. The differences between sales and income taxes in terms of the criterion of revenue stability over the business cycle are not great and could be moderated by adequate funding of a state "rainy day" or revenue stabilization fund. The primary advantage of a broad-based income tax is that it avoids the revenue shortages that occur over time under a sales tax that excludes several items, especially some services and government expenditures that have in recent years accounted for an increasing fraction of the economies of most states.

In addition, a state tax system that is closely related to the federal personal and corporate taxes would be simple in terms of compliance, administration, and enforcement. However, any significant reductions in lowering compliance, administration, and enforcement costs would occur only if the sales tax were replaced entirely with an income tax. This appears to be a rather unlikely proposition in most states.

TWO ALTERNATIVE APPROACHES

The vast majority of the analysis in this book focuses on a situation in which the only tax alternatives under consideration are state sales and income taxes. However, two alternative approaches to raising revenues at the state level are also briefly examined.

The first alternative approach is expanded utilization of user charges. Opportunities for the use of such fees are to some extent limited, both because user charges are not feasible (or prohibitively expensive to administer) for certain public services and because they are undesirable for those services that are explicitly designed to be redistributional. For many other types of services, however, user charges are an alternative means of finance that can be both equitable and efficient. Indeed, several prominent observers have argued that user charges should be utilized to the maximum extent possible at the state and local levels. Accordingly, it would generally be worthwhile for a state to examine systematically the possibility for increased utilization of user charges; in particular, states should identify at a highly disaggregated level those service functions for which cross-state comparisons suggest that increased utilization of user charges might generate significant revenues.

The second alternative approach is a different tax regime that would represent a rather dramatic change from current practice in all states. This approach, termed the Simplified Alternative Tax (SAT), consists of a business tax that allows immediate deductions or "expensing" for all business purchases (rather than deductions for depreciation), coupled with an individual tax on wages and pension receipts (and perhaps on the receipt of gifts and inheritances) that allows a standard deduction and personal exemptions and then taxes the remaining base at progressive rates. It results in a tax system that is progressive but, as a consumption-based tax, avoids most of the problems associated with income taxation. The SAT could very well be preferable to either a state income tax or the typical state sales tax structure. However, virtually all existing studies of a SAT-type tax view it as a national tax reform option, rather than as a tax system that might be adopted by a single state. Accordingly, a comprehensive analysis of the advantages and disadvantages of the SAT as a tax reform option at the state level is certainly warranted.

CHAPTER 2

Desirable Features

of a State Tax System

A wide variety of criteria have been used by public finance economists and policymakers in evaluating state tax systems. One particularly important criterion in the state (but not the national) context is exportability—the extent to which a state can shift its tax burden to out-of-state residents, either through deductibility against the federal income tax or through changes in the prices paid or returns received by such individuals.[1] Most of the other state tax criteria can be included under the familiar general headings of efficiency (defined to include the promotion of economic growth) and equity. These criteria are common to the evaluation of both state and national tax systems, although many special factors make the analysis of state taxes more complicated than national ones. In addition, revenue adequacy and stability are important issues, especially since the constitutions in most states in principle require a balanced state budget. Finally, the relative costs of administering, enforcing, and complying with alternative tax structures and the related issue of their differential effects on the "underground economy" are of interest. Each of these criteria is defined and discussed below.

Before proceeding, it will be useful to reemphasize one important point. Discussions of the desirable features of a state tax system, as well as debates regarding the relative merits of alternative tax structures, must necessarily take the existing federal income tax structure as given. That is, the focus of the analysis must be on the marginal impact of changes in the state tax structure (e.g., on individual or firm decisions) while holding constant the federal tax structure (rather than on coordinated policy changes at both the state and federal levels). This is the approach taken throughout the analysis in this book.

EXPORTABILITY

As noted above, one criterion that is applied primarily in the state (and local) context is exportability, or the extent to which the state tax burden can be shifted to out-of-state residents. Such exportability is generally viewed by state policymakers as highly desirable, since it allows state residents to enjoy public services at a lower effective cost.[2]

Taxes can be exported in one of two ways. The most obvious way is through the deduction of state and local taxes against federal tax liability. All business taxes, including sales taxes on business purchases (as well as user charges), are exportable in this sense. However, as a result of one of the more controversial provisions of the U.S. Tax Reform Act of 1986 (hereafter, TRA86), state sales taxes paid by individuals are no longer deductible against federal taxes and thus cannot be exported in this fashion; in contrast, state personal income taxes are still fully deductible.[3] The federal tax system thus has an obvious incentive for the use of personal income rather than sales taxes at the state (and local) level.

The second avenue for tax exporting is through tax-induced price changes, such as higher prices for goods consumed by out-of-state consumers or through the payment of lower returns to out-of-state factor owners. In general, however, there are relatively few markets in which business firms within a given state have significant power in national and international commodity and factor markets; thus, this avenue of exportation is quite limited by competitive forces.

EFFICIENCY

Efficiency is the criterion emphasized most in academic analyses of tax issues. The basic concept is that a tax system should be structured to minimize the aggregate loss in individual welfare associated with raising a given amount of tax revenue. Such losses are attributable to two factors—the obvious loss in welfare due to the transfer of funds to the government (net of the value of any benefits received) and the additional so-called excess burden induced by the distortions of individual and firm choices as these economic agents change their behavior in an attempt to reduce their tax liabilities. Since the first factor is common to all taxes, it is differences in excess burdens that give rise to differences in the efficiency properties of alternative taxes.

One problem that makes application of the efficiency criterion particularly difficult is that almost all taxes reduce economic efficiency; that is, virtually all tax structures are inefficient in the sense that they distort some type of individual or firm behavior. The central question then is not which state tax structure is efficient, but which is the least inefficient.[4] Any answer to this question necessarily involves a host of assumptions about both the nature of the state economy and its interaction with the national and international economies and the extent to which taxes affect individual and firm behavior. Accordingly, such answers will inevitably be controversial, and it is quite likely that a consensus regarding the "optimal" tax structure may not be reached, even if the only tax criterion were efficiency. Nevertheless, many economic analyses have discussed the inefficiencies associated with various tax structures, and the results of these analyses will be examined below. In addition, the efficiency issue is complicated by the fact that taxation distorts so many different types of decisions that it is difficult to construct an economic model that considers simultaneously the effects of all potential tax distortions.

For example, sales and excise taxes on consumption commodities typically distort individual consumption decisions as well as the choice between labor and leisure. Income taxes distort both savings and labor/leisure decisions.[5] Any business tax—including an income tax, a tax on net wealth, and/or a sales tax assessed on business purchases—distorts a wide variety of business decisions, such as the level and composition of investment and risk taking, the method used to finance new investments, decisions regarding the distribution of earnings, and the choice of organizational form.

In addition, a number of critical issues arise because any state economy is a relatively small component of the U.S. and the world economies, and because businesses and, to a lesser extent, individuals are in the long run relatively free to migrate into and out of a state in response to changes in the state's economic conditions, including its tax system. Thus, a state tax system can also reduce economic efficiency by distorting the location decisions of firms and individuals. This particular aspect of the efficiency criterion is typically translated as a requirement that "the tax system should be conducive to economic growth and development in the state."

The choice of tax structure may also affect decisions regarding the level of public services. For example, state or local governments that rely on the taxation of mobile capital may "underprovide" public services (relative to an efficient level) because they are concerned about driving capital out of their jurisdictions and thus reducing employment or the productivity of labor. On the other hand, as noted above, if states use taxes that can successfully be "exported" to out-of-state residents (or are perceived to be exported even if in fact they are not), there is a tendency toward overprovision of public services. More generally, benefit taxes, defined as taxes that are assessed to correspond to the benefits received from public services and thus are roughly analogous to prices in the private sector, are widely viewed as desirable on efficiency grounds. The rationale for this position is that benefit taxes promote efficient decision making in the political arena regarding the level of public services, since individuals bear the costs of funding services they utilize.[6] In marked contrast, under alternative tax structures that are not based on the benefit principle, individuals who do not bear the cost of services they consume are likely to support expansion of those services beyond the efficient level.

In the absence of benefit taxes, efficiency in public service provision is promoted by the use of highly "visible" taxes that ensure that citizens are aware of the costs of public services. This line of reasoning suggests that the use of income taxes and property taxes (and, to a somewhat lesser extent, sales taxes on consumption commodities) is desirable, while the use of sales taxes on business purchases and taxes on businesses is generally undesirable because the burden of these taxes is unclear (and indeed voters may be misled into thinking these sources of revenue are costless to them).[7]

Finally, note that a few types of taxes may actually improve efficiency. As discussed earlier, benefit taxes are efficient if structured appropriately. Taxes on activities that generate social costs (or create "negative externalities," in economic jargon) may change behavior in such a way as to increase efficiency; for example, properly structured taxes on emissions of environmentally harmful pollutants can improve economic efficiency by reducing production of pollution-intensive products or spurring firms to adopt less pollution-intensive production techniques. Similar arguments are sometimes used to justify so-called sin taxes on alcohol and tobacco; that is, such taxes may reduce behaviors that generate social costs. Thus, from an efficiency perspective, appropriately structured benefit taxes and taxes on activities that generate negative externalities are generally desirable since they may both improve the allocation of resources and raise revenue.

EQUITY

In some ways, defining the characteristics of an equitable tax system is even more difficult than identifying the features of an efficient one, as the concept of equity involves a host of philosophical and political considerations in addition to economic ones. Nevertheless, it is critical that a tax system be perceived to be fair by taxpayers; otherwise, taxpayer support of public expenditures will be reduced and taxpayer compliance with the tax system may decline.[8]

Two basic principles of equity have been suggested by public finance theorists. The first is the ability-to-pay principle, which argues that taxes should be assessed in terms of some measure of an individual's capacity to pay taxes. This principle in turn has two dimensions. First, horizontal equity requires that individuals with the same taxpaying capacity should pay the same amount of tax. Second, vertical equity requires that individuals with greater taxpaying capacity should pay a larger amount of tax. Unfortunately, it is difficult to apply these principles for at least two reasons. First, there is considerable disagreement about the appropriate measure of ability to pay, and, thus, there is disagreement about how "equals" should be defined for the purpose of applying the principle of horizontal equity. In particular, although annual income is commonly used as the indicator of ability to pay, many economists have argued that other measures (discussed below) are more appropriate. Second, even if there is agreement on the measure of ability to pay, the question of vertical equity is a very subjective and contentious one, as people have widely diverging views on how the tax burden should vary with ability to pay.[9]

The second (competing) notion of equity is the benefit principle, which argues that taxpayers should pay tax in accordance with their valuation of benefits received. This principle is difficult to implement in practice, because there are many problems in determining individual valuations of public services. In addition, application of the benefit principle is inconsistent with the goals of public expenditures explicitly designed to redistribute income. Nevertheless, a number of public services provided at the state and local levels are amenable to either taxes or user charges consistent with the benefit principle. Indeed, some have argued that income redistribution should be solely (or at least primarily) a function of the national government, and that state and local governments should avoid taxes based on ability to pay and should utilize benefit taxes to the maximum extent possible.

REVENUE ADEQUACY AND STABILITY

Another criterion used to evaluate alternative tax structures is revenue adequacy, which requires that the tax system raise an adequate amount of revenue in the presence of changing economic conditions; in other words, revenues should grow at approximately the same rate as the state economy, so that periodic rate increases are unnecessary. Note, however, that such growth implies that revenues would increase at a rate equal to the sum of the inflation rate and the real rate of growth in the economy. Although maintaining constant real revenues is generally desirable, one could argue that "automatic" increases in real revenues are undesirable because they reduce the need for periodic reexamination of the need for government programs and encourage the growth of government. Moreover, this argument is particularly relevant for tax systems that have a progressive rather than a proportional rate structure (especially if individual or firm real tax burdens increase with inflation), in which case the ratio of taxes paid to income grows automatically with income growth (and/or inflation).

In addition, revenue stability—relative invariance of revenues around their trend growth path in the presence of cyclical economic fluctuations—is generally perceived to be a desirable feature of a tax system. This is especially true for those state governments that are constitutionally required to balance their budgets each accounting period. Finally, alternative tax structures will differ in the extent to which they can help stabilize the economy. This factor is usually not deemed to be very important in the state context (although it plays an important role at the federal level).

LOW ADMINISTRATIVE, ENFORCEMENT, AND COMPLIANCE COSTS

Although difficult to quantify, low administrative, enforcement, and compliance costs are desirable features of any tax system. This criterion implies that the tax system should attempt to minimize both individual and firm compliance costs (including record keeping costs and fees paid to professional tax preparers), as well as the government's costs of administering, monitoring, and enforcing the tax system.

Another element of the enforcement issue is the way in which the tax system interacts with the illegal or so-called underground economy. There are two aspects of this interaction. The first is the extent to which the tax system is effective in obtaining at least some revenues from illegal activities. For example, a sales tax that applies to consumption commodities is somewhat more likely to generate revenues from those individuals engaged in underground activities than is an income tax, although this supposed advantage is often greatly overstated. The second aspect of this interaction is whether alternative tax structures have any impact on the size of the underground economy. For example, if certain types of taxes are easier or more likely to be evaded, then their use may increase the size of the underground economy.

CRITERIA NOT USED IN THIS STUDY

It may be useful to comment briefly on two criteria not used in this book but discussed in other studies. The first is balance—generally defined as roughly equal reliance on income, sales, and property taxes to raise revenues in a state.[10] However, as argued persuasively by Ladd and Weist (1987), balance is not by itself an appropriate goal for state tax policy. Rather, a balanced revenue structure should be viewed as desirable only if such a structure reflects the outcome of a process that weighs the various criteria noted above. A balanced revenue structure may in fact be desirable for a number of reasons. For example, since all tax options have both strengths and weaknesses, a combination of taxes may take advantage of the strengths of each while simultaneously avoiding problems associated with unusually heavy reliance on any single tax option. In addition, a balanced revenue system may be viewed as a "diversified" structure that reduces revenue instability and provides for smoother revenue growth. Nevertheless, such a result should be determined from a balancing of the goals noted above rather than assumed at the outset.

Similarly, broadness of base—also advocated in several state tax reform studies—is not really a separate criterion. Rather, broad bases are generally desirable because they promote both equity and efficiency, and are usually consistent with simplicity as well.

Public finance specialists typically use the wide variety of criteria described in this chapter to evaluate from an economic perspective the relative advantages and disadvantages of alternative tax systems. Unfortunately, there is not universal agreement about the precise definitions of these criteria or their relative importance. Nevertheless, such an evaluation process provides a useful framework for analyzing the desirability of tax reforms and is used in the following three chapters to analyze the relative merits of state sales and income taxes.

CHAPTER 3

Exportability and Efficiency

This chapter and the next, which comprise the bulk of this book, summarize the economic literature on the application of the criteria outlined in the previous chapter to the evaluation of alternative tax systems, including the state sales tax, perhaps coupled with a business level tax such as a corporate franchise tax, and a state income tax system that includes both corporate and individual income taxes. This chapter focuses on the issues of tax exportability and economic efficiency, while the following chapter considers the tax equity issue and a variety of other questions.

EXPORTABILITY

From a national perspective, "exportability" is generally an undesirable feature of a state tax structure on both efficiency and equity grounds. From the perspective of efficiency, if the residents of one state are able to export the burden of their taxes to the residents of another state, the government of the taxing state is likely to oversupply public services, believing that they are consumed largely by residents (and voters) of the state, while being paid for by nonresidents (and nonvoters). One can also argue that such tax exporting is inequitable, as it clearly violates the benefit principle of taxation, since the beneficiaries of public services are a group that is largely separate from those who are funding the services. Indeed, from a national perspective, tax exporting is desirable only to the extent that nonresidents of a state benefit from the state's public services, either directly as consumers of the services or indirectly in the form of "external benefits" that accrue to the region or to the nation as a whole.

Nevertheless, it is clear that from the perspective of an individual state, the ability to export a tax burden is commonly perceived to be highly desirable.[1]

Moreover, one could argue that the use of exportable taxes is required as a "defensive measure," since virtually all states attempt to export some of their tax burdens. Accordingly, this section assesses the two alternative tax structures on the assumption that tax exporting is highly desirable.

Exportability through Deductibility

The most obvious means of exporting part of the state tax burden is through the deductibility of state and local taxes against federal tax liability. That is, to the extent that a state tax is deductible, the effective tax price of state services declines as part of the tax burden is shifted to out-of-state federal taxpayers. The amount shifted depends on two factors—the fraction of taxes that is deductible (which is less than one since not all taxpayers itemize deductions) and the average marginal tax rate at which such taxes are deducted. Indeed, in the simplest models of the provision of state government services, the "tax price" of public services in the presence of deductibility equals one minus the product of the fraction of state taxes that is deducted against federal tax liability and the average marginal federal tax rate in the state.[2]

Differences in exportability do not arise for businesses, since all business taxes, including corporate income and franchise taxes and sales taxes on capital goods, are deductible against federal income taxes.[3] However, as noted above, individual sales taxes paid are no longer deductible under current federal income tax law while personal income (and property) taxes remain deductible. This implies that considerations of exportability argue unambiguously in favor of a state personal income tax over a state sales tax, as the former tax will maximize the extent to which the state tax burden can be shifted to out-of-state residents.

It is interesting to note that, contrary to the predictions of many observers, state utilization of sales taxes has in fact increased considerably since 1986. For example, Citizens for Tax Justice (1991) notes that twenty-six states increased their sales tax over the period 1986–91 while only two reduced it. Similarly, although the personal income tax was increased in eleven states over this period, it was reduced in twenty-eight states.[4] This behavior suggests that states have not responded as economic theory would predict to the incentives present under current law relative to the conditions prior to 1986. However, this is in fact not the case.

The paradox can be explained by a careful look at the relative "tax prices"—the net costs to residents of raising revenues using either the sales tax or the income tax, taking into account the advantages of deductibility—before and after passage of TRA86. As detailed by Pollock (1991), the explanation proceeds in two steps.

The first part of the argument notes that federal deductibility on average favored use of the income tax prior to 1986, even though both income and sales taxes were deductible. This occurred for two reasons. First, the fraction of taxes paid that was deducted was much smaller for the sales tax than for the income tax. Indeed, Pollock estimates that nationwide only 22.2 percent of individual sales taxes were deducted in 1986, while over 90 percent of individual state income taxes were deducted. This large difference occurred because sales taxes were more concentrated among lower income nonitemizers and because the IRS sales tax tables used by most itemizers significantly understated sales taxes paid, especially for high-income taxpayers. Second, sales taxes were typically deducted at a somewhat lower marginal rate than were income taxes, especially in those states that have a progressive state income tax rate structure. Pollock estimates that on average in 1986 income taxes were deducted at a marginal rate of 33.7 percent, while sales taxes were deducted at a marginal rate of 28.8 percent.

The second step of the argument is based on the fact that although the TRA86 increased the tax price of both sales tax and income tax finance at the state level, the increase in the tax price of income tax finance was proportionately greater. This occurred because the reductions in the amounts of state income taxes deducted, due to increases in the standard deduction and personal exemptions and the associated reduction in the number of itemizers, had a large impact on the average tax price of the state income tax. By comparison, the impact on the average tax price of the sales tax due to the analogous reductions in the amounts of sales taxes deducted as a result of the elimination of deductibility was relatively small, since only a small fraction of sales taxes were deducted prior to 1986 in any case. Similarly, the relatively large reduction in the marginal tax rate at which the average state income tax was deducted had a bigger impact on the tax price of the income tax than the analogous increase in the tax price of the sales tax attributable to the elimination of deductibility. As a result, on average across the nation, the attractiveness of the use of sales taxes relative to state income taxes actually increased in 1986. Pollock estimates that the tax price of a state income tax increased on average by nearly 15 percent, while the tax price of a state sales tax increased on average by only slightly more than 8 percent. Thus, increasing reliance on state sales taxes nationwide does not represent an anomaly, despite the elimination of the deductibility of state sales taxes under the TRA86.

Finally, note that deductibility coupled with the progressivity of the federal income tax implies that a progressive state personal income tax results in a tax burden that is actually less progressive than suggested by the nominal rate structure in a state. For example, suppose that the state rate structure specified rates of 2 and 4 percent, and that most households subject to the 2 percent rate were in either the zero or the 15 percent federal rate bracket, while most households subject to the 4 percent tax rate were in the 31 percent rate bracket. In this case, the net tax rates after deductibility would be either 1.7 or 2 percent for the first group and 2.76 for the second group. That is, deductibility under the federal tax system reduces the effective progressivity implied by a progressive state rate structure. A related point is that deductibility implies that the reduction in the cost of public goods is highest for high-income taxpayers who typically receive less in the way of public services per tax dollar and who are also likely to be more influential politically. Note also that the magnitude of this effect was increased somewhat by the passage of the income tax rate increases in the Omnibus Budget Reconciliation Act of 1993, which increased the top marginal income tax rate to 39.6 percent.

Exportability through Price Changes

In addition to exporting taxes by taking advantage of federal provisions for the deductibility of certain taxes, a state may be able to export its tax burden in two other ways. The first is through higher prices paid by consumers in other states, or by tourists or business visitors in the state. The second way is through lower returns to factors employed in the state but owned by out-of-state residents. This argument is usually cast in terms of taxing out-of-state capital owners and (to a lesser extent) landowners.

The critical question is the extent to which a state can in fact successfully export its tax burden in this fashion. Unfortunately—at least from the state's perspective—the potential for such exportation is likely to be limited. The sales tax on consumer goods can be exported to the extent that such goods are purchased by out-of-state residents—primarily tourists and business visitors.[5] This is not likely to be a very important source of revenue for most states. In any case, if opportunities for tax exporting in this area are deemed to be significant, they can be exploited through the use of special taxes on hotel/motel occupancy, car rentals, and, to a much lesser extent, on entertainment and admissions to amusements. Thus, the potential for tax exporting in this area does not appear to provide an important rationale in support of a state sales tax.

Most discussions of tax exporting focus on the extent to which business taxes can be exported either as higher prices to out-of-state purchasers of the state's output or as lower returns to out-of-state owners of capital and land. Such taxes include corporate income and franchise taxes, oil and gas severance taxes, and sales taxes assessed on business purchases. Indeed, many states attempt to structure their business tax systems to increase the extent to which their corporate or franchise taxes may be borne by out-of-state firms. This is accomplished mainly by choosing a weighting formula for allocating corporate income or the franchise tax base to the state that emphasizes sales (rather than payroll or property)within the state and is thus more likely to impact out-of-state firms.[6] The following discussion suggests that these avenues of tax exportation are quite limited when the long-run nature of the markets for exportable goods and capital is taken into account.

Consider first the exportation of business taxes to out-of-state purchasers of goods produced within a state. Exporting of state tax burdens in the form of higher prices (known as forward shifting of the tax burden) is likely to occur only in those markets in which in-state producers can exert a significant amount of market power—that is, in markets in which prices for products produced within a state can be raised without losing a significant amount of sales to producers in other states. There presumably are some industries in which cost advantages due to factors such as superior access to resources and economies of scale and/or agglomeration imply that the industries within any given state possess some market power that could be exploited for the purpose of tax exporting. More generally, however, one would expect that in most cases products produced in other states are close substitutes for those produced in any given state. In general, it seems very likely that opportunities for tax exporting through higher prices for goods purchased by out-of-state consumers are rather limited.

A similar argument applies for backward shifting of the burden of business taxes (other than those directly related to benefits received) to out-of-state factor owners, especially capital owners. In the context of the national market for capital, any particular state can reasonably be viewed as a small open economy in the long run; specifically, any changes in a state tax structure can be expected to have only negligible long-run effects on the national after-tax return to capital.[7] In economic jargon, any given state faces a nearly infinitely elastic supply of capital because capital is highly mobile across all states in the long run. This implies that any business tax initially borne by out-of-state capital owners will eventually be shifted either to in-state consumers in the form of higher prices or to the owners of less mobile factors of production in the state (primarily in-state labor and land). Moreover, the process by which the shifting occurs creates an excess burden, which is also borne by in-state factors. That is, perfect capital mobility implies that the imposition of a business tax has the long-run effect of driving capital out of a state until the before-tax return to capital increases by an amount sufficient to hold the after-tax return constant. As a result, the productivities of in-state labor and land decline, and these factors bear both the direct burden of the tax as well as the excess burden caused by the inefficient (less capital-intensive) production methods attributable to the tax-induced capital out-migration. Thus, there is no exporting of the business tax burden to out-of-state capital owners in an open economy context.[8]

An opposing view is provided by Pollock (1991), who argues that the potential for the exportation of state sales taxes is large. Based on the assumption of full forward shifting of sales taxes paid by businesses on items related to the production of goods sold in national markets, he estimates that Connecticut is able to export roughly 22 percent of its total sales tax burden.[9] Pollock suggests two main reasons why such extensive forward shifting to out-of-state consumers may be possible. First, he argues that some firms may have market power; however, as discussed above, the extent of such market power is far from clear. Second, he notes that since all states tax business purchases to some extent, the average level of such taxation would be expected to appear in the national prices of goods, while only differentials about this average would be shifted backward to local factors. However, note that the above open economy arguments, which apply to different degrees in all states, suggest that all business sales taxes that apply to goods sold in national markets are shifted backward to immobile factors of production; that is, the "average" national amount of forward shifting may very well be close to zero. This is even more likely to be true if the price of the national market good is in fact determined in an international market.[10] Thus, Pollock's rather high estimate of the potential for exporting of the state sales tax is quite suspect.[11]

In summary, the question of tax incidence—the nature of the shifting of tax burdens—is always one of the more vexing ones in public finance. Nevertheless, in the absence of demonstrable market power for the firms within a state, the view of Oakland, who argues that "the opportunities for exportation are extremely limited" (1992, p. 24), seems to be the most reasonable basis for an evaluation of state tax policy options.[12] Accordingly, the potential for tax exporting does not provide a compelling argument for the use of a sales tax on business purchases rather than a personal income tax.[13] If the firms within a state possess significant market power in a few industries in which tax exportation is feasible, selective excise taxes on those industries would be indicated. Such market power, unless it is pervasive across many industries, does not provide a compelling rationale for a general tax on business, either through sales taxation of business inputs or a tax on corporate income (or wealth).

ECONOMIC EFFICIENCY

As noted earlier, there are many ways in which any tax system chosen by a state will reduce the efficiency of resource allocation in the state economy. Indeed, apart from benefit taxes (such as user charges) or taxes that compensate for undesirable effects that are external to individuals or firms (such as pollution charges), any tax will distort economic decision making in an undesirable way and thus give rise to an "excess burden"—that is, an efficiency cost beyond the revenues raised by the tax. Since the revenue potential of user charges and pollution taxes is limited, a state tax structure that causes no efficiency losses is impossible to achieve; rather, the key to designing an efficient tax system is to structure it to minimize the efficiency costs of taxation. The following discussion will examine the two alternative state tax structures in terms of this criterion.[14]

Before considering a variety of specific issues, three important general points should be noted. First, efficiency costs increase with increases in the extent to which individuals or firms can change their behavior in order to avoid taxes. In economic jargon, one would expect the excess burden or efficiency cost of a tax on any activity to be large if the relevant elasticity of supply or demand is large.[15] This implies that the economic effects of any particular state (or local) tax can be expected to be quite different from the effects of the same tax enacted at the national level, since the mobility of factors is much more limited in the latter case. For example, a local tax on capital income will cause a large excess burden if the elasticity of supply of capital to the taxing jurisdiction is high—that is, if capital is very mobile in response to changes in its after-tax rate of return. This will be true even if the owners of capital are unable to escape a national tax on capital income.[16] Similarly, a local tax on labor income, especially a highly progressive one, will cause a large excess burden if labor, especially highly skilled and well-compensated individuals, is highly mobile across states.

Second, excess burdens tend to increase more than proportionately with respect to the tax rate. Indeed, in the simplest cases, the relationship is quadratic, so that a doubling of the tax rate will result in a quadrupling of the excess burden.[17] This suggests that wide tax differentials across different types of economic activities—unless justified by large differences in supply or demand elasticities—are undesirable on efficiency grounds.

Third, it must be remembered that efficiency is only one of the factors that must be considered in evaluating a tax system. In particular, considerations of efficiency and equity often imply very different prescriptions for tax policy. For example, consider a sales tax with differentiated rates. In this case, efficiency suggests that necessities should be taxed at high rates since it is difficult for consumers to substitute away from such commodities, while equity suggests that such goods should be taxed lightly or made tax exempt, since they are consumed disproportionately by the poor. Thus, efficiency considerations must always be balanced against the other criteria used to evaluate a tax structure.

Distortions of Capital Supply and Allocation

The tax distortion that receives the most attention in the context of state tax structures is the extent to which source-based taxes on capital and/or capital income (in excess of benefits from public services received by capital owners) reduce the supply of capital to the state; phrased alternatively, the question is whether tax reductions can be effective in attracting capital investment from out-of-state sources.[18] As noted above, the key factor in thinking about the efficiency costs of taxing capital income is that in the context of the national (and indeed international) market for capital, a state is effectively a small open economy—that is, the supply of capital is very likely to be highly elastic to the state in the long run. Another way of stating this proposition is that capital owners are free in the long run to invest in any state (or nation), regardless of their state of residence, and will do so in any given state only if the risk-adjusted after-tax rate of return to investment in the state is the same as the returns available elsewhere. This in turn implies that in the long run the after-tax rate of return to capital invested in any state will be virtually independent of the taxes on capital income in that state; for example, the imposition of a capital income tax will drive some capital out of the state, raising the rate of return on the remaining capital until it is the same as in the pretax equilibrium (and thus in the rest of the economy).

The implications of this analysis are striking—in the long run, the owners of capital in the state bear none of the burden of any source-based taxes imposed on capital. Instead, the tax burden is shifted forward to consumers in the form of higher prices or backward to relatively immobile factors of production—labor and land.[19] Moreover, not only do in-state consumers and owners of labor and land bear the burden of the tax, they also bear the excess burden of the tax in the form of lower wages and rents and/or higher prices as capital leaves the state, making the remaining factors of production less productive. Thus, in-state consumers and owners of labor and land should prefer a direct tax on themselves to a tax on capital. In either case, they bear the direct costs of the tax, but in the latter case they must bear the excess burden as well. Such considerations have led several authors to conclude that in a small open economy the optimal tax rate on capital income—other than benefit-related user charges or taxes on externalities—is zero.[20] (Note that this result also implies that subsidies to capital—or negative tax rates—are undesirable. Subsidies drive the benefits to local residents of an increased capital stock, which are subject to diminishing returns, below the cost of "purchasing" capital, which remains constant at the fixed, externally determined after-tax rate of return.)

This very strong result—a small open economy optimal capital income tax rate of zero—must be qualified in a number of ways. First, as suggested above, if some of the firms within a state have market power in the national market for their exports (or even only in the state market for goods that are not traded in national markets), a positive tax rate on capital can be an indirect means of sharing the economic rents associated with that market power on a statewide basis.[21] However, most firms are unlikely to have significant market power in most national and/or international markets. Nevertheless, there are no doubt some exceptions to this general rule, and there may be a significant number of firms with market power in certain state markets (for goods that are not traded in national or international markets).

Second, the analysis presented above ignores uncertainty of returns in different states and countries. Investors will wish to diversify widely their portfolios in order to minimize their exposure to state-specific risk. To the extent that a state provides unique diversification opportunities, it could in effect "charge" for diversification services by imposing a tax that would apply to out-of-state capital.[22] However, given the sizes of and diversification opportunities available in the economies of other states and countries, it does not seem likely that risk diversification considerations could justify a very large state tax burden on capital income.

A third commonly cited justification for a business tax applies only to the case of a corporate income tax in a state that has a personal income tax. Specifically, it is often argued that a corporate tax is necessary to prevent evasion of the personal income tax in the form of retention of earnings in corporate form.[23] This argument is valid for the federal income tax and for (typically relatively small) corporations owned exclusively, or at least primarily, by in-state residents. Nevertheless, one should note that this argument does not provide a solid rationale for general corporate taxation since, in the vast majority of cases, in-state corporations are owned primarily by nonresidents, and most of the corporate holdings of state residents are in out-of-state corporations. Thus, a state corporate tax is a rather poorly focused instrument to limit such evasion of a state personal income tax; in addition, it encourages residents to invest in out-of-state corporations. The goal of limiting evasion of the state income tax would be better met by requiring small corporations whose owners are primarily in-state residents to follow partnerships in "passing through" annual earnings to their owners for purposes of calculating the base of the state personal income tax. At the same time, it must be noted that some means must be found for taxing business purchases that are merely disguised personal consumption on the part of the owners or employees of the business (items such as fringe benefits, most food and entertainment expenses, some travel expenses, car and housing allowances, etc.). These items should either be taxed at the business level (by disallowing deductions for nonbusiness expenses) or be imputed to individual taxpayers and taxed at the individual level.[24]

A fourth possible justification for taxing capital in a small open state economy depends on the nature of the interaction between the state and federal tax codes. In the international context, the existence of foreign tax credits in many capital-exporting countries provides a strong rationale for capital-importing countries to tax foreign capital. Specifically, at least in the simplest cases, the crediting arrangement implies that a capital-importing country can use a source-based tax to obtain revenues effectively "from the foreign treasury" of the capital-exporting country with no deleterious effects on investment, as long as the domestic tax rate does not exceed the tax rate applied to the income by the foreign country and is thus fully creditable.[25] However, in the state case, this argument is much weaker, since only a tax deduction rather than a tax credit is allowed for state taxes by the national government. Nevertheless, it would appear that even a deduction would provide at least some justification for the taxation of capital income in a small open economy.

However, even this intuitively plausible argument for a source-based tax on capital income in a small open economy context does not hold up under further scrutiny. The small open economy assumption implies that the return to capital after federal taxes is constant; that is, it cannot be reduced by state taxes. It certainly is true that federal deductibility implies that the effective tax burden imposed by a state corporate tax at rate "s" is only $(1-f)s$, where "f" is the federal corporate rate. Thus, in the small open economy context, the return to capital after federal taxes must go up only by enough to cover state level taxation at an effective rate of $(1-f)s$. However, in order for this to occur, the gross return to capital must go up to cover the federal tax burden on these incremental earnings as well (since the increase in returns required to cover deductible state taxes is subject to federal taxes). The net result is that gross returns must go up by the full amount of the state tax rather than just the deductible portion.[26] This is simply another way of saying that the full burden of the state tax is shifted, as discussed above, and is likely to take the form of either price increases to consumers of state-market goods or backward shifting to state supplies of land and labor. Thus, tax exporting occurs only to the extent that state land and labor are owned by out-of-state residents, and is presumably fairly minor.

All of the above arguments suggest that source-based state taxation of business income is undesirable. Nevertheless, it is clear that all states in the United States utilize a significant amount of such taxes. There are many explanations for this phenomenon, apart from attempts to tax environmental externalities or capture some of the rents earned by firms with some monopoly power in national (or in-state) markets. The most convincing explanation is that businesses do not pay enough in the way of user charges to cover the benefits they receive from public services. As noted above, benefit taxes are highly desirable on efficiency grounds as they play a resource allocation role analogous to prices in private markets, and they are equitable in the sense that they ensure that public services are financed by their users. Accordingly, as detailed in chapter 6, a very strong case can be made for assessing user charges on firms to the maximum extent feasible. However, alternative broad-based taxes that are independent of benefits received do not function well as benefit taxes. Nevertheless, one potential justification for such taxes is that they may serve as at least a very rough proxy for benefit taxes or user charges.

A second rationale is that the incidence of business taxes is likely to be perceived as falling on the rich. Although the above discussion suggests that this perception is largely misplaced due to the pattern of shifting of business taxes, this perception undoubtedly is an important factor in the popular support for such taxes.[27] A related point is that business taxes are sometimes viewed as desirable on ability-to-pay grounds, that is, on the assumption that these taxes are imposed on high-income business owners. This assumption is highly questionable both on the grounds that state taxes on business are very likely to be shifted to individuals in ways that are not related to ability to pay, and that at least some and perhaps many owners of businesses may in fact not be high-income individuals (e.g., middle-income retirees, the owners of pension assets, and the owners of some small businesses). If taxation according to ability to pay is deemed desirable, a direct (individual-based) tax is the appropriate vehicle to achieve it.

A third possible explanation is that the arguments against business taxes presented above are largely long-run arguments, as the capital outflows required to produce the tax shifting described above would take a number of years after the imposition of a tax. To the extent that policymakers tend to think in short- run terms, they may very well believe such long-run arguments are not compelling, and may be attracted to the possibility of extracting tax revenues from firms that have made capital investments that are difficult to reverse in the short run. A related point is that taxes on capital already in place may be viewed as much less harmful than taxes on potential capital inflows, so that the use of business taxes involves balancing the benefits of taxing immobile capital against the costs of taxing mobile capital. Indeed, the use of business taxes coupled with exemptions for new firms, which is fairly common in many states, especially at the local level, reflects exactly this type of balancing.[28]

More generally, the tax shifting described above is "hidden" in the sense that the link between taxes paid by businesses and the resulting price increases or declines in factor returns is not an obvious one. As noted previously, the use of such hidden taxes is undesirable on efficiency grounds since taxpayers do not perceive the true cost of the public services they receive when such taxes are used, and thus they face an incentive to support public services in excess of efficient levels. Nevertheless, politicians and supporters of various public services are likely to find this feature of business taxes an attractive one.

Yet another potential rationale is that policymakers recognize the problems associated with business taxation, but they are also aware that serious efficiency problems arise in taxing individuals, especially high-income individuals who are relatively mobile. Moreover, the political costs of heavy reliance on individual-level taxation may be significantly greater than those incurred in a system that includes a significant business tax. Accordingly, some business taxes may be used in order to lower the direct tax burden on individuals.

A final potential rationale is that policymakers believe that the basic premise underlying the above analysis is faulty; that is, they believe that business location and investment decisions are not as sensitive to tax factors as implied by the open economy analysis. This perception would be supported by the early empirical literature on this issue, which suggested that tax factors play a fairly minor role in business location and investment decisions. However, more recent research calls this result into serious question. Since the effect of taxation on business location and investment decisions is such a critical (and controversial) issue, the empirical literature on this question is examined in some detail in the following subsection.

Taxes and Business Location and Investment Decisions

Researchers examining the effects of taxation on business location and investment decisions have focused on two types of studies—surveys of the business executives responsible for firm location and expansion decisions and econometric analyses based on both microeconomic (individual firm) and macroeconomic (aggregate) data.[29] The following discussion provides a brief and necessarily selective survey of this evidence; it draws on recent literature reviews by Blair and Premus (1987), Carroll and Wasylenko (1990), Wasylenko (1991), Bartik (1991, 1994), and Tannenwald (1993).

Most surveys have examined business location decisions, especially those regarding the openings of new manufacturing plants, focusing on identifying and ranking the factors that were perceived to be most important to the decision by those individuals responsible for the decision. For purposes of tax policy evaluation, the primary issue is usually interpreted to be whether overall tax burdens (as well as the availability of public services) are mentioned as factors important to the location or expansion decision. To a large extent, this approach is not especially informative, since it would not be surprising to find that factors other than taxes would be more important determinants of business location or expansion decisions, given that taxes typically represent a fairly small fraction of total costs. (Such factors include access to markets, wage patterns, the extent of unionization, relative prices of energy, land and other production inputs, transportation facilities, access to skilled labor and to a major university, etc.) Nevertheless, it could still be true that fiscal factors are quite relevant in that they have important effects on location and expansion decisions at the margin, holding these other factors constant. Moreover, taxes and expenditures are likely to be among the most important factors under the direct control of policymakers.[30]

In addition, survey analysis suffers from several other problems. Respondents may not respond truthfully if they believe that false responses may further their own policy goals. The way in which questions are posed by the researcher may seriously bias answers. Only existing firms can be surveyed, and the characteristics of the firms in the resulting sample may differ from those of the general population of firms considering relocation.[31]

Nevertheless, it is useful to examine briefly the results of the industrial location survey literature.[32] Virtually all of the early studies indicate that the "traditional factors" listed above are the critical ones for location decisions, and that taxes are not an important determinant. For example, Morgan's (1967) study indicates that taxes are ranked of "little significance" in thirteen studies, of "some significance" in three studies, and of "primary significance" in only one study. More recent studies affirm the importance of traditional factors, but find that other factors, especially environmental ones such as "quality of life," are also important.[33] Nevertheless, taxes and expenditures are seldom cited as critical determinants of location decisions.

Similar results were obtained by Tannenwald in a survey of the business consultants that advise firms on location decisions. Tannenwald reports that, "None of the consultants identified state and local tax differentials as being an important factor in locational choice" (1993, p. 28). However, the consultants also noted that taxes can be an important consideration under certain circumstances; for example, capital-intensive firms are likely to be particularly concerned about the taxation of business property. In addition, Tannenwald reports that educational levels and the availability of labor with the requisite skills are among the most important locational determinants, and that some clients of the consulting firms surveyed place particular emphasis on the quality of public education in a location.

In addition to the reasons noted above, the importance of these studies is open to question because it is impossible to estimate the quantitative significance of any effects that taxes or expenditures might have on location and investment decisions. For this reason it is extremely difficult to interpret survey results. For example, Schmenner (1982), who examined the location decisions of the Fortune 500 firms in 1972 and 1978, reports that only 1 percent of his sample cited avoidance of taxes as a primary factor in determining the location of a branch plant, but that 35 percent noted that low taxes were desirable and might influence a location decision at the margin.[34] Since survey evidence is inherently unable to provide quantitative information, the econometric evidence on this issue is at least potentially of considerably more interest.

Finally, two additional interesting points are raised by the survey evidence regarding industrial location. First, Schmenner (1982) stresses that relocations are rather uncommon, and that most increases in production capacity take the form of plant expansions and, to a lesser extent, new branches.[35] This strongly suggests that incentive policies geared solely to relocations may be misguided in the long run, and that any tax incentives that are granted should be made available to existing firms.[36] Second, personal or idiosyncratic factors apparently play at least some role in the site selection process. For example, Kieschnick (1981) reports that 69 percent of the respondents in his survey cited personal reasons as either a deciding influence or a moderately positive influence.[37]

ECONOMETRIC EVIDENCE: AN OVERVIEW

Although there is a sizable literature on the effects of taxation on business location and investment, the empirical evidence is sufficiently mixed that different observers can draw, and certainly have drawn, different conclusions. To some extent, this is not surprising, as the determination of the effects of taxes and expenditures on business location and investment decisions poses a formidable econometric problem for a number of reasons.[38]

First, it is difficult to model accurately the business location or expansion decision because it is inherently so complicated. As a result, the appropriate model specification for empirical work is not obvious. In particular, the precise way that taxes enter the location decision must be specified, and the effects of tax-financed expenditures must be considered as well. (Studies that focus only on tax effects are relevant only if a business receives none of the direct or indirect benefits of public expenditures.)

Second, it is difficult to measure many of the key economic variables. For example, it is hard to get accurate data on wages adjusted for skill level (rather than just average manufacturing wages or some similar average wage measure) and on the quality (rather than just expenditures) of public services. Similarly, it is difficult to calculate accurate measures of effective business tax rates that are applied to new investment, especially in the presence of any tax abatement programs.[39] Errors in measuring these variables will bias estimates of the effects of taxes on business location decisions.

Third, any analysis will inevitably omit some observable and/or unobservable variables that affect location decisions and vary across states. As a result, effects on business location decisions that are attributed by the analysis to tax factors may instead be caused by these omitted variables. Although various econometric techniques have been used in attempts to deal with this issue, each has its own set of problems.[40]

Fourth, causality is always difficult to establish unambiguously in such econometric analyses; that is, many important factors that affect location decisions and economic growth, including taxes, are also affected themselves by business relocations and economic growth. For example, a state or locality experiencing growth may be able to lower tax rates and still obtain a sufficient amount of revenue. In this case, the effect of taxes on business location decisions would be overstated by an econometric analysis explaining such decisions as a function of tax factors. On the other hand, a state or locality with low or negative growth may lower business tax rates in an attempt to attract business. In this case, the effect of taxes on business locations would be understated by the econometric analysis. Sorting out these effects also poses a difficult econometric problem.[41]

Finally, it is difficult to measure accurately the effects of current policies on location decisions, because such decisions are also affected by previous policies. For example, current business expansion in an area may be attributable in large part to a previous decision to locate in the area, which was in turn affected by the tax and expenditure structure existing at that time. Similarly, current location or expansion decisions may be affected by existing economies of agglomeration (lower costs due to a concentration of a particular type of business activity) that are also attributable to previous policies.

Taken together, these problems are sufficiently serious that it is not surprising that econometric studies have produced conflicting results. Moreover, the discussion above suggests that there is enough uncertainty in any econometric results that they should be viewed cautiously. Nevertheless, it will be useful to review briefly the large literature on the effects of taxes on business location and investment and on economic growth.[42]

ECONOMETRIC EVIDENCE: START-UPS, BRANCH OPENINGS

Two types of econometric studies are most directly relevant to the question of whether businesses are as responsive to taxes as suggested by the open economy assumption described above. The first uses microdata at the firm level to examine whether capital investment in the form of new firm start-ups or branch openings (usually for manufacturing firms) is responsive to tax differentials across states or localities. The second—discussed in the following subsection—analyzes aggregate data at the state level to examine whether total investment is sensitive to tax factors.

The very early empirical studies (conducted during the 1950s and 1960s) found very little evidence that taxes had significant effects on business location and expansion decisions.[43] However, the results of more recent studies are mixed, and some of the strongest tax effects have been found in the most recent, and most carefully done, studies.

Two papers that are consistent with the hypothesis of small effects are by Carlton (1979, 1983), who examines new establishment start-ups and new branch plants for three manufacturing industries over 1967–75 as a function of tax variables (such as the combined corporate and personal income tax rate and the property tax rate) and a variety of other variables. Carlton's results indicate that, after controlling for the effects of other variables, tax effects are either small or nonexistent. In contrast, Bartik (1985) finds that firm start-ups (for a sample that consists of Fortune 500 firms over 1972–78) are negatively affected by the presence of a corporate income tax. His estimates imply a tax elasticity of −0.2; that is, holding services constant, a 10 percent reduction in the state corporate tax rate (calculated as an average rate by dividing total corporate tax revenues by estimated total corporate income) should increase start-ups by roughly 2 percent. These results are partially reinforced by the research of Schmenner, Huber, and Cook (1987), who examine the same Fortune 500 data set and find that tax variables generally have only weak effects on location decisions but are critical for those firms that they can identify as being highly mobile and/or controlled by managers who have a strong sentiment for reducing taxes. Similarly, Deich (1990) uses data from the Census of Manufacturers to examine start-ups and branch openings by two groups—all manufacturers and the manufacturers in three smaller industry groups (food products, apparel, and printing)—as a function of average tax rates and other variables. He finds that taxes do not affect single-establishment start-ups, but that corporate and property taxes affect new branch openings in half of the cases he examines.

One of the more provocative recent studies in this area is by Papke (1991a). She argues that most studies of the effects of taxes on business location and/or investment—including those cited above—are seriously flawed because they miscalculate the tax variable. Specifically, economic theory indicates that the tax variable relevant to a location or expansion decision is the "marginal effective tax rate," that is, the tax rate effectively applied to the future returns generated by a marginal investment, taking into account all of the provisions of the tax code, including depreciation allowances, investment tax credits, interest deductions, and so forth, as well as the effects of inflation and the deductibility of state taxes against federal tax liability. In contrast, the average tax rates typically used in studies of taxation and business location/expansion decisions primarily reflect the effects of all previous tax structures (rather than the current structure, which would apply for a new investment). In addition, they do not capture tax differentials that exist across assets (and thus across business sectors) and across alternate locations within a state. Accordingly, Papke argues that average tax rates are an inappropriate variable for measuring tax effects on investment decisions, and that the absence of strong tax effects on investment in previous research may be attributable to the measurement error resulting from the use of average rather than marginal rates.[44]

Using a marginal effective tax rate approach, Papke analyzes new single-establishment start-ups using pooled cross-sectional time-series data for twenty-two states and five manufacturing industries over the period 1975–82. She finds relatively large tax effects—most of the estimated elasticities range from 2 to 10 in absolute value—in roughly half of the cases she analyzes. She concludes that taxes do play an important role in location decisions for certain industries.

ECONOMETRIC EVIDENCE: AGGREGATE INVESTMENT

A second type of empirical study focuses on the extent to which the allocation of aggregate investment across states (or localities) appears to be sensitive to tax factors. Plaut and Pluta (1983) examine the effects of various taxes on the change in the real capital stock in manufacturing in the forty-eight contiguous states over 1967–77 with tax variables constructed as average tax rates. They find that only the property tax variable positively affects the growth rate of the capital stock and conclude that firms may be attracted to regions that rely relatively heavily on the property tax rather than a corporate or personal income tax.[45]

However, the Plaut and Pluta analysis is also subject to the criticism that its tax rate variables are measured inaccurately because they are based on average rather than marginal concepts. Papke (1987) makes this argument and, as above, conducts an analysis based on marginal effective tax rates. She examines tax effects on capital expenditures per worker for twenty manufacturing industries in twenty states. Her estimates indicate that a tax-induced increase in the after-tax rate of return of 1 percent will increase new investment expenditures per worker by roughly 2 percent, which implies an elasticity (with respect to the tax rate) of roughly −0.2.[46] Moreover, she tests the sensitivity of her results to the choice of tax rate variable by reestimating her results with two alternative "average" tax rate variables and finds that tax effects on investment are negligible with these specifications. Papke argues that these results suggest that studies indicating that taxes have no effects on investment suffer from serious measurement error.

In addition, Papke (1991b) obtains similar results in an analysis of five manufacturing industries over 1975–82. In this study, new capital expenditures are sensitive to marginal effective tax rates in two of the five industries analyzed; the estimated elasticities in these two industries range from 6 to 8 (in absolute value). She again concludes that taxes play an important role in location decisions for at least some industries.

Finally, a recent paper by Hines (1993) analyzes the effects of alternative state tax structures on the location of foreign direct investment across states. Since such investment has surged in recent years, its responsiveness to tax factors is also important in assessing the extent to which the open economy assumption is a reasonable one. Hines carefully models state tax systems to include the effects of formula apportionment of tax bases across states and the interaction between state and foreign tax systems. He notes that under certain circumstances investors from countries that allow foreign tax credits are indifferent to the level of state taxes, while this is not the case for investors from countries that do not allow such credits. Hines finds that state tax systems have significant effects on foreign direct investment. Specifically, he estimates that a 1 percent reduction in a state's corporate tax rate will increase the share of manufacturing foreign direct investment from countries that do not have foreign tax credit systems, relative to countries that do allow such credits, by 7 to 9 percent. However, one problem with the Hines study is that state tax rates are assumed to equal statutory rates, rather than the marginal effective tax rates used by Papke.[47]

ECONOMETRIC EVIDENCE: EMPLOYMENT, OUTPUT, INCOME

Much of the empirical evidence on the effects of state and local taxes on business activity has focused on aggregate employment, output, and income effects. The results of this literature are even more mixed than those obtained in the studies examining tax effects on business relocations or capital investment.

An early example of an employment study is Plaut and Pluta (1983), who examine the effects of various tax variables on the percentage change in aggregate manufacturing employment over 1967–77 and find very few tax effects. At a more disaggregated level, Newman (1983) and Wasylenko and McGuire (1985) find that taxes have significant employment effects in certain industries (typically durable manufactured goods), but not in others. The importance of these results is clouded, however, by the fact that McGuire and Wasylenko (1987) could not replicate their results when the sample was extended to include more recent data. Mixed results—with effects of some variables in some industries but not in others (and not necessarily the same industries in each study)—are presented in Wasylenko (1988) and Wasylenko and Carroll (1989). In addition, Mehay and Solnick (1990), Munnell (1990), and Quan and Beck (1987) generally find significant employment effects, while Carroll and Wasylenko (1994) do not. Interestingly, Carroll and Wasylenko (1994) argue that tax effects were stronger in the 1970s than in the 1980s, and they suggest this result may obtain because tax differentials across states were larger in the earlier period.[48]

In general, studies that examine aggregate personal income tend to find negative tax effects. An often-cited study is Helms (1985), who analyzes state personal income growth as a function of state tax and expenditure variables in the forty-eight contiguous states over 1965–79 and finds significant negative tax effects. In addition, Helms finds that the effects of public expenditures on education and highways have even larger effects on income growth than do taxes. He concludes that an increase in state and local taxes used to finance public expenditures may very well raise personal income, but that the same effect would not occur for an increase used to finance transfer payments. Generally similar results are obtained by Quan and Beck (1987) who suggest that taxes have larger effects on income (and employment) in the Northeast than in the South and Southwest. However, much weaker results are obtained by Carroll and Wasylenko (1989).

Finally, several studies have analyzed state and local tax effects on various measures of aggregate economic activity. Plaut and Pluta (1983) find that aggregate manufacturing growth over 1967–77 was negatively affected by the overall level of taxation, but that, given the overall level of taxes, the levels of corporate, personal income, and sales taxes were not important. This suggests that it is the total tax burden (net of benefits received by businesses), rather than the choice between income and sales taxation, that affects the rate of economic growth.[49] In addition, Papke (1990), using the marginal effective tax rate approach for data on five manufacturing industries in twenty-two states from 1975–82, finds that taxes have a negative effect on gross state product in four of the five industries. The elasticities of gross state product with respect to the marginal effective tax rate in these industries vary from 1.1 to 14.7.

ECONOMETRIC EVIDENCE: SUMMARY

The econometric evidence on the effects of taxes on business location, investment, and other macroeconomic variables is sufficiently mixed that various observers have drawn different conclusions about its implications. For example, Bartik (1991, 1994) is one of the strongest proponents of the view that taxes have important negative effects on various measures of business activity. He reviews fifty-seven studies of tax effects across states or localities and notes that 70 percent of the studies have at least one statistically significant negative tax effect. This figure increases to 92 percent when the sample is limited to studies that made the appropriate econometric controls for unobserved nontax differences across states. Bartik concludes that the "recent research suggests a consensus on the likely magnitude of tax effects on business location decisions. The long-run elasticity of business activity with respect to state and local taxes appears to lie in the range of −0.1 to −0.6 for intermetropolitan or interstate business location decisions" (1991, p. 43).[50] Similarly, Blair and Premus conclude that, "until recently, the conventional wisdom has been that taxes— and, by implication, other fiscal variables—do not deter industrial locations or economic growth. . . . However, most recent studies show tax-expenditure variables to be important" (1987, p. 82).[51]

Other observers are more cautious in drawing conclusions from the existing literature. For example, McGuire concludes that "the effects of state and local tax policy are so uncertain that concern over this issue should not be a driving force in general fiscal policy decisions" (1992, p. 458), and Wasylenko concludes that the "findings for the fiscal variables from these studies are perplexing and do not leave us with a clear conclusion." Wasylenko does note, however, that the evidence of significant tax effects is strongest for capital investment decisions, and he acknowledges the superiority of Papke's marginal effective tax rate approach over the average tax rate alternative. (As described above, Papke's work strongly supports the existence of significant tax effects on a variety of business decisions.) Wasylenko concludes that, "given this evidence, it is increasingly difficult to argue that business climate, however broadly defined, does not influence interregional firm locations" (1991, pp. 26–28). Similarly, Tannenwald argues that, "It is still too early to draw strong policy conclusions from these new findings. However, one can no longer summarily dismiss the notion that business tax differentials affect interstate location" (1993, p. 4).

For purposes of this book, the primary implication of the above discussion is that it would be inappropriate to dismiss the notion that taxes affect business location and investment decisions. Indeed, the empirical evidence described above is, at least to some extent, consistent with the view that a reasonable assumption to make in thinking about state tax policy toward business is that any given state can be approximated as a small open economy. As described above in detail, such an assumption has important implications for tax policy.

In addition, note that even if the concept of significant tax effects on the level of business activities in a state is accepted, one must be very careful in interpreting the policy implications of such a result. In particular, the results described above estimate the effects of a tax increase on business, holding service levels constant. The net effect of a tax increase used to finance an increase in public expenditures depends on the nature of the expenditures and the efficiency of service provision. Thus, as stressed by Bartik, "Tax increases would have a less negative effect on an area's business activity—or even a positive effect—if public services were simultaneously changed in the same direction" (1991, p. 44).[52] The implication of the above literature is certainly not that business tax increases are necessarily bad; rather, the essential message is that tax increases that are not offset by public expenditures that benefit business are likely to have negative effects on business activity.[53] Thus, Bartik concludes that, "For business tax cuts to boost a state economy, they must be financed by increases in personal taxes or reductions in spending that does not provide services valued by business" (1994, p. 853).[54]

In terms of state tax policy, this discussion suggests that source-based taxes on capital used within a state should be avoided. The implications for the choice between state sales and income taxes, however, are not clear. Recall that the typical state sales tax has a large capital tax component, as business purchases comprise a significant fraction of the sales tax base, estimated by Ring (1989) to average roughly 40 percent. At the same time, for large multistate firms, formula apportionment implies that the state corporate tax is less a tax on capital income earned within the state and more a tax on the factors in the apportionment formula—some combination of sales, property, and payroll.[55] For such firms, the corporate tax is tax on capital used in the state only to the extent that (1) property is in the apportionment formula, and (2) sales are in the formula, to the extent that the firm's sales consist of purchases by other businesses.[56] It is thus quite possible that capital income is taxed more heavily under the state sales tax than under the state corporate tax, although this would have to be determined on a state-by-state basis.

Other Business Tax Distortions

At the outset, it should again be noted that efficiency questions are inherently difficult to answer, as any business tax distorts a wide variety of business decisions. The best approach to analyzing tax policy for any given state would be to construct a comprehensive "general equilibrium model" of the state economy and perform numerical simulations that would analyze the effects of alternative tax policies on the residents of the state.[57] Even in this case, however, uncertainty about the effects of various parameter values used in the simulations would lead to uncertainty about the relative merits of alternative tax structures in terms of the efficiency criterion. In any event, the construction of such a model is far beyond the scope of this book, which instead focuses on identifying the most important distortions caused by the alternative business tax structures considered and draws on the existing literature to obtain some intuition as to how important they might be.

DISTORTION OF THE CAPITAL-LABOR MIX

Taxation of capital income in an open economy will discourage the use of capital, result in a lower overall capital stock, and grant an inefficient tax preference to labor-intensive industries.[58] One estimate of the associated efficiency loss is provided by Diewert (1987), who finds that the efficiency cost of business income taxation varies from 0.44 to 9.45 percent of output (depending on tax rates and parameter values). Again, the implications for the choice between state sales and income taxes depend on the extent to which capital goods are taxed under the two alternative approaches.

DISTORTIONS OF RISK-TAKING

Popular discussions of tax policy often assume that taxation reduces risk-taking, since the government appropriates a portion of the return to successful investments as increased tax revenue. This argument is, however, incomplete as it ignores the role of the government in sharing the risk associated with the uncertain returns to investment, since an unsuccessful investment will result in lower tax revenues from the investment or losses that are deducted against ordinary income. Indeed, in the simplest models of individual portfolio behavior—characterized by proportional income taxation with full loss offset and only two types of assets (safe and risky)—taxation unambiguously increases risk-taking. The intuition behind this somewhat counterintuitive result is that taxation does not alter the relative risk-expected return ratio, but government risk-sharing does reduce the variance of returns, thus encouraging more total risk-taking by the individual. If the government, due to superior risk-spreading opportunities, can assume risk costlessly, or at least at a lower cost than the individual, then overall (individual plus government) risk-taking increases, and this increase is desirable from a social perspective.[59]

The effect of taxation on risk-taking becomes theoretically ambiguous—even assuming that the government can assume risk costlessly—when the strict assumptions of the basic model are relaxed to include features such as progressive taxation, assets of various types, limits on loss offsets, taxation of inflationary gains, and taxation of capital gains upon realization (rather than as accrued) with exemption of gains transferred at death. Nevertheless, the overall income tax system may still encourage rather than discourage risk-taking. For example, such a result is obtained by Haliassos and Lyon (1993), who simulate the effects of reducing capital gains taxes while increasing taxes on interest and dividend income. They find that excess burdens actually increase by roughly 3 to 6 percent due to reduced government risk-sharing. Alternatively, in models in which the government cannot absorb risk more easily than the private sector, investment tends to be unaffected by changes in taxation; for example, such a neutrality result is obtained in the recent analysis by Kaplow (1994).[60] At a minimum, such results suggest that income taxation is not likely to have a significant negative effect on risk-taking.

A related issue is the effect on risk-taking of a tax that is based on wealth (rather than on income). In general, any tax effects on risk-taking tend to be lower under a wealth-based tax than under an equal-yield income tax. This result obtains because the extent of government risk-sharing is much smaller under the wealth-based tax, since wealth is taxed regardless of the income (or loss) attributable to investment of that wealth.[61] Thus, a corporate income tax is arguably preferable to a wealth-based franchise tax in terms of encouraging risk-taking.

DISTORTIONS OF THE CHOICE OF ORGANIZATIONAL FORM
Another efficiency cost that has received much attention in the public finance literature is the distortion of the choice of organizational form attributable to the use of corporate taxes on income (or corporate franchise taxes) rather than taxes that apply to businesses generally. Some recent research suggests that the excess burdens of this distortion may be quite high. For example, Jorgenson and Yun (1991) estimate that the efficiency cost of the U.S. corporate income tax is roughly equal to 45 percent of revenues, while Gravelle and Kotlikoff (1993) estimate this cost to be on the order of 100 percent of revenues.[62]

This criticism obviously applies to a state corporate income tax and to a corporate franchise tax since all of these taxes apply only to corporations. On the other hand, since the business component of the sales tax applies to both corporations and noncorporate entities (although presumably at different effective rates), the sales tax should not give rise to large distortions across such entities. Thus, smaller distortions of the choice of organizational form are an important advantage of sales taxation.

Given the existence of a business tax, an inefficiency that has received a great deal of attention in the public finance literature is the distortion of production methods attributable to the differential taxation of the income earned by different types of capital assets and the resulting distortions across different business sectors or industries. Indeed, a desire to "level the playing field" by taxing capital income uniformly—the goal of "neutral" taxation—was one of the primary rationales underlying the passage of the Tax Reform Act of 1986 (TRA86).[63] Most observers agree that the recent reform reduced tax differentials across assets and across business sectors.[64] Nevertheless, significant tax differentials remain, especially between investment generally and investment in owner-occupied housing, and between investment in depreciable assets and investment in intangible assets that have long useful lives but are expensed rather than depreciated.[65] Thus, a state corporate tax based on the federal tax would exacerbate the existing distortions across assets and business sectors associated with corporate income taxation at the national level. Moreover, as noted previously, since state income taxes would be imposed in addition to the federal income tax, the marginal distortions and efficiency costs associated with state income taxation would be relatively high.[66]

The application of the sales tax to business purchases also introduces a wide variety of distortions in business production decisions. The use of inputs that are subject to tax is discouraged, especially for goods that are subject to multiple layers of sales taxation in the production process and thus face high effective tax rates (higher than the statutory rate). Moreover, as noted previously, these distortions may be particularly large—even if the sales tax rate is relatively low—because they are assessed on a gross concept (sales) rather than on a net concept (such as income); that is, the effective income tax rate associated with even modest taxation of sales can be quite high. Such distortions also encourage inefficient "vertical integration," as firms produce their own inputs or engage in mergers in order to avoid the taxation of transactions between firms. In addition, to the extent that these sales tax differentials are shifted forward in the form of higher prices, consumer decisions are distorted as well, as consumption of the goods that are produced with heavily taxed inputs is discouraged.[67]

Finally, note that recent moves to increase the number of services subject to the sales tax would exacerbate this problem to the extent that services used by businesses rather than by consumers are included in the tax base. Thus, to the extent that business rather than consumer services are included in the tax base, expansion of the sales tax in this direction could very well be undesirable on efficiency grounds. In addition, the use of a state corporate franchise tax under a sales tax regime also creates its own set of distortions across business sectors, because a franchise tax creates tax disadvantages for sectors characterized by capital-intensive firms.

DISTORTIONS OF THE FINANCING DECISION

Another criticism frequently made of the corporate income tax (and a net wealth–based franchise tax) is that it encourages debt finance over equity finance, since deductions are allowed for interest payments but not for dividends paid (and debt is deductible from the base of the franchise tax). As a result, the allocation of risk-bearing is distorted; in particular, firms are more likely to incur a costly bankruptcy. Gordon and Malkiel (1981) estimate that the cost of this distortion could be on the order of 10 percent of corporate tax revenues. Again, this distortion does not arise under the sales tax since that tax applies to business purchases whether they are financed with debt or with equity.[68]

Note that a state income tax system might be modified in order to reduce this distortion; for example, dividends received might not be included in the individual income tax base. This would reduce the extent to which the enactment of a state corporate tax would exacerbate the distortions of the federal corporate tax.[69] However, the main effect of such an approach would be to extend tax relief to dividends attributable to income earned out of state and thus not subject to the state corporate income tax. In addition, deviations from the federal tax base would increase administrative, compliance, and enforcement costs, and the tax exemption of an important component of capital income would likely be perceived as unfair.

DISTORTIONS OF PAYOUT DECISIONS

It should also be noted that the combination of a corporate income tax and a personal income tax distorts firm decisions regarding dividend payouts. Specifically, such a system favors retained earnings over dividends, since the latter are fully taxed as ordinary income while the former are taxed as capital gains and thus benefit from tax deferral and, in the case of gains transferred at death, complete exemption from tax.[70] A tax bias toward retained earnings creates inefficiencies in the allocation of capital if new and emerging firms, which typically have little or no retained earnings, have better investment prospects than established firms with significant retained earnings.

Individual Tax Distortions

The discussion above indicates that the alternative tax systems examined in this book distort a wide variety of business decisions. In addition, these tax systems, like virtually all others, distort a number of consumer decisions as well. The following discussion considers a number of these distortions of individual behavior, which are attributable primarily to the personal income tax in the case of a state income tax system and to the sales tax on consumer goods in the case of the typical state sales tax system.

DISTORTIONS OF INDIVIDUAL LOCATION DECISIONS

In general, the overall level of taxation, relative to benefits received, plays the largest role in affecting individual location decisions. It is generally assumed that individuals are considerably less mobile than is capital, and that high-income individuals are more mobile than are lower-income individuals. The latter consideration suggests that a highly progressive individual income tax—especially if the funds were used to finance transfer payments—would be undesirable at the state level because it would tend to drive high-income individuals out of the state.

DISTORTIONS OF CONSUMER PURCHASING DECISIONS

All of the tax alternatives will distort consumer purchasing decisions, although on balance it appears likely that the sales tax (on both consumer and business purchases) is somewhat more distortionary than the income tax option (including both a personal and a corporate income tax). In the latter case, any forward shifting of the corporate income tax implies that consumers will face artificially inflated prices for goods produced by the corporate sector, especially capital-intensive ones sold in state rather than national markets. In the case of the sales tax, inefficiencies arise because different goods are subject to tax at different rates. An obvious reason for this is that certain consumer goods are exempt (e.g., goods that are classified as necessities and many services, including those produced by the government). In addition, consumer prices will reflect sales taxation of business inputs at different effective rates. In particular, sales taxation of business inputs implies that tax cascading can occur since inputs may be subject to tax several times in the production process, giving rise to relatively high overall effective tax rates.

It is interesting to note that an efficient system of sales taxes does not require neutrality; rather, goods that are demanded relatively inelastically should be taxed relatively highly (because the possibilities for substitution are low).[71] In marked contrast, the pattern of exemptions in most states is based on equity considerations that generally result in exemptions (rather than relatively high rates) for goods with relatively low price elasticities (that is, necessities). This increases the likelihood that the efficiency costs of the sales tax system are relatively high, although it improves the equity properties of the tax.[72] Equally important, a large number of exclusions from the consumer portion of the sales tax base implies that the tax rate applied to that base in order to obtain any given level of revenue must be rather high, relative to the rate that must be applied to an income tax with a more comprehensive base.[73] As emphasized above, high tax rates lead to disproportionately large negative effects on economic efficiency.

In addition, the issue of cross-border purchases arises in the context of a state sales tax. Cross-border purchases, especially from mail order firms that do not have an established presence in a state and thus do not have to collect sales tax on purchases by in-state residents, are another potentially important source of economic distortions. The potential for such efficiency costs, as well as the loss in economic activity that arises from purchases diverted from in-state retail establishments, suggests that increases in the sales tax rate in a state might result in noticeable inefficiencies from this source.[74]

It should be noted, however, that the income tax distorts some consumption decisions as well. In particular, the very generous tax treatment of investment in owner-occupied housing and of various employer-provided fringe benefits distorts individual consumption decisions toward these tax-favored activities.

DISTORTIONS OF SAVINGS DECISIONS

One of the most telling criticisms of an income tax is that it distorts the present/future consumption choice; in other words, by taxing the return to savings, an income tax distorts individual decisions toward current consumption and away from saving. (Indeed, the combination of a personal income tax and a corporate income tax double-taxes certain forms of saving.) Some estimates of the size of this distortion are quite large. For example, simulation results presented by Summers (1981) suggest that a switch from an income tax to an equal-revenue cash flow consumption tax results in steady-state welfare gains that range from 11.3 to 11.8 percent of lifetime income. Simulations by Auerbach and Kotlikoff (1987), in the context of a similar but much more complicated model (with more conservative parameter values), indicate that a switch from an income tax to a cash flow consumption tax increases steady-state welfare by 2.3 percent of lifetime resources (including the value of leisure). On the other hand, some recent research, such as the studies by Hall (1988) and Skinner and Feenberg (1990), suggests that the sensitivity of savings to the real after-tax rate of return is fairly low. Nevertheless, much of the interest in direct taxation on the basis of consumption at the national level is attributable to a desire to eliminate the taxation of saving inherent in an income tax.

If a state sales tax applied only to retail sales, one could argue that it was a type of consumption tax and thus does not distort the present/future consumption or savings choice. However, as noted above, much of the base of the typical state sales tax is business purchases. As stressed by McDonald (1989), this suggests that the typical state sales tax has a base that is in a very rough sense similar to that under an income tax. Indeed, McDonald shows that, in a closed economy, a comprehensive income tax is by definition equivalent to a sales tax that is applied uniformly and comprehensively to both consumption and investment goods. This result obtains because the two tax bases, if defined comprehensively, are identical. Under these circumstances, the aggregate budget constraint for the closed economy implies that all income in a given time period (the comprehensive income tax base) must be spent either on individual consumption goods or saved by individuals and then spent by businesses on investment goods (the base of a comprehensive sales tax on both consumption and investment goods). This naturally implies that the incidence of a uniform and comprehensive income tax would be identical to that of a uniform and comprehensive sales tax applied to both consumption and investment goods. Alternatively, since saving and investment are equal in this simple model, the base of a sales tax that applies only to consumption goods would be equivalent to the base of a comprehensive income tax that allows a full deduction for all saving.[75]

This equivalence result does not hold precisely for a variety of reasons; in particular, no state even approximates a closed economy so that savings are not necessarily spent on in-state investment goods (and some consumption purchases are for out-of-state goods), and both the business and the consumer portions of the sales tax are neither comprehensive nor uniform. However, the large fraction of sales tax revenue typically collected from business purchases suggests that the indirect burden of the sales tax on saving may be quite large—perhaps even larger than would obtain under an income tax. As a result, it is impossible to say whether a state income tax or the typical state sales tax is worse in terms of distorting the savings decisions of consumers. It would be difficult, however, to make a convincing case that a state income tax would be significantly more distortionary than the typical state sales tax.

DISTORTIONS OF THE LABOR-LEISURE CHOICE

Both the sales tax and income tax options distort individual choices between labor and leisure, where leisure is defined broadly to include any type of non-market activity. These taxes discourage work effort in the marketplace either by reducing net wages or by increasing the prices of goods that can be purchased with labor income. In general, an income tax is less distortionary of the labor/leisure choice than is a consumption-based tax, because the income tax base is larger since it includes capital income and thus has a lower tax rate. However, consistent with the discussion in the previous subsection, the inclusion of a large fraction of business purchases in the state sales tax base makes this comparison ambiguous.

The recent empirical evidence on the effects of taxation on labor supply suggests that these effects are not as large as once believed. Hausman (1981) indicates that the federal income tax has large negative effects on labor supply and on economic efficiency, and that these effects are most pronounced at high income levels where individuals are subject to high progressive tax rates. More recently, however, Triest (1990) and MaCurdy, Green, and Paarsh (1990) have argued that Hausman's results are flawed and have concluded that the federal tax system has a fairly small effect on labor supply.[76] More generally, the labor economics literature suggests that the supply of labor is fairly insensitive to changes in net wages. In a sense, this is not too surprising since a wage change has two opposing effects on labor supply. For example, a wage increase encourages labor supply because the opportunity cost of leisure has increased (the "substitution" effect of the wage increase), but it also decreases labor supply because the individual has more income at any given level of work effort and elects to spend at least some of that income on additional leisure (the "income effect" of the wage increase). It is interesting to note that wage increases (or tax cuts) for individuals at high income levels appear to reduce labor supply; that is, for such individuals, the "income effect" of the wage increase apparently outweighs the substitution effect. The opposite is true at lower income levels, as increases in wages increase labor supply.[77] In the aggregate, the empirical evidence suggests that a proportional increase in net wages would have relatively little effect on total labor supply.[78] The message of this literature is that the labor supply effects of a proportional—or at most a very modestly progressive—state income tax would not likely be very large.

DISTORTIONS OF HUMAN CAPITAL ACCUMULATION DECISIONS
Finally, both sales and income taxes distort decisions regarding investments in "physical capital" (savings accounts, stocks, bonds, real estate, etc.), relative to investments in "human capital" (expenditures on education and training that are made in the hope that they will increase an individual's marketable skills and thus increase future earnings). It is difficult, however, to characterize the nature of these tax distortions (even if one assumes that the sales tax is a true consumption tax).

Most analyses of human capital accumulation decisions assume that the primary cost of increasing one's human capital is foregone earnings—the wages lost during the time spent on education or training (direct costs such as tuition, books, and fees are ignored). In this case, a standard result is that under proportional taxation, the returns to investment in human capital are effectively tax-exempt under both income and sales taxes. The intuition behind this result is that such investment is effectively treated very generously in that an implicit full "deduction" is allowed for the investment of foregone earnings, and the value of this up-front deduction offsets in present value terms the future taxation of the increased labor earnings attributable to the investment in human capital.[79] The key factor then is the taxation of the return to investment in nonhuman or "physical" capital. A proportional sales tax is neutral with respect to the human versus physical capital decision as the returns to both types of investment are untaxed. In contrast, a proportional income tax favors investment in human capital, since only the returns to investment in physical capital are subject to tax.

The distortionary effects of encouraging too much human capital formation under the income tax may be large. Driffill and Rosen (1983) estimate that the excess burden of a proportional income tax with a 20 percent rate is roughly 80 percent of revenues, and that most of this welfare cost (60 to 65 percent) is attributable to distortions of human capital accumulation decisions. In particular, distortions of human versus physical capital decisions result in much larger efficiency costs than distortions of labor supply decisions. They also suggest that a proportional consumption tax is considerably more efficient than an income tax once human capital accumulation decisions are taken into account. However, these results can be viewed as a short-run phenomenon, since they assume that interest rates are not affected by the level of investment. Davies and Whalley (1991) construct a model in which the increased investment in physical capital under the income tax reduces the interest rate in the economy, which in turn reduces the incentive to invest in physical capital to the point where decisions regarding human versus physical capital accumulation are no longer distorted in the long run.

This literature is, however, far from conclusive, as there are many ways in which these models of taxes and human capital accumulation might be extended to shed more light on the income tax versus sales tax debate. The effects of progressive rates could be analyzed; for example, human capital investment could be discouraged if foregone earnings are "deducted" early in life at relatively low tax rates with the associated income taxed at higher rates during prime earning years. Similarly, human capital investment may be discouraged if returns to investment in human capital are more uncertain than returns to physical capital. These latter two factors suggest that the income tax bias favoring human capital investment may be desirable—at least in the absence of expenditure policies explicitly supporting education, vocational training, and so forth. Hamilton (1987) argues that an income tax may be preferable to a consumption tax because it offsets the tendency toward underinvestment in human capital with relatively uncertain returns. Finally, the roles of direct costs and depreciation of human capital, both of which are generally nondeductible, need to be examined further; for example, Nerlove, Razin, Sadka, and von Weizacker (1993) argue that when all costs are nondeductible direct costs, the income tax discourages investment in human capital relative to investment in physical capital.[80] Thus, it is difficult to make an unambiguous case favoring either the income tax or the sales tax in terms of minimizing distortions of individual decisions regarding human capital accumulation.

Distortions of Government Expenditure Choices

The tax system affects choices regarding the level of state government expenditures in a number of important ways. All are related to the absence of an explicit link between government services received and taxes paid. The first is through the use of nonbenefit taxes. As noted above, some use of nonbenefit taxes is inevitable, as the benefits of many public services cannot be allocated in an unambiguous fashion and many other public services are explicitly intended to be redistributive. Nevertheless, it should be noted that the use of nonbenefit taxes creates incentives for inefficient levels of government service provision. These arise because individuals who benefit from public services without paying full price for them face an obvious incentive to support expansion of those services, while individuals who pay more in taxes than they receive face an obvious incentive to oppose government expenditures. In theory, either underprovision or overprovision of public services can result. However, many observers have noted that the benefits of public services are often highly concentrated, while the costs are usually spread out across the entire population.[81] The implication is that the recipients of public services face a strong incentive to support expansion of the public sector, while there is a much weaker incentive for the general taxpaying population to oppose such expansion. On the other hand, the recent trend toward highly vocal opposition of tax increases suggests that this paradigm may be less applicable than in the past. In any case, the main point is that the use of nonbenefit taxes creates all sorts of incentives for inefficient levels of government service provision and thus should be avoided when possible.

Another way that the choice of tax system affects the level of government services is through the different degrees of "visibility" of alternative taxes. In general, taxes that are highly visible in the sense that taxpayers must pay them directly, preferably only once or a few times a year, are believed to be desirable on efficiency grounds. The rationale is that taxpayers, who are the "consumers" of public services, should see clearly the social cost of providing those services, so that decisions regarding the allocation of resources from the private to the public sector can be made more rationally. This argument supports the use of highly visible taxes such as user charges, a personal income tax, and the property tax. It applies to a lesser extent to the retail sales tax, since it is paid in thousands of small "installments" and is thus less visible than a tax that must be paid on an annual basis. At the same time, this rationale argues against the use of business taxes, including corporate income and franchise taxes and the sales taxation of business purchases, on the grounds that the burdens of such taxes are hidden in the prices of consumption goods or in the form of lower factor payments to landowners and labor.[82] By comparison, "hidden" taxes are desirable only if there is a systematic bias in the political system against the provision of public services (especially those of a redistributive nature) so that any "encouragement" of an expansion of the public sector made possible with the use of such hidden taxes is desirable. This argument does not seem compelling.

A related point is that the use of multiple tax instruments—that is, both a state sales tax and a state income tax—may facilitate the growth of government. This argument relies on a type of "fiscal illusion," under which state residents are more likely to perceive their tax burdens accurately under a single tax than under a system that raises the same revenue but does so using two relatively smaller, and thus less noticeable, taxes. On the other hand, raising revenues with a modestly progressive income tax rather than the typical state sales tax might result in lower levels of expenditures, as the tax burden would be shifted to higher income individuals with greater political power to resist spending increases.[83] On balance, it seems unlikely that a change in the tax mix would have a significant effect on expenditure levels.

In addition, the time path of the growth of the revenues obtained from the tax system may influence the level of public services. Under a progressive income tax, revenues will increase with economic growth as individuals are pushed into higher income tax brackets. Although some have argued that such "automatic" increases in revenues are desirable because they make it easier to fund higher levels of government expenditure, the currently more popular view is that such expenditure increases lead to too much public spending and are thus undesirable (unless they are explicitly deemed desirable by the electorate). Accordingly, one can argue that efficiency in public service provision is most encouraged by a tax system that increases roughly proportionately with the size of the economy rather than at a faster rate. This suggests that a highly progressive rate structure is not desirable under an income tax, and that the income bracket widths that determine the income levels at which higher marginal rates become operative should increase with growth in the economy (unless a compelling case can be made that the ratio of government expenditures to state income should be increasing). Alternatively, the sales tax should be structured so that its base grows roughly proportionately with income.

Finally, the use of taxes on mobile capital—and to a lesser extent taxes on relatively mobile high-income individuals—may result in an underprovision of government services. The rationale is that the government is reluctant to drive out mobile factors of production through the use of nonbenefit taxes and thus cuts back on such taxes and the services they finance in order to avoid deleterious effects on the state capital stock and the productivity of the state labor force.[84] Again, this line of reasoning supports the use of benefit taxes (especially user charges) and taxes on relatively immobile factors, primarily local labor and/or consumers, rather than taxes on business capital. However, as discussed above, a countervailing force encouraging overconsumption of public services is present to the extent that taxes on capital are perceived to be exported to out-of-state residents.

CHAPTER 4
Equity and Other Issues

The previous chapter evaluated the state sales and income tax options in terms of the criteria of tax exportability and economic efficiency. This chapter continues the comparison of the two alternative approaches to state taxation, focusing first on the tax equity issue and then turning to a variety of other questions.

EQUITY

Equity: Tax Fairness and the Potential for Redistribution at the State Level

As discussed in chapter 3, two basic principles are commonly used to evaluate tax structures from the perspective of equity. The first is the benefit principle, which asserts that taxes should be assessed in accordance with the benefits received from public services. The second is the ability-to-pay principle, which asserts that taxes should be assessed according to an accurate measure of ability to pay, and that the tax burden should increase with that measure. At the national level, virtually all discussions of tax policy focus exclusively on the ability-to-pay criterion. This is the case for at least two reasons. First, the benefit principle would be exceedingly difficult to apply to most national government services, since such services are often "public goods" in the technical sense—they are consumed jointly with few or no congestion effects as the size of the population increases, and it is difficult or impossible to exclude individuals from enjoying their benefits.[1] Under such circumstances, determining the benefits of public services received and then assessing a national individually based tax that would correspond to benefits received would be virtually impossible. Second, income redistribution, which is commonly viewed as an explicit national policy goal of the federal tax system, is inherently incompatible with taxation according to benefits received. Accordingly, most analysts evaluate the fairness of the federal tax structure from an ability-to-pay perspective.

However, exclusive reliance on the ability-to-pay principle does not extend automatically to the state (and local) level. Indeed, the conventional wisdom, attributable to Musgrave (1959) and Oates (1968) among others, is that income redistribution should be the sole (or at least the primary) responsibility of the central government, and that subnational governments should rely on benefit taxes to the maximum extent possible. Another interpretation of this dictum is that state and local governments should focus their attention on efficiency in resource allocation, which is promoted by the use of benefit rather than ability-to-pay taxation, and leave the task of redistribution to the federal government. (Note that benefit taxes can in principle be progressive, regressive, or proportional, depending on how rapidly the demand for public services increases with income. Since there are very few data on this issue, it is difficult to determine the progressivity of a tax system based on the benefit principle.)

The primary rationale for the argument that redistributive efforts should be focused at the national level is the belief that individual mobility is sufficiently great to doom any subnational attempts to redistribute income. For example, if a single state (especially a relatively small one) attempts to engage in a significant amount of income redistribution, it will lose high-income individuals who will migrate to other jurisdictions in order to avoid a net fiscal loss. At the same time, the state will gain low-income individuals who are attracted by the state's redistributive policies. As a result, the tax base will shrink while the number of individuals qualifying for the transfers will increase, and the extent to which any redistribution is effected will be limited. In addition, note that these migratory effects will exacerbate after-tax income differentials to the extent that income levels are correlated with skill levels. That is, outmigration of high-income individuals will reduce the supply of high-skilled individuals and thus drive up their wages, while inmigration of low-income individuals will increase the supply of low-skilled workers and thus drive down their wages.[2] In addition, outmigration of high-skilled individuals may reduce the productivity of low-skilled individuals, further depressing their wages. These changes in the structure of gross wages will offset the reduction in the after-tax income differentials, which is the goal of taxation according to ability to pay. In the limiting case of perfect factor mobility—that is, when labor is so mobile that all wage differentials at a given skill level are eliminated entirely—the tax-transfer system will be completely ineffective in altering the after-tax income distribution.[3]

This point is stressed by Feldstein and Vaillant (1994), who recently conducted an empirical investigation of the extent to which states in the United States can redistribute income through the use of progressive income taxation. Feldstein and Vaillant examine the extent to which differences in progressivity in income tax rates, corrected to reflect the effects of federal income tax deductibility, are offset by changes in gross wages in such a way that the net distribution of income across states is left unchanged. In addition, they examine the speed of the adjustment to the new equilibrium. Their estimates indicate that the adjustment of gross wages to differences in progressivity is roughly complete and that this adjustment occurs quickly—within the space of a few years. Feldstein and Vaillant conclude that "states cannot redistribute income for a period of even a few years." This in turn implies that differences in the relative progressivity of state taxes "by altering the structure of employment in the state and distorting the mix of labor inputs used by the firms in the state, create deadweight.efficiency losses without achieving any net redistribution of income" (1994, pp. 29–30). They attribute redistributive policies on the part of many states to the illusion, held by politicians, voters, or both groups within a state, that such policies can be effective in altering the distribution of income.[4]

A related point is that local redistribution is viewed as undesirable because the changes in migration patterns described above inefficiently distort the allocation of resources across jurisdictions; that is, individual location decisions become partly based on fiscal considerations and are thus inefficiently altered by the system of redistributive taxation. Finally, some observers, such as Ladd and Doolittle (1982) and Peterson and Rom (1990), argue that support of low-income households is largely a national public good—that is, the benefits of income redistribution are national in scope—which implies that from a theoretical perspective, income redistribution policy should be carried out at the national level.

The implications of this point of view are twofold. First, to the extent possible, benefit taxes should be used to finance state services. In particular, user charges (discussed in detail in chapter 6) should be utilized to the maximum extent possible. Second, any redistributive tax and transfer policies should be limited due to concerns regarding migration effects and inefficient location decisions. For example, rough proportionality of the tax system might be viewed as a reasonable goal, and highly progressive state tax systems are likely to have negative consequences on the supply of labor to the state, especially highly skilled and well-compensated labor.

These very strong conclusions have not gone unchallenged in the literature. Pauly (1973) argues that income redistribution is to some extent a local rather than a national public good—that is, altruistic individuals are more concerned about the well-being of the poor in their neighborhoods than those who reside at more distant locations. Such preferences provide a rationale for income redistribution through the use of ability-to-pay taxes at the state and local levels. The final result will be that states whose residents are relatively altruistic toward the poor will tend to have more progressive tax systems. Similarly, Break (1980) notes that differences in tastes for income redistribution across states can be accommodated only if the states supplement federal tax and transfer programs with their own programs. Goodspeed (1989) uses an economic model of the individual location decisions within a metropolitan area to suggest that the efficiency losses attributable to ability-to-pay taxes at the local level may be relatively small. Chernick (1996) constructs an empirical model that suggests that mobility of high-income individuals is an issue only for states that are in close geographic proximity to high–income tax states. More generally, all analysts agree that the scope for redistributive taxation according to the ability-to-pay principle increases with the size of the taxing jurisdiction, since the costs of outmigration to avoid the tax increase correspondingly. Thus, the scope for redistributive taxation is greater in larger states than in smaller states. Note, however, that the opposite is true to the extent that redistributive tax and transfer programs in border states—especially Texas and California—would increase the immigration of potential recipients of transfer programs.[5] Finally, as noted in the previous discussion of the "exportability" of state taxes, deductibility of state income taxes against federal tax liability implies that the costs to high-income individuals of a redistributive tax and transfer system are smaller than suggested by the structure of marginal state tax rates.[6]

Equity: Distribution of the Tax Burden

The considerations noted at the end of the above discussion, when combined with popular perceptions regarding what constitutes fairness in taxation, suggest that even if application of the benefit principle is possible in some cases, ability to pay is very likely to be the primary criterion used to evaluate the fairness of a state tax system. Application of this criterion obviously assumes that ability to pay can be measured accurately. Most studies that analyze the equity of a tax system focus on the distribution of taxes paid as a function of measured annual income, examining whether a tax system is proportional, progressive, or regressive with respect to annual income. These results are reviewed briefly in this section. The discussion then turns to an important qualification of such results that has been stressed in some recent economic research. Specifically, several authors have argued that conventional estimates of the regressivity of the sales tax are overstated—as is the progressivity of the income tax—by calculations of tax burdens that assume that annual income is the appropriate measure of ability to pay. These studies argue instead that measures more closely related to lifetime income provide a better indicator of the ability to pay taxes. Since these arguments have important implications for the assessment of alternative state tax systems, including especially the choice between the sales tax and the personal income tax, they are described and discussed in some detail in this subsection.

CONVENTIONAL STATE TAX BURDEN ESTIMATES

The critical factor in the standard approach to estimating the distribution of the burden of a state tax system is that the statutory incidence of a tax—who legally pays it—may be very different from its economic incidence—who ultimately bears the cost of the tax once market adjustments have taken place. An incidence analysis determines the distribution of the tax burden among different groups of individuals, typically classified by measured annual income, given a set (or sets) of assumptions regarding the pattern of market adjustments to a change in a tax structure. Incidence analyses can be either short run, in which case certain types of market adjustments to changes in the tax system are ignored, or they can be long run, in which case all tax-induced market adjustments are taken into consideration. The latter case is the more relevant one for policy discussions of a fundamental reform of a state tax system and is thus the focus of the analysis below.

A LIFETIME VIEW OF TAX INCIDENCE

The result that a tax system that relies primarily on proportional consumption-based taxes is regressive with respect to annual income is of course entirely consistent with most of the incidence literature, since the ratio of consumption to income clearly declines with annual income. However, some recent studies have questioned the theoretical rationale underlying these results and have concluded that consumption-based taxes (such as general sales taxes) are in fact likely to be roughly proportional with respect to an improved measure of ability to pay.

These studies argue that the regressivity of sales taxes is overstated when annual income is used as the measure of ability to pay.[7] Three different arguments are used to support this contention. The first is based on an economic theory developed by Friedman (1957) known as the "permanent income hypothesis." This theory begins with the observation that annual income fluctuates considerably for a number of reasons. For example, in some occupations, such as those in which pay is partially or fully based on sales commissions or is otherwise closely related to either general or firm-specific business conditions, income fluctuations are simply a characteristic of the job. Similarly, income may fluctuate due to variations in bonuses or in overtime pay or will be temporarily low during periods of short-term unemployment.

The permanent income hypothesis postulates that individuals base their consumption plans on an estimate of permanent income—defined as average income over a moderately long time horizon—rather than on annual income. The key implication of the permanent income hypothesis is that, for any given level of income variation, fluctuations in consumption can be expected to be less pronounced. Thus, for example, an individual whose income declines temporarily from its average or permanent level will draw down savings to smooth consumption. Similarly, the theory argues that a significant fraction of an increase in income would typically be saved if that increase were expected to be temporary.

One implication of the greater stability of consumption relative to income is that measures of the regressivity of sales taxes based on annual income will be more pronounced than those that would be obtained if the measure were based instead on an estimate of average or permanent income. For example, if an individual's annual income is temporarily low, consumption and thus sales taxes will fall proportionately less than the decline in income. As a result, the sales tax system will appear to be more regressive than it would be, say, if income and consumption taxes were averaged over several years. That is, the individual will appear to be poorer than he or she is in terms of permanent income, which in turn implies that the sales tax burden will be artificially high. The same effect occurs if annual income is temporarily high and consumption and sales taxes do not increase proportionately as much as income; that is, the measured ratio of taxes paid to annual income will be artificially low.

The second argument used to support the contention that annual income measures of ability to pay overstate the regressivity of sales taxes is based on the "life-cycle" theory of consumption and saving. This theory in essence extends the permanent income hypothesis to an individual's entire lifetime and postulates three phases of consumption and saving over the life cycle. During each of these phases, consumption and savings decisions are assumed to be based on an estimate of lifetime income. In the first phase, individuals borrow to fund consumption early in life when earnings are relatively low, especially if they are obtaining schooling or other forms of job training. In the second phase, which covers the prime earning years, individuals save in order to retire debt accumulated during their youth and to fund retirement consumption (and perhaps the making of bequests). In the third phase of the life cycle, retirees consume primarily by drawing down the assets accumulated during the second phase (note that during this phase individuals who are quite wealthy can nevertheless have relatively low annual incomes). Under the life-cycle theory, the appropriate measure of current ability-to-pay taxes is thus not annual but lifetime income, defined as the present value of lifetime earnings plus the present value of inheritances and gifts received.

Some empirical support for these views is provided by the fact that annual income tends to fluctuate considerably more than annual consumption. In addition, Hall and Mishkin (1982) estimate that 80 percent of consumption is determined by lifetime income and the remainder by current income. Also, lifetime income endowments tend to be more stable than annual earnings, which in turn implies that distributions calculated using the former concept will be characterized by less inequality than those calculated using the latter measure. For example, Blomquist (1981) finds 32 to 42 percent less inequality in the value of lifetime labor endowments than in annual labor endowments.

If lifetime income is the appropriate measure of ability to pay, burden estimates based on annual income will, as in the case of fluctuating incomes, overstate the regressivity of a sales tax. For example, in the first and third phases of the life cycle (youth and the retirement years), an individual of any level of lifetime income will have a relatively low annual income, while consumption and thus sales taxes paid will be high relative to annual income. On the other hand, in the second phase of the life cycle (the prime earning and saving years), an individual of any level of lifetime income will have a relatively high annual income, while consumption and thus sales taxes paid will be low relative to annual income. Thus, a perhaps significant portion of the regressivity of the sales tax, when measured in terms of annual income, simply reflects life-cycle effects rather than a tax burden that declines in proportionate terms as ability to pay increases.[8] Indeed, Casperson and Metcalf (1994) show that, neglecting bequests and inheritances, a truly comprehensive consumption tax is by definition proportional with respect to lifetime income.[9]

Although most of the following discussion will focus on these two arguments, a third point, made by those who contend that the regressivity of sales taxes is overstated when annual income is used as the measure of ability to pay, should also be noted. This point arises because the measure of annual income used in most incidence studies is likely to be understated. For example, Schwab (1990) argues that the income levels reported in the Consumer Expenditure Survey are likely to understate true income levels by as much as 26 percent (while capturing the level of consumption expenditures much more accurately). Alternatively, some estimates of income are based on adjusted gross income (or some similar concept) as reported on federal tax returns, perhaps supplemented by additional information relevant to a calculation of net income. The problem with this approach is that any measure of regressivity based on federal tax return data will (unless adjusted) be subject to the same flaws in measuring annual income that characterize the federal tax base measure. Unfortunately, adjusted gross income falls considerably short of a comprehensive measure of annual income. This was especially true prior to passage of the TRA86, as a significant number of individuals who were not poor by any reasonable definition of ability to pay were nevertheless able to report very low or even negative annual incomes through the use of various tax "loopholes" or "shelters." Since such "low-income" individuals would typically pay a significant amount of sales taxes, their inclusion in the analysis would result in a considerable overstatement of the regressivity of a sales tax.

This point is recognized explicitly in many state incidence studies, but attempts to correct for such problems in measuring income accurately are not particularly satisfactory. For example, Fritz (1989) notes that the 1984 sample used in his incidence analysis attempts to exclude "tax sheltered" families by eliminating households with "sharply negative income." The average income of households deleted from the sample is $-\$28,000$. However, it would appear that such an approach captures only the most aggressive tax avoiders. Perhaps a significant number of families still included in the sample have measured income levels that are artificially low and thus have a ratio of sales tax burden to annual income that is artificially high.

A number of additional income measurement problems further complicate the issue. In many cases, measured income does not include transfers received. Although the inclusion of such items might seem counterintuitive, it is important to realize that such transfers must be included in any measure of ability to pay if horizontal and vertical equity comparisons are to be accurate. For example, it is clear that a family that earns $10,000 and has additional income or in-kind transfers with a value of $3,000 is better off than a family that has only an earned income of $10,000. However, in most incidence analyses, such items are at best only partially included in the measure of annual income used. Thus, to the extent such items are omitted from the income measure, the ratio of sales taxes paid to measured annual income is again artificially overstated.

In addition to the problems caused by tax shelters and uncounted income transfers, one could argue that income as reported for federal tax purposes is inaccurately measured in a wide variety of ways. For example, adjusted gross income does not include a variety of fringe benefits, unrealized capital gains, tax-exempt interest, the imputed rent from investments from owner-occupied housing, and various adjustments for inflation.[10] The net effect of all these omissions is difficult to judge, but it seems unlikely to reverse the conclusion that real economic income for those whose reported annual income is very low relative to their consumption is likely to be understated.

Finally, note that income reported for federal tax purposes by definition does not include income earned in the "underground economy." Although such tax evasion occurs at all income levels, it seems likely that at least some of the regressivity of the sales tax is attributable to underreporting of income by those whose annual income appears to be very low.

Some recent research has focused on the construction of alternative measures of ability to pay and tax incidence that deal with the first two problems—and to some extent with the third as well.[11] Two alternative approaches, each of which attempts to construct a measure of ability to pay that is more closely related to permanent or lifetime income than annual income, have been utilized. The first simply uses annual consumption as the measure of ability to pay, on the grounds that the permanent income hypothesis predicts that annual consumption is based on an individual's estimate of permanent income (or indeed lifetime income), and thus serves as a better measure of ability to pay than does annual income.[12] The second approach uses data on individual age, wages, and asset holdings to estimate a lifetime earnings path and to calculate an estimate of lifetime income.[13] In each case, the regressivity or progressivity of various taxes is calculated with respect to the "improved" lifetime measure of ability to pay, and the results are compared to calculations using the traditional approach based on annual income.[14]

The results of these studies call into serious question the conventional wisdom that sales taxes are highly regressive with respect to ability to pay. One set of results examines the effects of excise taxes on items such as motor fuels, alcohol, and tobacco. For example, Poterba (1989) follows the first of the two approaches described above—that is, he assumes that annual consumption is a reasonable proxy for permanent or lifetime income, and that the latter provides a much better indicator of a household's economic status than does annual income. He first obtains the standard result that each of these three excise taxes will be highly regressive relative to annual income because the income share devoted to purchases of the taxed good declines with income. For example, the income share of gasoline for the lowest quintile in his sample averages 15.0 percent and declines uniformly to 2.8 percent for the highest quintile. In marked contrast, when measured as a share of total consumption expenditures, gasoline and alcohol purchases are a roughly constant fraction of income over the first four quintiles, with a relatively small decline for the fifth quintile. For gasoline, the consumption share of the lowest quintile is 6.0 percent, ranges between 6.6 and 7.2 percent for the next three quintiles, and then drops to 3.9 percent for the top quintile; a similar pattern obtains for alcohol consumption. Interestingly, although most of the regressivity of gasoline and alcohol taxes is eliminated when consumption is used as the measure of ability to pay, taxes on tobacco remain regressive (although the degree of regressivity declines). Specifically, the annual income share of tobacco expenditures declines uniformly from 4.6 to 0.5 percent, while the annual consumption share declines uniformly from 2.2 to 0.7 percent. That is, it appears that tobacco consumption declines with income regardless of whether an annual or a lifetime measure of income is utilized. In summary, Poterba concludes that from the perspective of lifetime incidence analysis, "these taxes are therefore much less regressive than is usually thought" (1989, p. 326).[15]

A similar conclusion is reached by Lyon and Schwab (1995) who use the alternative approach of estimating lifetime income (including transfers received) from the age, income, asset, and other characteristics of a sample of households taken from the PSID survey. They conclude that the regressivity of alcohol taxes is reduced when a lifetime perspective is adopted, but the regressivity of tobacco taxes is quite similar regardless of whether a lifetime or an annual measure of income is used. In addition, Lyon and Schwab show that incidence estimates are little affected if income averaged over a five-year period is used (rather than annual income) as a measure of ability to pay; accordingly, they conclude that most of the differences in the estimates of the regressivity of the alcohol tax are due to life-cycle effects rather than transitory income fluctuations. This in turn implies that life-cycle effects, not transitory income fluctuations, provide the primary justification for using a lifetime rather than an annual approach to tax incidence analysis.

The second set of results focuses on the regressivity of a general sales tax. For example, Metcalf (1994) assumes that annual consumption is an adequate proxy for lifetime income and thus is the best measure of ability to pay. Metcalf's model accounts for the federal income tax deductibility of state income taxes and sales taxes (prior to the passage of the TRA86). He notes that the use of annual consumption as the measure of ability to pay does not necessarily imply that general state sales taxes will be proportional. Since there are typically many exemptions from the sales tax base, rates are not necessarily proportional (especially when excise taxes on motor fuels, alcohol, and tobacco are considered), and bequests are not included in the tax base.[16] Nevertheless, Metcalf's results indicate that although state sales taxes (taken in the aggregate) are quite regressive with respect to annual income, they are actually slightly progressive when annual consumption is used to measure ability to pay. Indeed, his estimates yield the striking result that in 1989, aggregate state personal income taxes were no more progressive than were aggregate state sales taxes. In addition, Metcalf shows that progressive personal income taxes also appear less progressive when viewed in a lifetime rather than an annual income context. This occurs because relatively low rates are applied to the life-time rich in their youth and old age, and relatively high rates are applied to the lifetime poor during their prime earning years.

Similar results are obtained by Fullerton and Rogers (1991, 1993), who estimate lifetime earnings from PSID data. Their model is more complex than the previously cited research in that it includes a full-scale economic model of the responses of individuals and firms to changes in tax policy.[17] Their results indicate that state sales taxes are considerably less regressive or roughly proportional (depending on the treatment of leisure) when viewed from a lifetime income perspective rather than as a fraction of annual income.[18]

Finally, these results are confirmed and extended by Casperson and Metcalf (1994), who analyze the regressivity of a national value-added tax on the assumption that it is fully shifted forward to consumers. First they use annual consumption expenditures as the measure of ability to pay, and then they construct an estimate of lifetime income using PSID data. They find that although a broad-based VAT is quite regressive with respect to annual income, it is roughly proportional with respect to annual consumption and only mildly regressive with respect to their estimates of lifetime income. They also analyze a VAT with zero ratings for food, housing, and health expenditures. In this case, the VAT is less regressive (than a comprehensive VAT) with respect to annual income, roughly proportional with respect to their estimates of lifetime income, and moderately progressive with respect to annual consumption. For example, in the third case, the median tax burden rises from 1.27 percent for the poorest decile to 2.34 percent for the richest decile. Casperson and Metcalf conclude that concerns over the potential regressivity of a value-added tax are misplaced.

In concluding this section, it must be noted that the use of lifetime rather than annual income in tax incidence analysis is still quite controversial, and the annual income approach is still the standard approach in incidence analysis.[19] Supporters of the use of annual income argue that the assumption of life-cycle behavior may be inappropriate, and that annual income is the better indicator of ability to pay in the presence of capital market imperfections. The latter argument is particularly relevant in the case of liquidity constraints, especially in light of the difficulties experienced by the young in borrowing against the value of their current and future "human capital." In such cases, the assumption that current consumption is a good indicator of lifetime consumption (utilized in some of the lifetime incidence studies described above) may be a rather poor one. In addition, Barthold (1993) notes that those politicians who tend to focus on the short-term effects of policy changes will not find the lifetime approach an appealing one, and the U.S. Joint Committee on Taxation (1993) notes that lifetime incidence assumptions can be very sensitive to the choices of parameter values.

Moreover, the various proxies used for lifetime income may be inaccurate so that known current annual income may better reflect ability to pay than any proxy of expected lifetime income. In particular, annual consumption may not be an accurate indicator of lifetime income, especially for the very wealthy (and, as noted above, for individuals who are liquidity constrained). Nevertheless, the use of a proxy for lifetime income has a great deal of intuitive appeal, and, as noted above, studies based on annual income commonly make a variety of adjustments (or note that such adjustments should in principle be made) to reflect life-cycle considerations. Accordingly, it is reasonable to argue that direct use of an approach based on lifetime income is preferable to ad hoc adjustments to an analysis based on annual income. At the least, as argued by Fullerton and Rogers (1994), lifetime incidence analysis should be used to supplement annual incidence studies, especially in those cases in which the focus of the analysis is the long-run distributional effect of alternative tax policies.

If one finds such reasoning persuasive, the studies outlined above have a clear implication for discussions of the relative equity properties of state sales and income taxes—conventional estimates of the regressivity of state sales taxes are very likely to overestimate the degree of regressivity of such taxes. Indeed, given the exemptions of necessities that characterize most state sales taxes, it is likely that they can be characterized as roughly proportional relative to a measure of lifetime (rather than annual) income. Of course, these statements must necessarily be viewed as suggestive; for any given state, a more definitive statement could be made only with a detailed lifetime incidence analysis of the actual state sales tax system.

Nevertheless, these results do strongly suggest that the terms of the equity debate should be redefined—or at least modified. Specifically, a state sales tax on consumer purchases is undesirable on equity grounds if the residents of a state believe that a system that is roughly proportional relative to a lifetime measure of ability to pay is inherently unfair because it requires such a tax payment even from those at the lowest income levels. In this case, equity concerns imply that it would be desirable for the tax system to completely relieve low-income individuals from tax (with the tax system then being proportional or somewhat progressive once income exceeds the tax-free levels). Such tax relief for low-income families is accomplished much more efficiently through the use of personal exemptions and standard deductions under an income tax than by exempting commodities consumed disproportionately by the poor under a sales tax. In particular, the latter approach (1) involves administrative difficulties in identifying which goods qualify for exemption, and (2) is poorly targeted since all consumers benefit from an exemption for a particular commodity, with the size of the benefit increasing with income (although less than proportionately if the commodity is consumed disproportionately by the poor). The latter problem in turn implies that the commodity exemption approach has a high revenue cost and results in higher tax rates than would the more targeted income tax approach. Such high sales tax rates are undesirable because they cause large economic distortions and create incentives for tax evasion and avoidance. Thus, on this view of what constitutes a fair tax system, considerations of equity, efficiency, and ease of administration all favor the income tax over the sales tax.[20] Note, however, that this equity rationale for an income tax is quite different from the commonly articulated argument that the state sales tax is a highly regressive tax that is inherently unfair because it deviates significantly from a proportional tax system.

The validity of this argument clearly depends on one's views regarding the nature of an equitable state tax system. The citizens of a state may instead believe that all its residents should contribute to the financing of state public services, regardless of income level. In this case, tax burdens that are roughly proportional to lifetime income are likely to be perceived as quite fair, as would the use of sales tax finance.[21] Indeed, under this view of equity, one might even argue that the case for sales tax exemptions for commodities consumed disproportionately by the poor is not particularly compelling.

Note that one additional point related to the life-cycle theory is quite relevant to the choice between income and sales taxes. Specifically, life-cycle theory suggests that the elderly finance a significant amount of consumption by drawing down assets accumulated during their earning years. Such consumption is subject to tax under a sales tax, but is not taxed under an income tax.[22] This effect is exacerbated to the extent that the elderly tend to finance consumption out of tax-exempt capital income such as state and municipal bond interest and untaxed capital gains on owner-occupied housing. Thus, one can argue that the sales tax is preferable to an income tax on equity grounds because it reaches consumption by the elderly. This argument is reinforced to the extent that one is concerned about a general pattern of redistribution of wealth from young to elderly generations as a result of U.S. fiscal policy. Auerbach, Gokhale, and Kotlikoff (1991) forcefully argue that the net fiscal impact of all government programs is considerably less favorable to current young and future generations than it is to the current elderly.

Perceptions of Equity

Finally, since considerations of equity are always subjective, survey data attempting to discern individual notions concerning what constitutes an equitable or fair tax system should be taken into account. The research cited most often in this regard is the annual *Changing Public Attitudes on Government and Taxes* survey of taxpayer opinion conducted by the U.S. Advisory Commission on Intergovernmental Relations (ACIR). However, between 1972–91, the surveys indicate relatively little difference in the perceived fairness of state income and sales taxes. For example, in 1991, 12 percent of the public surveyed perceived the state income tax as being the least fair tax in comparison to 19 percent who viewed the state sales tax as being the least fair tax. These data suggest that the state income tax is popularly perceived to be a somewhat fairer tax than the sales tax alternative, although the definition of fairness used by the respondents in unclear.

ADDITIONAL ISSUES

A number of additional issues arise in discussions of alternative tax structures. These come under the general headings of (1) the relative stability of tax revenues over time, and (2) the relative complexity of alternative structures in terms of compliance costs and monitoring and enforcement costs, including the effects of the tax system on the underground economy.

Revenue Stability

There are two critical aspects of revenue stability—stability over time in the presence of economic growth and stability over the business cycle.

STABILITY AND GROWTH OVER TIME

A critical revenue stability issue is the way in which tax revenues increase over time in the presence of economic growth. In a growing economy, a progressive income tax will automatically result in a higher ratio of revenues to income.[23] In contrast, a comprehensive sales tax tends to increase proportionately with the economy, while a sales tax that undertaxes elements of the economy that are growing in relative (as well as absolute) terms will result in revenues that decline as a fraction of economic activity, which in turn will imply chronic revenue shortages.

As noted above, an open question is the nature of the optimal behavior of tax revenues over time as the economy grows. Although some support the automatic revenues increases that occur under a progressive income tax, the currently more popular view is that unless such expenditure increases are explicitly deemed desirable by the electorate, they are likely to lead to too much public spending. Accordingly, one can argue that efficiency in public service provision is most encouraged by a tax system that increases roughly proportionately with the size of the economy—or even simply at the rate of inflation—rather than at a faster rate. This suggests that a highly progressive rate structure is not desirable under an income tax, and that the income bracket widths that determine the income levels at which higher marginal rates become operative should increase with growth in the economy (unless a compelling case can be made that the ratio of government expenditures to state income should be increasing). Alternatively, the sales tax should be structured so that its base grows roughly proportionately with income.

STABILITY OVER THE BUSINESS CYCLE

Many observers have noted that revenue stability over time is also a desirable feature of a state tax structure, as it minimizes the extent to which the levels of essential services must fluctuate or additional revenues must be raised (through undesirable temporary rate increases or changes in tax bases) in response to cyclical variations. Recall from the above discussion of the life-cycle model of individual behavior that consumption is more stable over time than is income, as individuals draw down assets in response to temporary declines in income and accumulate more assets than usual in response to transitory increases in income. Moreover, any progressivity under an income tax will also act to accentuate the variations in revenue attributable to income fluctuations. Accordingly, a comprehensive tax based on sales will generally be more stable than a tax based on income. This in turn implies that the revenue growth that is obtained under an income tax, relative to a general sales tax, is to some extent obtained at the cost of greater revenue instability.

However, as demonstrated by Dye and McGuire (1991), this general characterization may be inaccurate for some states, as there is considerable variation in the growth and stability characteristics of the various components of income and sales tax bases. Indeed, revenue growth and stability can even be positively related for some tax base components.[24] Thus, the revenue growth and stability characteristics of any particular state tax revenue system depend on the details of its revenue structure. For example, Dye and McGuire find that although the tax bases of a typical broad-based sales tax and a typical more narrowly based tax (one that excludes food for home consumption, personal and repair services, recreational services, and motor vehicle fuels) exhibit roughly the same trend growth rates, the latter base exhibits nearly twice as much variability (as measured by the standard deviation of revenues around the trend growth path). In addition, their data are consistent with the conventional view that increases in the progressivity of an income tax result in both higher revenue growth and greater revenue instability; in particular, they show that increases in progressivity result in fairly modest increases in revenue growth but are accompanied by significant increases in revenue variability. Most important, Dye and McGuire show that a relatively flat rate and broad-based income tax can result in both a modestly higher trend growth rate and a lower degree of variability than a narrowly based sales tax. They conclude that one must be quite careful in generalizing about the revenue growth and stability properties of the income tax and sales tax alternatives.

The notion of a trade-off between revenue growth and revenue stability has been formalized in the "optimal state tax portfolio" literature. Recent examples include Gentry and Ladd (1994), Harmon and Mallick (1994), and Perdue and Weed (1991).[25] This approach involves the calculation of an "efficiency frontier" that describes the revenue growth/stability trade-off for a particular state as it alters its tax mix, given the structure of its tax bases. Specifically, each point on the efficiency frontier is the tax mix, which, given a particular revenue growth rate (as well as constraints on other characteristics of the tax system, such as its equity characteristics and some measure of the competitiveness of its tax system relative to other states), minimizes revenue instability. These optimal combinations, which reflect the optimal amount of "diversification" across revenue sources, given their different characteristics, can then be compared to the actual tax mix in the state to determine the direction of future reforms.

The results of these studies must be interpreted with caution. Most important, they generally focus on only the revenue growth/stability trade-off in determining the optimal tax mix. As a result, the other characteristics of the tax system (including all of the other desirable features of a tax system described above) are either held constant, subject to arbitrarily determined limits, or simply ignored. The degree to which the resulting tax mixes are in fact "optimal" is thus open to debate. In addition, the measures used to characterize various tax systems are to some extent arbitrary and the incidence assumptions made in the analyses, especially regarding business taxes including the business portion of the general sales tax, are of course also subject to debate. Finally, as stressed by Gentry and Ladd, the policy prescriptions that result from an optimal state tax portfolio analysis in one state cannot automatically be applied to other states, since other states will differ in the nature of their economies, the details of the revenue structure, and the relative valuations that the citizens of the state place on different tax policy goals.[26]

Nevertheless, the results of such studies are of interest, especially in terms of thinking about the relative revenue growth and stability properties of state sales and income taxes. Most relevant to the current discussion is that a general message of the two optimal state tax portfolio studies cited above—Gentry and Ladd (1994) for Massachusetts and North Carolina and Harmon and Mallick (1994) for New York—is that the optimal tax mix in these particular states calls for significant reliance on a personal income tax, somewhat greater than under the state tax mix existing at the times the studies were conducted. Since these models stress the advantages of diversification (without considering its costs, such as those associated with administering multiple-tax systems), one would expect that they would prescribe a mix of taxes with different revenue and stability characteristics. However, the optimal degree of reliance on the income tax obtained in these two studies is particularly large primarily because, given the existing tax structures in these states, the income tax is characterized by both higher revenue growth and lower revenue instability.

More generally, the importance of these considerations depends on whether one places more weight on revenue stability or on the extent to which revenues grow as the economy grows. Although it is possible that the revenue stability criterion would provide an argument in support of use of the relatively stable state sales tax rather than a state personal and corporate income tax, this is far from clear. (Note that this argument is much stronger to the extent that the consumer portion of the sales tax base is comprehensive and business sales are excluded from the base.) Moreover, the importance of the revenue stability criterion may be overstated. In particular, to the extent that a state has a "rainy day" fund, the impact of economic fluctuations on the level of funds available to the state government can be reduced. Furthermore, the level of resources devoted to such a fund can always be increased if deemed necessary. Thus, to the extent that such a fund has adequate financing, the issue of revenue stability over the business cycle will be a much less important one. In addition, one could argue on both equity and efficiency grounds that it is only appropriate that at least some public services be included in the cutbacks associated with a cyclical economic downturn.

Accordingly, it is arguably the case that the more critical revenue issue is that of adequate revenue growth—that is, a state should focus on avoiding chronic revenue shortfalls attributable to the structure of the tax base. In this case, a broad-based income tax is generally preferable to the sales tax, especially if the base of the latter largely excludes some relatively rapidly growing sectors and thus tends to grow more slowly than the state economy.[27]

Finally, it is important to note that the stability of consumption relative to income that makes a comprehensive sales tax preferable to an income tax in terms of increased revenue stability over the business cycle also implies that a comprehensive sales tax tends to exacerbate economic fluctuations to a greater extent than does an income tax. That is, taxes fall more under an income tax than under a consumption-based tax, so that after-tax incomes fall proportionately less during a cyclical downturn—the income tax is an "automatic stabilizer" from a macroeconomic viewpoint, while the sales tax tends to accentuate business cycles. This effect is magnified if the income tax has progressive rates, as individuals are likely to move into lower (higher) tax brackets during an economic downturn (boom).[28] However, this effect is reduced to the extent that the sales tax base includes a considerable amount of business purchases, which are subject to the same type of fluctuations as is income.

Costs of Compliance and Administration

COMPLIANCE COSTS

For individuals, compliance costs under either a state sales tax or a state income tax would be quite small. In the case of the state personal income tax, compliance costs are typically not much of a problem, because the state income tax is typically based to a large extent on the federal personal income tax. The most extreme forms of this dependence occurs when the state tax liability is a simple multiple of the federal tax liability or the state rate structure is applied to some federally defined concept of income, such as taxable income. However, even in less pronounced cases, the calculation of state liability typically begins with some federal income concept and then makes a relatively small number of modifications—often using information already required for the federal return. For example, the U.S. Advisory Commission on Intergovernmental Relations reports that thirty-six out of the forty-three states that tax personal income base their tax on the federal definitions (perhaps modified) of adjusted gross income (25 states), taxable income (8 states), or tax liability (3 states).[29] It seems unlikely that the compliance costs associated with such a state personal income tax are very high, especially if the modifications are largely confined to high-income taxpayers who would have relatively little trouble complying with them.

In the case of the sales tax, individual compliance costs are virtually nil, since assessment and collection are solely the responsibility of the selling firm. However, the costs of complying with the sales tax are quite high for those firms that must collect the tax, as they must determine which goods or services are subject to tax, assess the appropriate rate, and keep the requisite records on sales and revenues collected. These compliance costs are presumably disproportionately important for small firms with limited access to accounting help and computerized record-keeping processes, which implies that a state tax system indirectly creates a tax bias against such firms.

Compliance costs under a state corporate income tax are also presumably fairly small, provided again that the calculation of the state tax burden is closely based on federal tax liability. Such an approach is a fairly common practice. The U.S. Advisory Commission on Intergovernmental Relations reports that thirty-eight of the forty-five states that tax corporate income base their tax on a modified version of the federal definition of corporate income.[30] However, businesses incur some additional compliance costs, including those associated with employee tax withholding for the state as well as the federal personal income tax. In many cases, including those involving small operations, firms that currently have no responsibility for the collection of state sales taxes would have to comply with the provisions of a state income tax, and compliance costs for such firms would inevitably increase. In addition, if the state tax involved significant additional computations beyond those required for the federal tax, compliance costs would increase as well.

MONITORING AND ENFORCEMENT COSTS

Effective monitoring and enforcement of the sales tax is fairly difficult, as there are hundreds of thousands of vendors who sell goods or services subject to the tax. Moreover, audits are complicated by the fact that there are no purchaser records for sales taxes assessed on consumer goods. Nevertheless, compliance with the sales tax is probably quite good, at least on the part of large vendors. One potential area of concern is that continued expansion of the sales tax base to include more services is likely to encounter various costly administrative problems.[31]

Once again, monitoring and enforcing a state corporate income tax is facilitated to the extent that the state tax is closely related to the federal tax. Audits can be coordinated with federal agencies, as can other exchanges of information, including information relevant for the determination of taxes due from residents of other states. Finally, as noted by McDonald, "If to violate the state tax law one must violate the federal law also, one will do the former less lightly" (1989, p. 517).

Effects on the Underground Economy

Much concern has been expressed recently about the magnitude of the illegal or "underground" economy that operates largely on a cash basis and pays little in the way of taxes. State income tax systems typically are not very successful in obtaining revenues from such individuals and firms. Similarly, it is presumably very difficult to collect sales taxes on purchases made by firms that operate in the underground economy. However, even participants in the underground economy must purchase commodities and presumably some business inputs from taxpaying firms and thus bear at least some of the burden for the public services they enjoy. This argument would appear to provide considerable support for the sales tax over the income tax. However, this argument is quite misleading, as firms and individuals who charge market prices (inclusive of sales tax) for the goods and services they sell but then do not pay the sales tax will have enough additional income to pay the sales tax on their own purchases.[32] Thus, as long as individuals are willing to evade taxes, their real incomes will not be reduced by either tax. Note also that under an income tax, state enforcement efforts can be coordinated with federal efforts and may thus be more effective in reducing the extent of tax evasion in the state.[33]

The previous two chapters have discussed the relative advantages and disadvantages of state sales and income taxes in terms of a wide variety of criteria that are typically used by public finance specialists to evaluate alternative tax systems. Not surprisingly, this discussion demonstrates that there are strong arguments both for and against each of the two alternative tax options. The following chapter attempts to weigh these arguments and thus provide some perspective on the state sales versus income tax debate.

CHAPTER 5

The Bottom Line: The Sales Tax versus the Income Tax

The discussion thus far has identified the criteria typically used by public finance economists to evaluate alternative tax systems, including the state sales and income tax options. This discussion quite naturally identified numerous arguments that could be used to support each of the two options. This chapter reviews and attempts to weigh the arguments for and against both state tax options.

EXPORTING TAX BURDENS THROUGH DEDUCTIBILITY

The most unambiguous argument in the state sales versus income tax debate supports the use of a personal income tax over the consumer portion of a state sales tax. Specifically, under current federal law (which seems relatively unlikely to be changed in this respect at any time in the near future), state income taxes are deductible from an individual's federal tax liability, while state sales taxes are not. Thus, under the income tax, the deductible portion of a state's tax burden is effectively "exported" to taxpayers in other states, while such tax exporting does not occur under the consumer portion of a state sales tax.

Just as important, the cost of public goods to high-income taxpayers, who typically receive less in the way of public services per tax dollar and are likely to be more influential politically, is significantly lower under a deductible state income tax. For example, taxpayers who itemize deductions and are in the 31 percent federal tax bracket (in 1995, couples with taxable income in excess of $94,250 and single individuals with taxable income in excess of $56,550) would face a tax price of only sixty-nine cents on the dollar. Similarly, high-income taxpayers in the 36 percent federal tax bracket (in 1995, couples with taxable income in excess of $143,600 and single individuals with taxable income in excess of $117,950) would face a tax price of only sixty-four cents on the dollar.[1]

In addition to lowering the effective cost of public services, the ability to export the burden of taxation to out-of-state residents through federal tax deductibility is important because it mutes the effects of any progressivity in the income tax rate structure. That is, the benefit of federal deductibility ranges from zero for low-income taxpayers who pay no federal tax or for those who do not itemize deductions to 39.6 percent for very high income taxpayers. Accordingly, since the benefit of deductibility generally increases with income, a modest degree of progressivity can be built into a state income tax rate structure while maintaining rough proportionality of the effective state income tax burden.

Thus, federal rules regarding the deductibility of state taxes provide a clear argument in support of a personal state income tax over a sales tax. Note that deductibility plays no role in choosing between the various business taxes, since all such taxes are deductible.

EXPORTING TAX BURDENS THROUGH PRICE CHANGES

The issue of tax exportability arises in a second important context. Specifically, taxes on business are often justified on the grounds that they can be exported to nonresidents. However, the discussion in chapter 3 argues that the ability of a state to export tax burdens through price changes is rather limited, and that most business taxes will be borne in the long run either by relatively immobile factors (labor and land within the state) or by in-state consumers. In addition, owners of these factors and/or consumers will bear the "excess burden" of the tax—the additional cost due to the tax-induced outflow of capital that reduces the productivity of a state's labor and land resources.[2]

The implications of this analysis are twofold. First, the potential for tax exportation does not provide a compelling argument for either of the two tax reform options, even though both include an important business tax component. Rather, the analysis suggests that, apart from benefit-related user charges on businesses, taxes on externalities such as pollution and taxes on personal consumption disguised as business purchases, business taxes should be limited to specific excise taxes on the outputs of those industries believed to have substantial national or international market power.

The second implication is that direct taxes on the state's residents are preferable to business taxes. The rationale is that the direct burden of such taxes is roughly similar to that under a business tax, but a direct tax on individuals is characterized by a lower excess burden. Moreover, some recent evidence supports the idea that business location decisions are sensitive at the margin to tax factors. Such mobility in response to differences in after-tax rates of return is consistent with the argument that business taxes are largely borne by local factors of production and/or consumers.

These factors suggest that business taxes are often counterproductive. Businesses should be charged for the services they use (whenever such user charges are feasible) and for any external costs, such as environmental pollution, they impose on the residents of a state. Moreover, business purchases that are really disguised personal consumption of firm owners or employees should be taxed at either the firm or individual level. Apart from such provisions, however, the small open economy argument made earlier suggests that the use of both corporate income (and franchise) taxes as well as sales taxes on business purchases is undesirable. More generally, given that it is obviously unlikely that any state would entirely eliminate such taxes on business, this argument implies that the tax that results in the relatively smaller tax burden on business is the more desirable one. Although one might normally assume that this would be the sales tax, the discussion above suggests that the opposite could very well be the case in states in which the sales tax applies to a large fraction of business purchases, especially if such a tax is also accompanied by a corporate franchise tax.

EFFICIENCY CONSIDERATIONS

The relative merits on efficiency grounds of the two alternative tax systems are difficult to resolve. The following discussion summarizes the relevant business and individual tax issues.

Business Tax Issues

It is clear that the haphazard sales taxation of business purchases that characterizes the typical state sales tax suffers from many deficiencies. The burden of such a tax varies across industries—some businesses use inputs that bear low taxes or are tax exempt, while for other businesses pyramiding of the sales tax results in relatively high burdens (since the effective tax rate is greater than the statutory rate on inputs that are subject to tax at more than one stage of the production process). Such differential tax burdens distort a variety of business production decisions—including those regarding goods produced, the capital/labor mix, and the extent of vertical integration—and thus lower the productivity of in-state factors of production. Moreover, these distortionary effects may be quite large since a relatively low-rate sales tax can translate into a significant increase in the effective tax rate applied to business income. This suggests that a comprehensive income tax would result in more efficient taxation of business than would the typical state sales tax.

Unfortunately, the typical state corporate income tax system is far from a comprehensive tax on business income. There are two primary reasons why this is clearly the case. First, the typical state corporate tax is based on the federal corporate income tax and thus, in general, shares and indeed magnifies all of its many flaws. These include preferential tax treatment of investments in certain types of assets and business sectors, distortions of choices regarding organizational form (corporate vs. noncorporate), and distortions regarding the method of finance used to finance investment (debt vs. equity).

Second, for large multistate corporations with operations in many states, the system of formula apportionment of national corporate profits among the states currently used in the United States implies that for any given state, its corporate income tax is primarily a tax on the property, payroll, and sales of the firms that are located within the state (depending on factors in the state's apportionment formula and their respective weights), rather than a tax on the income generated by the firm's operations in the state. As a result, for such businesses, the distortions of the state corporate tax are more like those associated with property, wage, and/or sales taxation than those associated with the federal corporate income tax. Thus, the property component of the tax still impinges upon capital owners, but in the form of a general tax on capital rather than a tax on equity capital income. Nevertheless, it still exacerbates most of the distortions associated with capital taxes described above. In marked contrast, the payroll component of the tax is effectively a tax on labor, and thus tends to discourage business use of labor rather than capital. Finally, the sales component of the formula-apportioned state corporate tax is the most complicated to analyze, as it applies not only to retail sales but to total corporate in-state sales, including all sales between businesses—without any provisions for exemptions of sales of goods for resale or for goods used in the production of other goods. The share of business purchases in the sales component of the corporate tax would thus typically be significantly larger than the rather large business share of purchases subject to the state sales tax. Thus, formula apportionment tends to mitigate the extent to which a state corporate tax is a tax on capital income—to the extent that payroll and the consumer portion of sales are in the apportionment formula, but this effect is limited to the extent that property and the business portion of sales are in the formula. In addition, the use of formula apportionment creates its own set of distortions, including distortions of decisions regarding mergers and the distribution of production and sales across states.[3]

An assessment of the net effect of all these distortions would in principle require the analysis of the two tax alternatives in the context of a full-scale general equilibrium model of a state economy that would include the effects of both federal and state tax structures in all of the dimensions noted above. However, in the absence of such an analysis, it is clear that both taxes result in significant distortions of firm decision making. A state sales tax results in inefficiencies due to differential sales taxation of various business inputs. By comparison, a state corporate income tax compounds the various distortions of the federal tax and, in the case of large multistate firms, formula apportionment implies that the corporate tax results in distortions similar to those that arise under property, payroll, and sales taxes, including sales taxation of business purchases. Accordingly, it appears that it is difficult to construct a strong argument for either of the two state tax alternatives on efficiency grounds in terms of their relative effects on business decision making.

Individual Taxes

In contrast, the efficiency case for a personal income tax over the consumer portion of a typical state sales tax is fairly clear. By exempting various items, including necessities and various consumer services, the typical state sales tax distorts consumption choices and encourages out-of-state mail order sales. Such distortions would be largely eliminated under a personal income tax. Both types of taxes distort labor/leisure choices and the present/future consumption choice to roughly the same extent. (Recall that the sales tax distorts savings decisions indirectly through the taxation of business purchases.) Similarly, both taxes distort individual location decisions, although the effect of the income tax on relatively mobile high-income individuals is likely to be larger. This in turn suggests that a highly progressive state income tax is undesirable. On balance, a sales tax is likely to be more distortionary of consumer choices than is a personal income tax, especially if the latter is at most mildly progressive.

Government Services

Finally, a small state business tax burden is desirable in that it should result in improved political decision making regarding the allocation of resources to the public sector, since the extent to which the tax burden is "hidden" is relatively small. In general, this argument would seem to favor the sales tax option. However, this argument is rather suspect because the typical state sales tax applies to a significant amount of business purchases. Thus, to the extent that it would result in a smaller tax burden on businesses, the income tax option may well be preferable in terms of improving political decision making. This effect is reinforced by the fact that the personal income tax is probably more visible than is the sales tax on consumer purchases.

EQUITY CONSIDERATIONS

Business Taxes

Equity arguments for either of the two approaches to business taxation are inevitably rather murky, since the incidence of such taxes is far from clear, and the "fairness" of business taxes—beyond benefit taxes for services received, taxes on externalities generated by the business, and taxes on business expenditures that represent personal consumption of firm owners or employees—is largely in the eye of the beholder. As discussed previously, relatively little of the business tax burden is exported to residents of other states. Business taxes are borne either by in-state labor and land, in which case incidence is roughly proportional to income attributable to those factors, or by consumers of "state market" goods, in which case incidence is roughly proportional to such consumption. In any case, it is difficult to make a strong case that either of the business taxes is inherently fairer than the other. The most compelling argument is that businesses should pay taxes in accordance with benefits received. This provides a strong rationale for the utilization of user taxes, but it also provides a weak argument for the use of a tax based on wealth or production within the state—as a very rough proxy for services received in excess of other taxes paid—rather than one based on income.[4]

Individual Taxes

At one level, any equity comparison of alternative state tax structures could be viewed as irrelevant. Specifically, as noted above, Feldstein and Vaillant (1994) argue that individual mobility is sufficiently great that the states are powerless to redistribute income. Their empirical evidence suggests that (1) any differences in progressivity in income tax rates, corrected to reflect the effects of federal income tax deductibility, are offset by changes in gross wages in such a way that the net distribution of income across states is left unchanged, and (2) fairly little time—on the order of several years—is required for gross wages to adjust to such differences in state tax progressivity. Although their results are controversial, Feldstein and Vaillant conclude that state efforts at income redistribution are completely offset by market adjustments, and that redistributive policies only cause efficiency losses by distorting the allocation of labor across states (e.g., as an inefficiently low level of skilled workers employed in relatively high tax states).

If, however, one believes that states can be at least somewhat effective in redistributing income, the equity arguments in the case of the two personal taxes are more important and more controversial than in the case of business taxation. A common complaint is that the sales tax is regressive, and that a progressive income tax is an inherently fairer way to raise revenues to finance government services. The discussion in chapter 4 argues that equity arguments should take into account differences in the relationship between consumption and income over the life cycle (as consumption typically exceeds income during youth and old age, and income typically exceeds consumption during the prime earning years) as well as the effects of transitory income fluctuations. The implications of taking these considerations into account are that (1) at least some—and probably a significant portion—of the measured regressivity of the typical sales tax is due to the use of annual income as a measure of ability to pay, (2) alternative measures that attempt to capture lifetime income, including annual consumption, are a preferable measure of ability to pay, (3) the typical state sales tax is probably roughly proportional with respect to lifetime income, except for the highest income classes where some regressivity is likely to obtain, and (4) progressive income taxes are in fact less progressive than they appear when their incidence is evaluated from a lifetime perspective.

This analysis suggests that the equity issue should be rephrased. Specifically, the primary issue is whether it is desirable to structure a state tax system in such a way that low-income individuals are entirely exempt from tax, or whether such individuals should bear a tax burden that is roughly proportional to consumption or lifetime income. If one's views regarding equity are consistent with the former approach, an income tax is the more desirable option. In contrast, if the latter view of equity is seen as more reasonable (e.g., because everyone should contribute to the provision of public services), the comprehensive sales tax is the preferred option.

In addition, it must be emphasized that reducing tax burdens on the poor under the typical sales tax has a rather high cost. Specifically, excluding various items from the tax base on the grounds that they are consumed disproportionately by the poor does reduce the regressivity of the tax, but only at the cost of dramatically reducing the size of the tax base. As a result, the tax rate required to achieve any given level of revenue is relatively high. In contrast, under a personal income tax, a given level of consumption can be excluded through the use of personal exemptions and standard deductions. Such an approach is more targeted than sales tax exemptions, which apply to all purchases of the exempt items whether they are made by the poor or reflect the relatively high consumption levels of the rich.[5] As a result, the tax rate under the income tax can be lower, which reduces the distortions associated with achieving any particular equity goal.[6]

An interesting complicating factor is that since the use of an income tax at the state level reduces or eliminates the tax burden on low-income individuals, it simultaneously reduces or eliminates the primary objection to the use of benefit taxes or user charges for public services in those cases in which such taxes are feasible. As noted above, user charges are highly desirable both because they promote efficiency in resource allocation to the public sector and because they are consistent with the benefit view of equity. The use of an income tax that exempts or greatly reduces taxes on low-income individuals offsets the regressive impact of such charges and makes them both fairer and more feasible on political grounds.[7]

However, two other (arguably more minor) equity arguments favor the use of the sales tax over the income tax. First, the use of an income tax reduces the tax burden borne by the elderly to the extent that they fund consumption with withdrawals of principal from savings and/or tax-exempt forms of income. Such consumption would generally be included in the sales tax base. Thus, only the sales tax will be effective in taxing the elderly who are wealthy but have relatively little current taxable income. Second, only the sales tax is likely to result in at least some tax burden on tourists and business travelers (who are also consumers of public services and thus, according to the benefit principle, should pay at least some tax). As noted above, this effect can instead be achieved by selective excise taxes on goods and services consumed disproportionately by such individuals.

ADDITIONAL POINTS

Several additional points should be noted. The differences between the sales and income tax options in terms of the criterion of revenue stability over the business cycle are not great and can be moderated by adequate funding and appropriate use of a state's "rainy day" revenue stabilization fund. The primary problem with the typical state sales tax is that it excludes the most stable elements of the consumption base (necessities) and thus is not as stable as total consumption. In addition, state sales tax bases often exclude various items, especially some services and government expenditures, that have in recent years accounted for an increasing fraction of the economies of most states. Under these circumstances, the sales tax base grows less than proportionately with the state economy, which can result in chronic revenue shortages. This problem does not arise under a broad-based income tax that grows proportionately (or more than proportionately if it is progressive) with the state economy.

Note, however, that many observers reasonably argue that a progressive income tax is undesirable because it results in an increasing ratio of revenues to income in the presence of economic growth and thus tends to lead to a higher level of services than would occur in the absence of such an easy source of revenue. This suggests that a highly progressive rate structure is not desirable under an income tax, and that bracket widths (which determine the income levels at which higher marginal rates become operative) should increase with growth in the economy unless a compelling case can be made that the ratio of government expenditures to state income should be increasing.

Finally, a state tax system that is closely related to the federal personal and corporate tax system is simpler than a sales tax in terms of compliance, administration, and enforcement. However, any significant reductions in lowering state compliance, administration, and enforcement costs would occur only if a state sales tax were replaced entirely with an income tax, which appears to be a rather unlikely proposition in most states.

CHAPTER 6

Two Alternatives: User Charges and a State SAT

The discussion thus far has assumed that the only tax instruments available to a state government are sales and income taxes. This assumption is relaxed in this chapter. Specifically, this chapter considers (1) the case for increased utilization of user charges at the state level and (2) the case for a direct consumption-based tax system referred to as the Simplified Alternative Tax (SAT).

THE CASE FOR USER CHARGES

User charges are probably the best "real world" example of a tax based on the benefit principle. As noted in the discussion of equity in taxation, the benefit principle is very relevant at the state and local levels, despite the fact that the ability-to-pay principle is virtually the sole equity criterion applied in practice to the evaluation of federal taxes. Moreover, the use of benefit taxes in the form of user charges is generally desirable on efficiency grounds as well. Indeed, several prominent observers have argued that benefit taxes or user charges should be used to the maximum extent possible at the state and local levels. Since such arguments may be counterintuitive, it will be useful to examine the theoretical case for user charges as well as their revenue potential.[1]

In those cases in which user charges are technically feasible, a strong case can be made for their use as a revenue source on both equity and efficiency grounds. However, note that user charges should be utilized only where their administration and compliance costs are not excessive, relative to the total costs of alternative revenue sources and to the efficiency and equity gains attributable to their use. In addition, note that, as in the case of sales taxes on consumer goods, an argument against user charges is that they are not deductible against individual federal income taxes and thus cannot be "exported" to residents of other states.

Equity Considerations

There are several rationales underlying support for user charges at the subnational level. The equity rationale is simply that in those cases in which the consumers of public services (including nonresidents and tax-exempt institutions) can be identified, they should be taxed on the basis of the level of their consumption; conversely, individuals who can clearly be identified as nonbeneficiaries of a particular service should not be forced to pay for it.[2] The primary problem with this rationale is of course that it implicitly assumes that the distribution of income—after federal taxes and transfers—is acceptable from a social viewpoint, so that an individual's ability to pay taxes is irrelevant. This argument can be a troublesome one, especially since local public services are in many cases essential ones. Thus, it is clear that user charges should not be utilized for services that are explicitly designed to redistribute income and thus augment the redistribution effected by federal tax and transfer programs. However, as discussed in chapter 4, such concerns should be addressed to the extent possible with explicit redistributional policies at the national level, perhaps supplemented by modest income redistribution at the state and local levels. If such redistribution is insufficient and it is deemed desirable to subsidize local public service consumption, every attempt should be made to provide financing from general revenues only for inframarginal units and to charge benefit taxes for marginal purchases. If it can be implemented, such an approach is clearly preferable to the overexpansion of the public sector implied by an artificially low (or zero) price, which is a costly and highly inefficient means of achieving distributional goals.[3] In addition, note that relative to the use of general revenues, the utilization of user charges may actually decrease the tax burden on the poor for services that are used primarily by middle- and upper-income taxpayers. Finally, any adverse distributional effects of user charges could be mitigated by making the charges income-conditioned or by providing a minimum level of services free and assessing user charges on additional purchases, although such an approach would greatly increase the complexity of a system of user charges.

A second equity rationale for the utilization of user charges is that they appear to be perceived as a very fair means of obtaining revenue. In particular, the annual *Changing Public Attitudes on Government and Taxes* survey of taxpayer opinion conducted by the U.S. Advisory Commission on Intergovernmental Relations (ACIR) indicates that, if local revenues are to be increased, taxpayers prefer user charges to other tax alternatives by large margins. For example, in a 1987 ACIR poll, user charges were preferred by 33 percent of the respondents; the sales tax, which was favored by 20 percent of the respondents, was the second most preferred option.

Efficiency Considerations

A wide variety of efficiency arguments can be made in support of user fees. The most important is that the likelihood of achieving an outcome approximating an efficient allocation of resources between the private and public sectors (and within the public sector) is greatest if state and local taxation follows the benefit principle, and user fees are the best example of a benefit-related tax. Most important, user charges imply that consumers of public services must pay the true cost of providing those services. As in the private sector, such information promotes efficient decision making in both consumption and production decisions. In particular, voters are aware of the true costs of providing services and are precluded from supporting public services that benefit themselves but are to be financed by others.[4] Such charges thus provide an important constraint on the demand for public services. Indeed, only under such circumstances are voters or special interest groups likely to limit their support of local public services to levels that are efficient from a social standpoint. In the absence of explicit charges, "shortages" of public services attributable to the fact that marginal units are provided at zero cost will be accompanied by political demands for increased service provision.[5]

In addition, benefit taxes provide the government with an indication of individual preferences in the form of information on consumers' willingness to pay for local public services. This in turn enables governments to make more informed decisions regarding the supply of public services in both the short and long runs. Also, knowledge of the true costs of providing local services and of differences in the costs of services across jurisdictions (including those who have privatized certain services) or between the public and private sectors provides consumers with an indicator of the relative costs of local services. This increases the extent to which local officials may be held accountable by voters for their cost effectiveness in providing local public goods (and, from a national perspective, it also enhances locational efficiency). Similarly, the prospect of losing residents should provide local governments with an incentive to produce local public goods in a cost-efficient manner.[6] Moreover, the problem of underprovision of public services motivated by governmental concern that nonbenefit taxes will drive out mobile capital and/or high-income individuals does not arise under a user-charge regime.[7] Finally, the utilization of user charges implies that increases in other distortionary taxes, such as those on income, sales, or property, can be avoided. The marginal excess burdens caused by increases in such taxes may be relatively high.

The Optimal Structure of User Charges

Suppose, in light of the equity and efficiency arguments made above, that benefit taxes are to be used to finance at least some public services. In this case, the optimal structure of benefit taxation depends on the extent to which the local public good being provided is characterized by the two essential properties of a "pure" public good: (1) "nonrivalness" in consumption, that is, a good for which the marginal cost of provision to another resident is zero (such goods are also said to be not "congestible") and (2) "nonexclusion," that is, a good for which it is technically impossible or prohibitively expensive to exclude a nonpaying resident from enjoying the benefits of the public good. In addition, the optimal structure of benefit taxation depends on the presence or absence of quantity restrictions on its consumption.[8]

USER CHARGES FOR PUBLICLY PROVIDED PRIVATE GOODS
Suppose first that the local public service is a "publicly provided private good"—one for which the costs of provision are proportional to the size of the population being served (with economies of scale exhausted once a relatively small population size is attained). Such goods are sometimes described as "completely rivalrous" in consumption, as the marginal cost of providing the service to another resident equals the average cost of providing it to all current residents. As a result, it is possible to identify the individual receiving the benefit of a public service. Most empirical evidence suggests that this particular case roughly approximates reality for most services that are provided at the local level.[9] In addition, exclusion is generally entirely feasible for such goods.

In this case, the nature of the optimal benefit tax structure depends on whether the public good is provided at a uniform level (the more common situation) or if individuals can purchase differing levels. In the former case, efficiency requires that each individual face a marginal cost or tax price equal to the marginal benefit received. This tax price will vary across individuals depending on their relative demands for the good. The optimal expenditure on the public good reflects the standard "Samuelson" condition for resource allocation to the public sector—that is, the optimum occurs at the level of expenditures at which the sum of the differing marginal benefits equals the marginal cost of provision.[10] Also, it is important to note that since average and marginal costs per capita are equal by assumption, such a system of benefit taxes generates sufficient revenue to cover all costs of the public service.

The structure of the benefit taxes implied by this rule depends on the nature of private demands for local public services. In general, one would expect that demand would increase with income but decrease as the tax price increased, so that benefit taxes might be regressive, proportional, or even progressive. Indeed, in the simplest case, it is possible to show that the tax system implied by the application of the benefit principle should be progressive (proportional, regressive) if the income elasticity of demand for the public good exceeds (equals, is less than) the own-price elasticity.[11] Since empirical estimates suggest that the income elasticity exceeds the price elasticity for most local public goods, this suggests that benefit taxes might be mildly progressive when a single level of the public good is provided to all residents. Note that the logic of this argument implies that if the cost of providing the service to different groups of individuals varies, the structure of user fees should reflect these cost differentials.

In the alternative case in which individuals can choose their level of consumption of the public service, the appropriate benefit tax or user charge simply equals the marginal cost of providing the good. Under this alternative scenario, all individuals should pay the same price for the good, and quantities consumed vary according to demand. This situation is clearly analogous to a private market in that all payments are voluntary.

USER CHARGES FOR PURE LOCAL PUBLIC GOODS

Consider next the situation in which the local public good is a "pure" public good, as it is characterized by both nonrivalness in consumption and nonexclusion. Note that the latter assumption precludes the use of standard benefit-related taxes. Under these circumstances, a source-based tax on an immobile factor within the jurisdiction is required for locational efficiency, which in turn suggests that land taxes should be used to finance pure local public goods. Indeed, it can be shown that under the appropriate circumstances, full taxation of all land rents generates precisely the amount of revenue needed to pay for the efficient level of pure local services—the so-called Henry George Theorem.[12] Moreover, there is an equity rationale for such a tax, as land values may increase to reflect some or even all of the benefits of the provision of pure local public goods; that is, such a tax can be viewed as an indirect form of benefit taxation. Note that a residence-based tax, such as an income tax or a head tax, cannot be a benefit tax since the level of services received is not related to the tax burden under these taxes.

USER CHARGES FOR CONGESTIBLE PUBLIC GOODS

Consider next the intermediate case in which the local public good is subject to some congestion effects, but the congestion problem is not so serious that consumption is completely rivalrous. As would be expected, the optimal benefit tax structure in this case reflects a combination of the two approaches used above. Specifically, a residence-based tax—ideally a benefit tax or user fee—should be charged to ensure that all residents pay the full marginal costs (net of any external benefits associated with their consumption of the public good) of providing them with local public services. This charge, sometimes referred to as a "congestion charge," should then be combined with a source-based tax on an immobile factor in the jurisdiction to cover the remaining cost of the public service, which is attributable to providing the "public" portion of the local public good.

Two additional questions arise in the application of the benefit principle. The first is whether the most obvious example of benefit taxes—user fees—can in practice raise significant revenues. The second question is whether broad-based taxes can be used in such a way that they can be viewed as "quasi-benefit" taxes, that is, as a proxy for benefit taxes. These two issues are considered in the following two subsections.

Revenue Potential of User Charges

User fees are defined as charges paid by the residents of a local jurisdiction that are directly related to the consumption of a public good provided by that jurisdiction. Since user fees are the textbook example of a benefit tax, the above discussion implies that they are in principle a highly desirable source of own revenue for state and local governments. Moreover, since many state and local services are not "pure" public services, and in fact are often best characterized as "publicly provided private goods," they are by nature conducive to the application of user fees.

However, the revenue potential of user fees is an obvious issue. Experience in the United States provides at least some guidance in this regard. Downing (1992) notes that over the past twenty years, user fees have become a very important source of municipal funds. In many cities, user fees provide more revenue than does the local property tax. On average, the extent of "user charge reliance" in the United States, defined as current user fees divided by own revenue (excluding utility fees in both cases), has increased dramatically from 17.5 percent in 1967 to 25.9 percent in 1987.

The degree of reliance on user fees naturally varies with the type of service. It also varies tremendously depending on whether the state generally tends to be aggressive in its utilization of user fees. Indeed, for cities that rely heavily on user fees, Downing shows that such fees regularly approach or even exceed total own expenditures for services such as sewerage, sanitation, parking, parks and recreation, hospitals, and airports.

Moreover, Downing argues that the full potential for user fees is far from realized in the United States for at least three reasons. First, many governments hesitate to utilize such fees for political or other reasons (an obvious source of additional revenue would be increased utilization of user fees by such governments). Second, user fees commonly do not cover the long-run marginal cost of providing local public services, as they typically are set equal to average direct costs, neglecting the costs of capital and land in providing the service. For example, parking fees might cover the cost of personnel and maintenance, but ignore land and capital costs. (Note also that increasing fees to reflect marginal costs accurately should reduce consumption demand, reduce total expenditures, and thus increase the fraction of such expenditures that is financed with user fees.) Finally, a variety of innovations in user fees have appeared in recent years but are currently utilized very sparingly. In particular, Downing cites the use of "fiscal impact fees," under which new residential developments pay direct compensation for the capital costs of providing these developments with local services, as a potentially important source of user fee revenue.

Proxies for Benefit Taxation

Although benefit taxation is most readily achieved by instituting a system of user fees, income, sales, or property taxes might be viewed as rough proxies for benefit taxation to the extent that the burden of taxation corresponds to the receipt of the benefits of local public services. However, this link is rather tenuous for two reasons.

First and most obvious is that the relationship between taxes paid and benefits received is much less direct than in the case of user fees. In particular, unlike in the case of a true benefit tax or user fee, receipt of the benefits of local public services is not conditional on payment of the tax. For example, under a retail sales tax, an individual living near the border of a jurisdiction will still receive the benefits of its local public services even if he or she makes retail purchases in a neighboring jurisdiction. This suggests that such taxes are more likely to approximate benefit taxes if they are used by larger jurisdictions rather than smaller ones, and that avoidance opportunities should be considered when selecting a state or local tax structure. However, it is important to note that even if avoidance is limited, the efficiency-enhancing direct link between tax payments and the quantity of services received does not exist under such quasi-benefit taxes.

Second, all of the broad-based individual taxes noted above, especially property taxes, may be shifted to other taxpayers, in which case the advantages of taxation on a benefit basis may not obtain. For example, by reducing the capital component of housing structures, capital owners can shift the burden of the property tax in a single jurisdiction to landowners and/or consumers of housing and to owners of nonresidential capital. Although such shifting is at least partly irrelevant in the case of owner-occupied housing (to the extent that the consumer and the owners of the land and capital are identical), this is not the case for rental housing. Thus, residential property taxes are benefit taxes only in special cases, as in Hamilton (1975) where strict zoning restrictions result in jurisdictions that are homogeneous with respect to house value, which precludes the shifting mechanism described above. This suggests that the linkage between taxes paid and benefits received is tenuous under the property tax, especially when nonresidential property is included in the base.[13]

THE CASE FOR A STATE SAT

Another alternative to state income and sales taxes—one that admittedly would represent a drastic departure from the status quo in all states, but which could very well be preferable to both of the standard options—is the Simplified Alternative Tax.[14] It has been recommended elsewhere as an alternative to a national income tax, but the potential for the use of an SAT by a single state has not been examined.[15] A full exploration of the advantages and disadvantages of adopting a state SAT is of course far beyond the scope of this book and is left to future research. Nevertheless, it may be useful to present some preliminary thoughts on the desirability of a state SAT, drawing on the literature that analyzes the tax in a national context. Accordingly, the following discussion describes the structure of the SAT (including some of the issues raised by its use at the state level) and outlines briefly the advantages and disadvantages of such a tax system.[16]

The Structure of the SAT

The SAT is an integrated system of direct business and individual taxation. Although it is broadly similar in structure to an income tax system, the SAT is a consumption-based rather than an income-based tax.[17] In that sense, it is similar to the consumption-based value-added tax (VAT) used in Europe. However, it cannot be emphasized too strongly that the SAT is very different from a value-added tax in that it is a direct tax assessed on individual firms and households (rather than an indirect tax on business transactions), and thus it can be structured to avoid any equity problems that might be associated with the VAT. Specifically, the SAT includes a standard deduction and personal exemptions so that no tax is assessed on the very poor. Moreover, the SAT has a progressive marginal rate structure, so that concerns about the vertical equity of the tax system beyond the tax treatment of the poor can be addressed directly. (Note, however, that the arguments presented above in support of only mild tax rate progression at the state level apply with full force to the SAT, as does the discussion of the importance of measuring tax incidence relative to lifetime or permanent income.) The following discussion outlines the structure of the SAT, considering first the business tax component and then the individual-level tax (additional details can be found in Zodrow and McLure [1991]).

THE BUSINESS COMPONENT OF THE SAT

The business component of the SAT is a tax on business cash flow. The tax base includes all nonfinancial receipts, and firms are allowed deductions for wages and salaries, contributions to pension plans, and all nonfinancial business purchases, including those of depreciable assets and additions to inventories. Both borrowing and the repayment of loan principal and interest have no effect on the tax base.[18] Thus, the biggest differences between the SAT and a corporate income tax are that (1) immediate expensing is allowed for purchases of depreciable assets and additions to inventories, (2) there are no deductions for interest expense, and interest income, dividends, and capital gains on financial assets are not subject to tax, and (3) all businesses (rather than just corporations) are subject to the tax. In addition, the business component of the SAT is similar to a subtraction-method VAT, under which the tax base is basically nonfinancial receipts less capital expenditures and all other nonlabor inputs.[19] However, the SAT differs fundamentally from the VAT in that it allows deductions for wages and salaries, which are then taxed at the individual level, as described in the following subsection.

In an open economy context, the main issue raised by the SAT is the appropriate treatment of interstate trade and multistate businesses. Like most analyses of an SAT-type tax (and of a state VAT), the following discussion will assume that the SAT would be based on the "origin" principle, which implies that all production occurring within a state would be subject to tax. Specifically, under an origin-based SAT, export receipts are included in the tax base, and firms receive deductions for the purchase of imported inputs (and imported consumer goods are not subject to tax).[20] Another interpretation of the origin principle is that there are no special provisions allowing credits or rebates for tax paid on goods exported out of state, and no attempt is made to apply tax to firm purchases of inputs or consumer purchases of goods from out of state.[21] Under such an approach, the business portion of the tax base, which consists of economic rents and returns to risk-taking, is taxed in the state in which the output is produced.

THE INDIVIDUAL COMPONENT OF THE SAT

Wages, salaries, and pension receipts are included in the individual tax base of the SAT, but all forms of capital income, including interest receipts, dividends, and capital gains, are exempt from tax.[22] Individuals would qualify for a standard deduction and personal exemptions. The remaining tax base would then be subject to tax at (presumably mildly) progressive rates. To address concerns regarding tax-free transmission of wealth across generations, gifts and inheritances received could be included in the tax base. On horizontal equity grounds, it would be desirable to include transfer payments in the tax base (subject of course to the standard deduction and personal exemptions of the SAT).

The Consumption-Based Nature of the SAT

As noted above, the SAT—at least in the case of a closed economy—is best described as a consumption-based tax. Since the appropriateness of this description is not obvious, it will be useful to elaborate on this point, as well as on the appropriate characterization of the nature of an SAT in an open-economy context.

Note first that the individual tax base is labor compensation—wages, salaries, and pension receipts—plus perhaps inheritances and transfers. Most consumption tax plans, such as the cash flow taxes proposed by the U.S. Department of the Treasury (1977) and by Aaron and Galper (1985), allow a current · deduction for saving with full inclusion in the tax base of all withdrawals for consumption purposes of both the original amount saved and all earnings. Such a tax, which corresponds to allowing unlimited individual retirement accounts (IRAs), is clearly a tax on consumption. However, the primary result of such treatment is that capital income is effectively exempt from tax; specifically, the value of the deferral of tax due to the deduction for saving is equal in present value terms (under the appropriate assumptions, including a constant tax rate) to the subsequent taxation of withdrawals of principal and interest. Accordingly, the tax system can achieve the same "consumption-type" result by simply ignoring capital income. This is the approach utilized under the individual component of the SAT.[23] This method of implementing a consumption-based tax is sometimes referred to as the "individual tax prepayment approach"; that is, relative to a cash flow consumption tax, the individual prepays tax by forgoing the deduction for saving, and thus capital income need not subsequently be subject to tax. Note that since the individual component of a state SAT would be assessed on all state residents, the characterization of the SAT as a consumption-based tax is roughly appropriate for this component of the tax—for those individuals who remain residents of the state over their entire life cycle.[24] In contrast, the link between consumption and wage income is weaker for individuals who move to or from the state during their lives (although it still exists to some extent since pension receipts are included in the individual tax base). For example, individuals who spend their earning years in a given state but retire elsewhere would bear a larger tax burden in the state in which they worked under the SAT than they would under a cash flow–type consumption tax.

In addition, the SAT includes a business tax. Since businesses do not consume, the need for such a tax is not obvious under a tax that is supposedly based on consumption. However, the business component of the SAT provides an important complement to the individual tax and is often referred to as a "consumption-based" business tax. This categorization follows from the fact that the net effect of allowing expensing, rather than deductions for depreciation, is that the income from marginal capital investments—those that earn the normal market rate of return—is not subject to tax under the SAT. In the terminology used in chapter 4, the marginal effective tax rate on investment is zero with expensing of all purchases of capital equipment, as allowed under the SAT.[25] This implies that the government earns no net revenue on such marginal investments, so that the primary element of the SAT base is the consumption taxed under the individual component of the tax. It is also important to note, however, that investments that earn economic rents or above-normal returns are taxed on such rents. As a result, the government will earn positive revenues in present value terms from the business tax.[26] Similarly, the government shares in both the return and the risk to risky ventures, and this risk-sharing should also result in positive revenues in present value terms, assuming that the aggregate return to risky investment is positive.[27] Such revenues will supplement those earned from the taxation of consumption under the individual tax.

In addition, to the extent that the business tax can be designed to prevent firms from disguising personal consumption as business expenses, it plays an important role in ensuring that the consumption base of the SAT is as comprehensive as possible. For example, firms might be denied any deductions for meals and entertainment expenses (only 50 percent of such deductions are allowed under current federal income tax law) and for employer-provided fringe benefits, including health insurance premiums. In general, as under an income tax, deductions should not be allowed for the personal component of business expenses.[28]

Note, however, that in an open-economy context, the business component of an origin-based SAT cannot be characterized as a consumption-based tax. Rather, as stated above, the tax base is production that occurs within the state, as exports are included in the tax base and imported inputs are fully deductible. Thus, the tax base of the business component of the SAT, which includes economic rents and the return to risk-taking, is production-based rather consumption-based.[29] Nevertheless, since most of the tax revenues of a state SAT would presumably arise from the individual component of the tax, the characterization of the tax as one that is based on consumption within the state may be a reasonable approximation to reality (although the accuracy of the approximation obviously cannot be determined without an explicit analysis of the issue).

Evaluation of an SAT as a State Tax Reform Option

The SAT has many desirable features, as well as a few undesirable ones. These are explored in the following discussion, although it must be noted that virtually all of the existing literature on the SAT and similar taxes analyzes them in the context of a national or closed economy. The discussion generally follows the order used in chapter 2.

EXPORTABILITY THROUGH DEDUCTIBILITY

The business component of the SAT would be deductible against federal tax liability as a business expense. Moreover, the individual component of the tax is broadly similar to the personal income tax in that it is structured as a direct or personal tax that includes standard deductions, personal exemptions, and progressive marginal rates. Thus, the individual component of the SAT presumably would be deductible against individual federal income tax liability as well, as it seems unlikely that the federal government would attempt to characterize a direct tax like a state SAT as a nondeductible sales tax. As discussed at length above, this advantage does not obtain under a state sales tax.[30]

EXPORTABILITY THROUGH PRICE CHANGES

The potential for tax exporting of the SAT through increased prices for exported goods or lower returns to factors owned by nonresidents depends on the precise treatment of such exports. This discussion assumes that the origin principle is applied to exports so that they are included in the tax base. Under any circumstances, however, there are two reasons why tax exporting is not likely to be much of an issue. First, as argued above, real opportunities to export state tax burdens are likely to be rather limited in any case. Second, the SAT is largely a wage-based tax, and its burden would most likely be borne largely in the form of reduced after-tax wage income. Accordingly, the imposition of an SAT should have little effect on consumer prices, and thus there should be fairly little opportunity for tax exporting either in the form of higher prices to out-of-state customers or as lower returns to factors other than labor.[31]

EFFICIENCY

The SAT eliminates many of the distortions that characterize either or both the sales tax and the income tax. Most important, the marginal effective tax rate on capital income is zero; that is, the SAT does not tax at the margin the income earned by capital. As a result, it does not create an incentive for mobile capital to leave the state, as do both the income tax and the sales tax (through the taxation of sales to businesses). The discussion of the theoretical aspects of the taxation of capital income presented above stresses that such tax treatment of mobile capital is highly desirable in the context of a small open economy, and that recent empirical research has supported the notion that the location of business investment is sensitive to tax factors. Thus, the application of a zero marginal effective tax rate to business investment is the most prominent advantage of a state SAT.

Another important advantage of the SAT is that it eliminates the problem of inadvertent taxation of business inputs that plagues the sales tax, since it allows deductions for all business-related purchases.[32] In addition, since the SAT is basically a tax on consumption, it results in a relatively low tax burden on saving and thus does not distort the present/future consumption choice as much as the income tax (or, for that matter, the state sales tax since it includes so many sales to businesses in the base).[33] Thus, the imposition of a state SAT would not exacerbate existing tax disincentives against saving under the current federal income tax.

Moreover, since the SAT applies an effective marginal tax rate of zero to the income from all types of capital investments, its use will not exacerbate any of the interasset or intersectoral distortions of the existing income tax. Similarly, since all businesses are treated identically, the corporate/noncorporate distortion of the existing federal income tax will not be worsened by the state tax system. In addition, since debt and equity finance are treated identically under the SAT (there are no firm-level deductions for either dividends or interest, and all capital income is untaxed at the individual level), firm decisions regarding the choice of finance as well as the choice of paying dividends or retaining earnings will not be distorted by the state tax system. Note also that the taxation of economic rents under the business component of the tax provides a relatively nondistortionary source of revenue and that the risk-sharing aspect of the business tax could result in more of an incentive for risk-taking than a conventional income tax.

At the individual level, the taxation of labor income under a state SAT will distort the labor supply decisions of the residents of a state, as they will be encouraged to engage in more nonmarket activity and leisure. In addition, to the extent that labor (especially highly paid labor) is mobile across state boundaries, the supply of labor in a state that uses an SAT will be reduced, and production will be inefficiently capital intensive. Of course, these problems also arise under both a state income tax and a state sales tax system; however, they are more pronounced under the SAT, since labor income bears more of the tax burden under the SAT than under either of the two alternative tax systems. These results reflect the inescapable fact that virtually no tax is free of economic distortion.[34] In addition, since the implementation of an SAT should have relatively little effect on consumer prices, it should be less distortionary of consumer choices than either a sales tax or an income tax (to the extent that a corporate tax would be shifted forward as higher prices for goods sold primarily in state markets).

Finally, since the SAT is certainly not a benefit tax, it will not remedy the problems associated with determining appropriate public service levels in the absence of benefit taxation. On the other hand, the SAT is a highly visible personal tax and thus should not encourage the overspending that might occur with a less visible tax.

EQUITY

One of the primary advantages of the SAT is that it has sufficient flexibility to meet most equity concerns, especially in comparison to alternative indirect consumption-based taxes like the VAT or a retail sales tax. In particular, if deemed desirable, poor families can be made entirely exempt from tax through the appropriate choices of the standard deduction and personal exemptions, or they can be made subject to a relatively low tax rate. In contrast, the various exemptions, credits, and refunds that characterize attempts to relieve the tax burden of sales taxes on the poor are complicated, poorly targeted (and thus expensive in revenue terms), and often of questionable effectiveness.

In addition, the possibility of progressive marginal tax rates under the SAT provides policymakers with considerable leeway in determining the distribution of the burden of the tax. Indeed, even if one believes that the ability to pay taxes should be measured by annual income, the burden of any particular state income tax structure can be replicated, on average, across income classes (although not for each household within an income class) by choosing the SAT rates appropriately.

The primary equity problem with the SAT is that the exemption of ordinary returns to capital from the tax base is often perceived to be inequitable. Note, however, that the discussion of lifetime income measures of ability to pay implies that such treatment of capital income is entirely appropriate. Indeed, consumption tax proponents argue that for any given level of lifetime income, the taxation of ordinary returns to capital unfairly penalizes those who earn relatively early or consume relatively late in their lifetimes and thus save to a disproportionately large extent.[35] Nevertheless, since most individuals are not accustomed to thinking about ability to pay in terms of lifetime income, they often perceive the treatment of capital income under the SAT as inherently unfair. Note, however, that the above discussion suggests that any problems with the exemption of ordinary returns to capital can be reduced to at least some extent by making the tax rate structure somewhat more progressive than it otherwise would be. The resulting system could thus achieve the efficiency gains described above, while having roughly the same equity properties as any particular state income and/or sales tax system. In addition, it must again be emphasized that the exemption of capital income that characterizes the SAT refers only to "ordinary" or "normal" returns to capital; above-normal returns to capital are in fact taxed under the business component of the SAT. To the extent that such above-normal returns accrue disproportionately to the wealthy, the SAT is more progressive than it might appear.[36]

A final equity consideration is of interest. Although the SAT is largely a consumption-based tax, it is also a comprehensive direct tax and as such should apply to all individuals and to all firms. As a result, it would be more equitable than an indirect tax system that excludes or provides preferential treatment to certain industries or business sectors. In particular, the business component of the SAT can readily be applied to most services, and the individual component applies to the wage and salary income of all workers, including those in the service and government sectors.[37]

REVENUE STABILITY

Since the base of the SAT is wages and pensions (above exempted amounts) plus any economic rents and returns to risk-taking captured under the business tax, it differs from an income tax base primarily in that it excludes normal returns to investment. The two taxes are thus sufficiently similar that it is difficult to make a compelling argument that either one would be more stable over the business cycle than the other.[38] Also, since the rate structure of the SAT is progressive, one could argue that the bracket widths that determine the tax base levels at which higher marginal rates become operative should increase with growth in the economy in order to avoid unlegislated increases over time in the ratio of government expenditures to state income.

Disadvantages of the SAT

There are four main disadvantages with the use of the SAT as a source of revenue at the state level. These are (1) difficulties in the treatment of interstate sales/purchases and of multistate firms, (2) difficulties in taxing certain industries and types of transactions, (3) complexity in administration and compliance, relative to a system that can "piggyback" on the existing federal individual and corporate income taxes, and (4) the lack of experience with the SAT. Each of these issues is discussed in turn below.

TREATMENT OF INTERSTATE SALES/PURCHASES, MULTISTATE FIRMS
The discussion above suggests that a state SAT should be implemented following the origin principle—export receipts should be included in the base and purchases of imported inputs would be deductible. However, such treatment would raise several problems.

The primary difficulty would be that the exports of a state that utilized the SAT might become somewhat less competitive on national markets due to the imposition of the tax.[39] However, since the SAT is most likely to be borne primarily by labor rather than by consumers, fairly little forward shifting of the tax should occur, so this should not be a major problem.

In addition, deductibility of business inputs imported into the state might create potential problems in two areas. First, production inputs imported into the state would be tax-favored over similar products that were produced in state and thus subject to the SAT. This problem should be relatively minor since (1) the SAT should be characterized by fairly little forward shifting of the tax into higher input prices, and any input price increase would be deductible against the firm's SAT liability, and (2) if the SAT were shifted forward, the prices of imported inputs would also be likely to reflect some forward shifting of the taxes in the state in which the inputs were produced. Thus, the implementation of the SAT would be problematical only if policymakers believed that a significant fraction of the burden of the tax would be shifted forward in the form of higher prices and that such shifting would place in-state firms at a competitive disadvantage relative to out-of-state producers, who are subject to taxation in their own jurisdictions.[40]

Second, the appropriate treatment of multistate firms poses problems for a state SAT. Under the origin principle, goods produced within the state and then transferred out of the state in an intercompany transfer should be included in the tax base at their fair market value. Similarly, inputs transferred between different components of a multistate firm must be valued. However, the determination of such "arm's length" or "transfer" prices is among the most troublesome issues in international taxation and would similarly be difficult to implement in a state SAT. In particular, multistate firms would have an incentive to overstate (understate) the prices of inputs transferred from (outputs transferred to) related companies located in relatively low tax rate states, and monitoring such transactions would be very difficult.[41]

One potential solution to these transfer pricing problems is to follow the approach used under current state corporate income taxes by utilizing an apportionment formula to determine state SAT liability. Under this approach, multistate firms would calculate their tax liability as if the SAT were applied in all states, and then the state SAT base would be determined by applying an apportionment factor to the "national" tax base. In principle, the apportionment formula should attempt to capture the fraction of total national economic rents generated in state.[42] Since in practice, economic rents are impossible to determine, the apportionment formula would presumably be based on economic variables such as those used in current tax apportionment formulas—sales, payroll, and property. The primary problem with such an approach is that it would be only an approximation to the SAT base that would be calculated under the more accurate (but difficult to implement) separate accounting approach. As a result, one of the main advantages of the SAT—the beneficial effects on capital allocation to a state of the application of a zero marginal effective tax rate to ordinary capital income coupled with taxation of economic rents at the statutory business tax rate—would be reduced to some extent, as the differential taxes effectively assessed on various factors of production through their inclusion in the apportionment formula would distort factor allocation decisions.[43]

PROBLEMS IN TAXING CERTAIN TRANSACTIONS

In general, one of the features of the SAT that greatly simplifies tax compliance and administration (relative to an income tax) is the fact that loans and interest income and expense are ignored under the SAT. However, this treatment does give rise to several problems.[44]

The most obvious is that since interest income (and other forms of capital income) and interest expense are ignored under the SAT, financial institutions would entirely escape taxation on the interest rate "spread" between their earnings and their cost of funds. Such treatment would very likely be deemed undesirable. One solution would be to apply cash flow (rather than prepayment) treatment to financial transactions made by financial institutions. Such an approach would, however, add to the complexity of the SAT. Another problem (which also causes difficulties under the income tax) is that financial institutions often combine low-interest payments to individual depositors with underpriced or "free" services; the low or nonexistent prices reduce the tax bases of the financial institutions and thus their tax liabilities, while the low-interest payments have no effect on individual tax liabilities under the SAT.[45] These problems suggest that financial institutions might be made subject to a special separate tax.

More generally, any firm might try to avoid tax by arranging simultaneous tax-reducing purchase/loan transactions with an entity not subject to the SAT. Such schemes would effectively trade reduced prices on the firm's sales for a higher interest rate on a "tied" loan the firm makes to the purchaser. In this case, the firm reports lower receipts while the purchaser is indifferent to the relabeling of payments. Alternatively, a business that is buying inputs from a firm not subject to the SAT could arrange to purchase the inputs at inflated prices and simultaneously borrow money from the seller at a below-market interest rate. The potential for abuse is significant, since all out-of-state firms (at least those which are not subject to a state SAT) potentially could engage in such transactions. Although theoretical solutions to such problems can be designed, they are not particularly attractive, especially from an administrative standpoint, as they involve difficult-to-enforce interest rate ceilings/floors, interest imputations, or restrictions on borrowing.[46]

COMPLEXITY

In general, the SAT is considerably simpler in structure than an income tax. In particular, the business tax avoids various complex "timing" issues (such as the calculation of economic depreciation) and the problems of inflation adjustment. The individual tax is a straightforward tax on labor compensation, and various troublesome issues of capital income measurement do not arise. However, from the perspective of a single state, the institution of an SAT is considerably more complicated than a state income tax system that piggybacks on the federal taxes on individual and corporate income by making state tax liability a simple function of federal tax liability.[47] This is inevitable, since the SAT tax base does not correspond to the federal tax base. On the other hand, most firms will already have all the information needed to calculate SAT liability. Nevertheless, added compliance costs might be considerable for small noncorporate firms, especially providers of services and other firms that typically are not subject to the state sales tax system. In addition, the introduction of individual-level taxation under the SAT (as under the personal income tax) would result in new compliance and administration costs.

THE "NOVELTY" EFFECT

A final problem associated with attempting to implement the SAT might be termed the novelty effect. Specifically, even though SAT-type taxes have been examined at length in the theoretical literature, no country or state has ever adopted such a tax. There is a natural reluctance to adopt a tax system that has not been tested in the "real world"; in particular, there may be a wide variety of problems that academic proponents of SAT-type taxes have not anticipated. This is especially true in the state context, since virtually all of the academic literature on SAT-type taxes has focused on their implementation at the national level. On the other hand, as suggested by the above analysis, the problems associated with state income and state sales taxes are well known and considerable, and many of them are easily handled by the SAT. Accordingly, it is difficult to know how much weight should reasonably be attached to the novelty argument.

The discussion thus far has examined four state tax options—sales and income taxes, user charges, and the SAT—in a general context applicable to all states. In the following chapter, the analysis turns to a case study of the tax structure of a particular state. Specifically, the question of tax reform in the state of Texas—including the especially contentious issue of the desirability of the introduction of a state income tax system—is analyzed, drawing on the information presented in the first six chapters of the book.

CHAPTER 7

An Application to the Case of Texas Taxes

Texas provides an excellent example of a state that is currently facing the problem analyzed in this book—choosing between a sales tax and an income tax. Indeed, since Texas is one of the relatively few states that has neither an individual income tax nor a corporate income tax (at least in name), a perennial issue in the state is whether it should adopt an income tax system—a personal tax on individual income coupled with a business tax on corporate income. This question has been a highly controversial one for many years, permeating discussions of proposals to reform the state tax structure, to provide local property tax relief (including efforts to increase the state role in education finance), or to expand state services.[1] It has been addressed in recent years by two blue ribbon state commissions. Perhaps not too surprisingly, given the degree of controversy surrounding the income tax issue in the state and—as discussed at length above—the many arguments for and against a state income tax, these bodies reached different conclusions. Specifically, the Select Committee on Tax Equity (SCOTE) recommended in 1989 against the income tax option although it urged continued "debate and dialogue concerning the tax," while a narrow (7 to 5) majority of the Governor's Task Force on Revenue (GTFR) in 1991 recommended implementation of a personal and corporate income tax system.[2] Moreover, it seems unlikely that this controversy will subside in the near future. Indeed, the recent passage of a constitutional amendment that requires voter approval before a state personal income tax can be implemented in Texas suggests that extended public discussions of this controversial issue are likely.

It is clear that a state income tax is anathema to most, if not virtually all, Texas politicians.[3] Nevertheless, this chapter follows the rest of the book in ignoring these well-established political concerns and focuses instead on the economic issues involved in the tax reform debate. As applied to the case of Texas taxes, the question posed by this book is straightforward—would the introduction of a state income tax in Texas be preferable to expansion of the current state tax system (a sales tax coupled with a corporate franchise tax, as described below) in terms of the standard criteria used by public finance economists to evaluate alternative tax systems?

The central implication of the analysis presented thus far is that from an economic perspective the case against the implementation of a state income tax in Texas—as compared to expansion of the existing sales/corporate franchise tax system—is not nearly as clear-cut as would be suggested by the virtually unanimous political opposition to an income tax. Rather, there are strong arguments both for and against an income tax, all of which should be fully aired in any debate about reform of the existing tax system. In my view, the implementation of a flat rate or a modestly progressive income tax in Texas is preferable to an expansion of the current tax system. The rationale underlying this position is not that income taxation is inherently desirable; in fact, as discussed in the preface, my general view is that taxation on the basis of consumption is preferable to income-based taxation. Instead—although it is clear that, after weighing the various arguments presented in this study, reasonable people could disagree with this particular policy prescription—my view is that the current tax system in Texas is plagued by more than enough serious problems that, given the existence of the current federal income tax, a state income tax is preferable to increased reliance on the current tax system. The rationale underlying this position is detailed below.

The rest of the chapter is organized as follows. I begin with an overview of the revenue system in Texas and compare it to the systems in other states. I then analyze the existing Texas state sales/corporate franchise tax system and the income tax alternative in terms of the criteria outlined earlier in the book. Next the two alternative sources of revenues discussed in chapter 6—user charges and a SAT—are discussed in the Texas context. Finally, I conclude with some directions for further research—most of which are relevant not only for Texas but for other states considering reforms of their tax structures.

AN OVERVIEW OF THE TEXAS REVENUE SYSTEM

This section examines the state revenue system in Texas. No attempt is made to be comprehensive, as the description stresses those aspects of the tax system that are particularly relevant to the issues discussed in this book. For complete descriptions of the state revenue system, see the SCOTE and GTFR reports and Texas Comptroller of Public Accounts (1995a, b). Some comparisons of the tax system in Texas with those in other states are also drawn in this overview.

The Sales Tax

The primary source of state tax revenue in Texas is the sales tax, with revenues of $10.26 billion in 1995, which represent 54.4 percent of state tax revenue of $18.86 billion.[4] The state sales tax rate is currently 6.25 percent. Add-on taxes imposed by counties, municipalities, and/or metropolitan transit authorities can increase this by a maximum of 2 percent. The state sales tax rate is the fifth highest in the nation; tax rates in other states range from 3 to 7 percent, with a median rate of 5 percent.[5]

Although commonly perceived to be a tax on retail sales to individual consumers, the sales tax in Texas is like that in most states in that a significant fraction of the tax is in fact assessed on sales between businesses. This fraction was estimated to be as much as 49 percent in 1992, but has declined in recent years with the phasing in of the exemption from the sales tax base for equipment used in manufacturing, processing, or fabrication. Full elimination of the taxation of such equipment, implemented on January 1, 1995, should reduce this fraction by roughly 3 percentage points, to approximately 46 percent.[6] The business tax burden under the sales tax arises primarily due to the taxation of office furniture and computers and some office equipment, some services, fuels, various intermediate goods, certain machines and tools, and certain raw materials. In addition, although purchases of structures are not taxed explicitly, they are subject to an implicit tax since sales taxes are paid on the purchases of many of the components of business structures and are thus incorporated in their prices. The sales tax thus imposes a significant burden on Texas businesses. Note that this occurs despite several provisions explicitly designed to reduce this burden (in addition to the equipment exemption noted above), including the exemption of goods sold for subsequent resale, property that becomes a component of a manufactured product, and property that will be consumed in manufacturing or processing.

As noted above, Texas is not unusual in this regard, as all state sales taxes include in their bases at least some items sold to businesses. However, the fraction of the total tax base accounted for by business sales in Texas is relatively large. For example, Ring (1989) estimates that in 1979 the consumer share of the sales tax in Texas was 46 percent, in comparison to a national average of 59 percent. His estimates indicate that Texas ranked thirty-eighth in the consumer share of sales taxes paid among the forty-five states that levy a state sales tax.[7] Joulfaian and Mackie (1992) stress that Ring's estimate that roughly 40 percent of state sales taxes are paid by businesses implies that a substantial amount of revenue is raised from state sales taxes on business purchases. Specifically, they note that, when aggregated at the national level, total state sales tax revenues obtained from businesses are about 40 percent as large as total federal revenues obtained from the corporate income tax.

This point has rather dramatic implications for the analysis of the relative desirability of state sales and income taxes. Specifically, to the (considerable) extent that the state sales tax applies to business purchases, it cannot accurately be characterized as a tax on consumption and thus does not in fact share the many advantages of consumption taxation. In particular, the Texas state sales tax differs from a true consumption-based tax in that it distorts business decisions regarding the level and the allocation of investment.

The consumer portion of the sales tax base includes most consumption commodities, with the main exemptions being food for home consumption, prescription medicines, and utilities for residential use. In addition, many services are not subject to the sales tax, although Texas, like many other states in recent years, has attempted to increase the sales tax base to include some services.[8] For example, services subject to tax include most nonautomotive repairs, amusements, laundry and dry cleaning, cable television, nonresidential repairs and remodeling of real property, telecommunications, data processing, security services, landscaping and lawn maintenance, janitorial and extermination services, garbage removal, credit reporting and debt collection, certain information services, land surveying, and certain insurance services.[9] Due and Mikesell describe the taxation of consumer services in Texas as "relatively extensive" (1995, p. 89), although still falling somewhat short of the coverage obtained in several other states. More generally, the state sales tax base, including selective excise taxes (discussed below), is reasonably comprehensive, as Texas ranks nineteenth among the forty-five states that levy a state sales tax in the degree of comprehensiveness of its sales tax base.[10]

The Corporate Franchise Tax

The corporate franchise tax in Texas raised revenues of $1.42 billion in 1995, which represents 7.5 percent of tax revenue in the state. The tax is assessed on corporations that have a Texas charter as well as on out-of-state corporations. "Corporation" is defined relatively broadly to include subchapter S-corporations, banks and savings and loan associations, and professional corporations; however, partnerships (including limited liability partnerships) and professional associations are not subject to the tax. For multistate firms, the

TABLE 7.1. NET REVENUES FROM CORPORATE
FRANCHISE TAX, 1984–95 ($MILLION)

Year	1984	1985	1986	1987	1988	1989	1990	1991	1992	1993	1994	1995
Rev.	607	856	901	874	933	680	587	597	1090	1193	1261	1423
% Chg.	9.3	41.0	5.3	−3.0	6.7	−27.1	−13.6	1.6	82.7	9.4	5.7	12.8

Sources: Texas Comptroller of Public Accounts (1994b, p. 36) and (1995a, p. 12).

fraction of the total tax base that is subject to taxation in Texas is equal to the fraction of the firm's total sales that occur in the state; that is, the tax base is apportioned using a "single-factor" formula, where that factor is in-state sales.

In general, the corporate franchise tax equals the larger of 0.25 percent of taxable equity capital (a deduction for debt is allowed), or 4.5 percent of net taxable earned surplus, which is defined as the corporation's net taxable income reported under the federal corporate income tax plus compensation paid to officers and directors of corporations that have more than thirty-five shareholders.[11] Roughly 76 percent of revenues raised by the corporate franchise tax comes from firms paying tax according to the latter income-based calculation method rather than the former wealth-based approach.[12] Thus, in a very real sense, Texas already has a corporate income tax, as more than three-quarters of the revenues under the current state corporate franchise tax are currently obtained under the income-based component of the tax. However, the corporate tax rate of 4.5 percent is low by comparison to those in other states. Only two states with flat rate taxes—Indiana and Kansas—have lower tax rates, and of the states that have graduated schedules, only eight have their lowest rate below 4.5 percent, and all of these have the top rate above that level.[13] Note that the inclusion in the tax base of compensation of officers and directors implies that Texas also indirectly imposes a state income tax at a rate of 4.5 percent on such individuals (who may not be residents of the state).

A number of recent court challenges to the net taxable wealth portion of the corporate franchise tax have reduced the revenues collected from this component of the tax. The primary points of dispute in these cases were (1) the choice of accounting methods to be used for tax purposes, (2) the tax status of reserve accounts, and (3) the treatment of undistributed preacquisition earnings of newly acquired subsidiaries.[14] As a result, revenues from the franchise tax have been extremely unstable in recent years, as documented in table 7.1, which shows that annual changes in revenues have varied from an increase of nearly 83 percent to a reduction of more than 27 percent. The Texas Comptroller of Public Accounts argues that "for the most part these issues have been settled" (1993b, p. 6). In any case, as long as the corporate franchise tax continues to be largely based on the net taxable surplus calculation, the issue of the definition of net taxable wealth will be less important from an overall revenue standpoint.

Oil and Gas Production Taxes

Oil production taxes provided $0.38 billion in revenues in 1995. Natural gas production taxes raised $0.51 billion. Together, these two taxes accounted for 4.7 percent of state tax revenues. By comparison, oil and gas production taxes accounted for 28 percent of state tax revenues as recently as 1981. The dramatic reduction in revenues from these sources, attributable to declines in state production levels and in oil and gas prices, has of course played a major role in the recent revenue crises that have plagued the state.[15]

Selective Excise Taxes and Other Taxes

In 1995, excise taxes on motor fuels (at twenty cents per gallon) raised $2.24 billion, or 11.9 percent of state tax revenues. Excise taxes on motor vehicle sales, assessed at a 6.25 percent rate, and on vehicle rentals raised $1.79 billion in 1995, or 9.5 percent of total taxes. Excise taxes on cigarettes, tobacco, and alcoholic beverages accounted for $1.05 billion, or 5.6 percent of 1995 state tax revenues.[16] Other taxes, including those on insurance premiums, utilities, inheritances, and hotel and motel occupancies resulted in $1.22 billion, or 6.5 percent of state taxes.

Other State Receipts

Other receipts totaled $19.82 billion in 1995. Thus, total tax revenues ($18.86 billion) accounted for 48.8 percent of total revenues available to the state government of $38.68 billion. By far the largest component of other receipts (57.5 percent) was federal grants at $11.41 billion. In addition, interest and dividends provided revenues of $1.71 billion, or 8.7 percent of other receipts. Net lottery proceeds accounted for $1.66 billion, or 8.4 percent of other receipts. The remaining sources of other receipts, which include a wide variety of fees, permits, fines, penalties, land income, and other items totaled $5.04 billion, or 25.4 percent of other receipts.

Local Revenues

Since state and local tax issues are related in many important ways, it will be useful to examine briefly the local revenue structure in Texas. Indeed, any comparison of Texas finances with those of other states must consider both state and combined state and local taxes and expenditures, as the revenue sources and functional responsibilities of state and local governments vary considerably across states. In particular, the fraction of total state and local revenues collected at the state level in Texas has been lower than the national average since the beginning of the 1980s. For example, in 1992, the state share of total state and local tax revenues was 51.9 percent, while the average state share in the nation was 59.0 percent. Thus, an exclusive focus on state level taxes and expenditures will understate the relative magnitude of the combined state and local government sectors in Texas.

The property tax is by far the largest source of local revenue in Texas, accounting for 81.6 percent of local tax revenues in the state, or $12.9 billion in 1992. In fact, the property tax is the single largest source of tax revenue in Texas, generating 39 percent of total state and local tax revenue in 1992.[17] It is levied by cities, counties, and special districts, the most important of which are local school districts.[18]

The other major source of local taxes is the general sales tax. As noted above, local taxing authorities can piggyback on the state sales tax with revenues collected by the state and distributed by the Comptroller of Public Accounts to the appropriate local government or governmental agency. The local sales tax generated 12 percent of total local tax revenue in 1992. However, taxes only make up 45.1 percent of total local revenue. Another 29.9 percent comes from intergovernmental aid, which is mostly from the state, while the remaining 25.0 percent comes from user charges and miscellaneous revenue sources.[19]

Recent Tax Trends in the State

The following discussion summarizes recent tax trends in Texas. A more complete description can be found in Texas Legislative Budget Board (1995) and Texas Comptroller of Public Accounts (1994b).

Table 7.2 indicates that state taxes per capita increased from $215 in 1973 to $1,010 in 1995, and fluctuated considerably over that period. However, the ratio of state taxes to personal income has remained fairly constant, ranging within the relatively narrow band of 4.5 to 5.1 percent. The ratio of state taxes to personal income was estimated to be 4.9 percent in 1995.

The state tax mix has changed considerably over the last twenty years. Table 7.3 indicates that the share of total tax revenues attributable to the general sales tax has increased from 35.8 percent in 1973 to 54.4 percent in 1995. The tax share of the excise tax on motor fuels has followed a U-shaped pattern, reaching a maximum of 14.9 percent in 1973, a minimum of 5.7 percent in 1984, and then increasing to 11.9 percent in 1995. Not surprisingly, given the nature of price fluctuations in the international oil market as well as the evolution of oil and gas production in the state, the opposite pattern occurs for the tax share of oil

TABLE 7.2. TRENDS IN TEXAS STATE TAX COLLECTIONS, 1973–95

Fiscal Year	State Tax Collections ($billions)	Resident Population (millions)	Per Capita Tax Collections ($)	Percentage Change of Per Capita Tax Collections	Taxes as Percentage of Personal Income
1973	2.6	12.0	215	7.9	4.8
1974	3.0	12.2	247	14.8	4.9
1975	3.4	12.5	269	8.7	4.9
1976	3.9	12.9	304	13.3	4.9
1977	4.4	13.2	336	10.4	5.0
1978	5.0	13.5	374	11.3	4.9
1979	5.4	13.8	389	4.2	4.6
1980	6.3	14.3	444	14.1	4.7
1981	7.7	14.7	527	18.5	4.9
1982	8.7	15.2	567	7.7	4.9
1983	8.5	15.7	542	−4.5	4.6
1984	9.3	16.0	582	7.5	4.6
1985	10.7	16.2	660	13.3	4.9
1986	10.2	16.5	620	−6.1	4.5
1987	10.3	16.6	618	−0.3	4.5
1988	12.4	16.7	742	20.1	5.1
1989	12.9	16.8	768	3.6	5.0
1990	13.6	17.0	801	4.2	4.9
1991	14.9	17.3	862	7.6	5.0
1992	15.8	17.6	899	4.4	5.0
1993	17.0	18.0	946	5.2	5.0
1994	18.1	18.3*	988	4.4*	5.0*
1995	18.9	18.7*	1010	2.3*	4.9*

*estimated

Sources: Texas Comptroller of Public Accounts, (1992a, p. 15) and (1995a, p. 19).

and gas severance taxes; specifically, the tax share of oil and gas severance taxes was 13.0 percent in 1973, increased steadily to a maximum of 28.3 percent in 1981, and subsequently declined steadily to a share of only 4.7 percent in 1995. The tax share of excise taxes on cigarettes and tobacco declined fairly steadily over this period, as it was 9.5 percent in 1973 but only 3.4 percent by 1995. The corporate franchise tax had been fairly stable at roughly 5 percent of revenues until the past few years when, due in large part to the effects of the court rulings noted above, it has fluctuated considerably. For example, the tax share

Year	General Sales Tax	Excise Tax on Motor Fuels	Motor Vehicle Sales and Rental Taxes	Cigarette and Tobacco Taxes	Taxes on Alcohol	Corporate Franchise Tax	Oil and Gas Severance Taxes	Insurance Occupation Taxes	Other Taxes
1973	35.8	14.9	7.6	9.5	3.2	5.2	13.0	3.0	7.8
1974	37.2	12.9	6.5	8.2	3.9	5.1	17.1	2.8	6.3
1975	37.6	11.7	6.0	7.8	3.8	4.9	19.7	2.7	5.8
1976	37.8	10.9	6.9	7.2	3.5	5.5	20.3	2.6	5.3
1977	38.2	10.0	7.4	6.5	3.6	5.4	20.4	2.7	5.8
1978	40.2	9.5	8.0	6.0	3.4	5.2	19.0	2.8	5.9
1979	40.3	9.1	8.0	5.7	3.4	5.4	19.0	3.1	6.0
1980	39.7	7.6	6.9	5.1	3.2	5.4	24.0	2.8	5.3
1981	38.5	6.2	6.6	4.4	3.1	5.4	28.3	2.4	5.1
1982	40.0	5.8	6.7	4.0	3.1	5.6	27.4	2.3	5.1
1983	38.9	5.8	6.9	4.2	3.2	6.5	26.5	2.6	5.4
1984	40.7	5.7	7.7	3.7	3.1	6.5	23.8	3.9	4.9
1985	39.1	9.2	8.3	3.5	3.1	8.0	20.2	3.4	5.2
1986	42.3	9.9	8.5	3.7	3.4	8.8	15.1	4.0	4.3
1987	45.0	12.4	7.8	3.6	3.2	8.5	11.5	4.1	3.9
1988	50.5	11.9	7.7	3.4	2.6	7.5	8.5	4.4	3.5
1989	53.6	11.6	7.9	3.3	2.5	5.3	9.1	3.4	3.3
1990	55.7	11.1	8.0	3.2	2.4	4.3	8.0	3.8	3.5
1991	55.3	10.1	7.2	4.3	2.5	4.0	9.0	4.0	3.6
1992	54.0	12.3	7.7	3.7	2.4	6.9	6.4	3.3	3.4
1993	53.6	12.3	8.4	3.6	2.3	7.0	6.9	2.7	3.2
1994	54.2	12.0	8.9	3.2	2.2	7.0	5.1	4.2	3.3
1995	54.4	11.9	9.5	3.4	2.2	7.5	4.7	3.2	3.2

Sources: Texas Comptroller of Public Accounts (1974a–1995a)

TABLE 7.4. STATE TAX REVENUE IN THE TEN
MOST POPULOUS STATES, 1993

State	State Tax Revenue Per $1,000 of Personal Income ($)	State Tax Revenue Per Capita ($)	State Percentage of State-Local Tax Revenue FY 1991–92
North Carolina	80.05	1,404.87	72.7
California	73.04	1,561.58	64.0
New York	71.59	1,719.59	47.1
Michigan	70.97	1,390.29	55.0
Pennsylvania	67.18	1,377.87	61.9
New Jersey	63.82	1,653.21	56.0
Florida	61.82	1,199.45	56.0
Ohio	61.32	1,153.04	56.8
Illinois	57.33	1,239.62	52.6
Texas	**55.91**	**1,011.63**	**51.9**
50-State Average	69.03	1,415.59	59.2

Source: Texas Legislative Budget Board (1995).

of the corporate franchise tax was 8.8 percent in 1986, 4.0 percent in 1991, and 7. 5 percent in 1995. The tax shares of the other taxes listed in table 7.3 have been relatively stable over the last twenty years.

A Brief Comparison with Other States

This subsection compares the overall level of taxation and the tax mix in Texas to those in other states. It also includes the results of a recent ranking of the states in terms of various indicators of "tax competitiveness" in attracting business.

THE LEVEL OF TAXATION AND TAX MIX

Using 1992 data, Texas ranks thirty-fourth among the fifty states in terms of combined state and local tax revenue as a percentage of personal income.[20] As noted previously, local government revenues are disproportionately important in the state/local revenue structure. In terms of the ratio of state tax revenue to personal income, Texas ranks forty-sixth out of the fifty states.[21] Table 7.4 shows per capita state tax revenues and state tax revenues as a percentage of personal income for the ten most populous states in 1993, as well as the state percentage of total state and local tax revenue for fiscal year 1991–92. State taxes in Texas were $55.91 per $1,000 of personal income, which is below the fifty-state average of $69.03. Similarly per capita tax revenue in Texas was $1,011.63, considerably below the U.S. average of $1,415.59. Note that Texas ranks last among the ten most populous states in terms of state tax revenue as a percent-

TABLE 7.5. PERCENTAGE DISTRIBUTION OF STATE TAX REVENUE BY MAJOR TAXES IN THE TEN MOST POPULOUS STATES, 1993

State	Total Sales Tax	General Sales Tax	Selective Sales Tax	Licenses	Personal Income Tax	Corporation Income Tax	Other
California	44.3	34.2	10.1	5.1	35.3	9.7	5.6
Florida	77.5	56.7	20.9	7.7	0.0	4.6	10.2
Illinois	50.5	30.1	20.4	5.8	33.2	7.6	2.9
Michigan	36.7	26.3	10.4	5.8	39.5	14.0	4.0
New Jersey	52.0	28.0	24.0	4.6	33.4	7.3	2.7
New York	36.1	20.1	16.1	3.1	48.9	8.4	3.5
North Carolina	43.2	24.1	19.0	6.3	40.9	7.3	2.3
Ohio	50.1	31.1	19.0	6.9	36.9	5.3	0.8
Pennsylvania	46.9	29.1	17.8	10.6	28.1	8.9	5.6
Texas	79.5	50.1	29.4	13.3	0.0	0.0	7.2
50-State Average	49.3	32.5	16.8	6.6	31.9	6.9	5.4

Note: The Texas corporate franchise tax is classified under the "Licenses" category.
Source: Texas Legislative Budget Board (1995).

age of personal income and per capita state tax revenues, and that only New York has a lower level of state taxes as a percentage of total state and local tax revenue.

The primary factor that distinguishes the tax mix in Texas from that in most other states is of course that Texas has neither a personal income tax nor (nominally) a corporate income tax. Only six other states do not have a personal income tax—Alaska, Florida, Nevada, South Dakota, Washington, and Wyoming. In addition, New Hampshire and Tennessee have only a limited tax on interest and dividend income. Other than Texas, only four states in the United States do not utilize a corporate income tax—Nevada, South Dakota, Washington, and Wyoming.[22]

The tax mix in Texas is thus characterized by heavy reliance on sales taxes. The general sales tax is a very common tax instrument among other states, as only Alaska, Delaware, Montana, New Hampshire, and Oregon do not utilize the sales tax.[23] However, in 1992, only four states—Florida, South Dakota, Tennessee, and Washington—had a greater share of state tax revenue attributable to the general sales tax.[24] In addition, severance taxes have played an important role in the Texas revenue structure, although they have become increasingly less important since the early 1980s.

To make these comparisons more concrete, table 7.5 compares the percentage distribution of state tax revenue by major taxes for the ten most populous

	Income Taxes	General Sales Taxes	Property Taxes	Other Taxes	Total Taxes	Charges and Misc. Sources	Inter-governmental Transfers
U.S. Average	14.2	13.5	18.3	11.0	57.1	24.5	18.4
Texas	0.0	18.5	22.8	16.6	57.9	25.6	16.5

Source: U.S. Advisory Commission on Intergovernmental Relations (1994, pp. 86–87).

TABLE 7.7. U.S. AVERAGE STATE TAX REVENUE BY SOURCE, PERCENTAGE DISTRIBUTION, SELECTED YEARS 1970–1990

Year	Individual Income Taxes	Corporation Income Taxes	Sales and Gross Receipts Taxes	Other Taxes
1970	19.1	7.8	56.8	16.2
1975	23.5	8.3	54.1	14.2
1980	27.1	9.7	49.5	13.7
1985	29.6	8.2	48.9	13.4
1990	32.0	7.2	48.9	11.8

Source: U.S. Advisory Commission on Intergovernmental Relations (1992b, p. 116).

states. Texas clearly relies relatively heavily on sales taxes, as nearly 80 percent of total tax revenue in the state is generated by general or selective sales taxes—the highest figure among these states and considerably higher than the national average of just over 49 percent. By comparison, the national average for the percentage of state tax revenues derived from the personal income tax is nearly 32 percent, while Texas does not have a personal income tax.

In addition, table 7.6 compares Texas to all other states in terms of the tax mix for combined state and local revenue for 1992. These data demonstrate that Texas places relatively heavy reliance on general sales and property taxes, as the revenue share of each tax is roughly 4 to 5 percentage points greater than the national average. Note that the share of total taxes in total revenues (57.9 percent) is very close to the national average share (57.1 percent).

Table 7.7 shows how the average mix of state taxes has changed over time. From 1970 to 1990, nationwide reliance on personal income taxes increased from 19 percent to 32 percent of total state tax revenues, while during the same time period, reliance on sales and gross receipts taxes declined from almost 57 percent to just under 49 percent. By comparison, table 7.3 shows that during this period Texas became increasingly reliant upon sales taxes, while avoiding the use of a personal income tax.

BUSINESS COMPETITIVENESS

Many discussions of state tax policy focus on the role of taxes in economic development, specifically the extent to which the tax system of a state might discourage business investment—in the form of either new plants or the expansion of existing facilities. Several researchers have attempted to quantify this feature of a tax system by constructing measures of the relative "competitiveness" of the tax structures of various states.

A good example of such a study is Tannenwald (1993), who uses 1991 data in providing rankings of the fifty states in terms of various indicators of "tax competitiveness" in attracting business.[25] For example, in terms of the level of total state and local tax revenue relative to personal income, Texas ranks thirty-third among the fifty states. The effective total tax rate of 10.2 percent in Texas falls slightly below the national average rate of 10.9 percent.[26] These figures, however, combine individual and business level taxes and are probably not as relevant to business decisions as data on taxes that have a direct impact on firms. Accordingly, Tannenwald also calculates the share of total state and local taxes—including estimates of the business shares of sales and property taxes—with an initial impact on business. Texas' ranking in terms of this criterion (sixth) is relatively poor, primarily due to the state's relatively heavy reliance on property taxes and a significant severance tax burden.[27]

However, Tannenwald notes that the share of total state and local taxes with an initial impact on business can be a misleading indicator of competitiveness for a number of reasons. Most obviously, this measure does not include any information about the absolute level of taxes with an initial impact on business. Thus, a state with a high business impact tax share might still have a relatively low absolute business tax burden. In addition, differences in business impact tax shares across states can arise from a number of factors not directly attributable to differences in the taxation of business income, including differences in the capital intensity of production, the level of personal income, the importance of extractive industries subject to severance taxes, and the importance of agriculture (which tends to be taxed relatively lightly).

Tannenwald argues that two other measures are much better indicators of tax competitiveness. The first is the tax burden on high-income individuals, which Tannenwald argues is likely to be an important element of a state's tax competitiveness because such individuals are relatively mobile and thus more likely than lower-paid workers to demand salary increases to compensate for a relatively high tax burden in a state, and because the individuals who are responsible for firm location decisions generally receive high salaries and thus have a personal interest in a state's tax burden on high-income individuals. Texas appears to be quite competitive in terms of this criterion. For example, its total state and local tax burden on high-income families ranked forty-fifth among the fifty states.[28]

The second measure is an analysis of the net effects of the tax systems in cities in different states on the rate of return earned by a "representative firm" making a "representative investment."[29] This approach is very useful because it allows detailed analyses of the effects of the tax system on the incentives for future investment, although it is limited in the sense that it considers only a finite number of types of investments in a finite number of cities. Tannenwald cites the work of Brooks (1993), who examines potential investments by representative firms in five industries in fifteen cities, including El Paso (the only Texas city considered in the analysis). In all cases, El Paso is reported to be the most competitive city—that is, the city with the highest after-tax rate of return on the representative investment. Tannenwald attributes this result primarily to the absence of a state corporate income tax in Texas. This result is suspect, however, because the calculations do not consider the burdens of state sales taxes on business purchases, which, as stressed above, are relatively large in Texas.

These various measures of competitiveness suggest that the overall tax burden in Texas is lower than the national average, even though the share of taxes with an initial impact on businesses is quite high. Note that none of the calculations provides any comparisons regarding differences in government service levels across states.

THE STATE SALES VERSUS INCOME TAX DEBATE: THE CASE OF TEXAS TAXES

This section applies the analysis presented in the rest of the book to the case of Texas taxes. Specifically, it compares the relative merits of the current Texas sales/corporate franchise tax system with the alternative of an income tax system consisting of a personal and a corporate income tax. The evaluation thus uses the criteria detailed in chapter 2 and applies the analyses presented in chapters 3 through 6 to the tax reform debate in Texas.

Exporting Tax Burdens through Deductibility

As described at length in chapter 3, the current federal tax system provides an unambiguous incentive for the use of a state income tax rather than a sales tax because only the former is deductible against individual tax liability at the national level.[30] A critical question is the magnitude of this incentive. One way of examining this issue is by estimating the amount by which the residents of a state could reduce their effective state tax liability, holding revenues constant, by a partial or complete switch from a nondeductible sales tax to a deductible personal income tax. A very rough estimate of the amount of this "deductibility savings" for Texas can be obtained as follows.

For Texas, total state sales tax revenue in 1995 was $10.26 billion, or 54.4 percent of total state tax revenue of $18.86 billion. Following the discussion above, assume that 60 percent—or $6.16 billion—of this amount is paid by individuals. Suppose for the sake of argument that all of this amount was instead raised using a deductible state personal income tax. The fraction of this amount that would be deductible depends of course on the details of the state and federal income tax laws, including the extent to which the state income tax is paid by those who itemize (and thus actually deducted against federal tax liability) and the relevant state and federal income tax rates. However, to obtain a rough estimate, note that Pollock (1991) estimates that about 75 percent of state income taxes were deducted in 1991 and that the average marginal tax rate applied to these deductions was 26.5 percent. If these nationwide averages were applicable to a state income tax, the gain for Texas from switching to a deductible income tax would be approximately 20 percent of personal sales tax revenues or a little over $1.2 billion dollars. However, this figure should be reduced by roughly 25 percent—to 15 percent of personal sales tax revenues or $920 million—to reflect the fact that items that are potentially deductible are less likely to be deducted in Texas than in the nation as a whole because state taxpayers itemize deductions on their federal tax returns to a smaller extent than the national average.[31] This represents about 9.0 percent of total sales tax revenues and 4.9 percent of total state tax revenues. This figure may be an overestimate, since it ignores the fact that average incomes, and thus tax rates, are lower in Texas than in the nation as a whole. On the other hand, adoption of a state income tax would increase the fraction of Texas taxpayers who itemize, since potential deductions would increase, and this in turn would tend to increase the gain from using a deductible tax rather than a nondeductible one.[32]

Thus, the marginal effective cost to Texas taxpayers of financing state services could be reduced by something on the order of 10 percent if the state were to introduce a personal income tax and reduce reliance on the general sales tax.[33] If the only goal were to take advantage of the deductibility of a state income tax, this tax change could be structured in such a way as to replicate on average the burden of the current general sales tax, taking into account the fact that the total burden of any state income tax structure (holding state revenues constant) would be reduced by the ability to export some of the tax burden through federal deductibility. In addition, the benefits of deductibility are more important for higher income individuals, since they are more likely to itemize deductions and they face higher marginal tax rates. Thus, a modestly progressive state income tax could be structured so that its net effect, taking into account deductibility, would on average be roughly proportional across all income classes.

Exporting Tax Burdens through Price Changes

As also described in chapter 3, competition at the national and international levels implies that the other avenue of exportability—increasing prices to out of state consumers or lowering returns to out of state factor owners—is not likely to be important under either an income tax or a sales tax. For example, in an analysis of Texas state and local taxes under the assumptions that business taxes are shifted forward and severance taxes are borne by landowners, Fritz (1989)—following the methodology used by Phares (1980)—estimates that only slightly more than 3 percent of all Texas state and local taxes are exported to out-of-state consumers.[34]

Note that this analysis applies even to oil and gas production, which is of course a critical industry in Texas. Early analyses suggested that Texas was in a position to export a significant fraction of its tax burden in the form of higher prices for oil and natural gas, which reflected severance taxes on oil and gas production. For example, Phares (1980) estimated that 75 percent of the severance tax burden in 1976 was exported to out-of-state residents. However, most recent analyses suggest that since the prices of oil and, to a slightly lesser extent, natural gas are determined in an international market, the potential for tax exporting is very limited. For example, McDonald (1980) argues persuasively that since the world price of oil is independent of production levels in Texas (and indeed in the United States), any severance taxes assessed by the state must be borne as lower factor returns—most likely as lower land rents, since oil-producing land is immobile. Thus, except to the extent that such land is owned by nonresidents, Texas oil and gas severance taxes are ultimately borne by in-state landowners.

Efficiency Considerations

In the Texas context, the most compelling efficiency argument for a state income tax system is rather counterintuitive—the adoption of such a reform would probably lower the overall state tax burden on business relative to the current tax system. The allocation of tax burden across businesses and individuals would, of course, depend on the specific income tax structures that would ultimately be adopted. Nevertheless, it is quite possible that the total business tax burden would decline, relative to the current system, because under current law a substantial fraction of business purchases is subject to the sales tax and a significant portion of corporate income is subject to tax under the corporate franchise tax. By comparison, under a state income tax system, sales taxation of all business purchases would be eliminated, leaving businesses subject only to the corporate income tax. In addition, under the current single-factor (sales) apportionment formula for the state corporate tax, some of the burden of the tax falls on sales to consumers. As a result, a lower overall tax burden on businesses would appear to be likely, although this obviously depends on the corporate tax structure. The arguments presented above suggest that such a reduction in business tax burden would be desirable.

In addition, it is clear that the haphazard sales taxation of business purchases that occurs under the state sales tax suffers from many deficiencies. The burden of such a tax varies across industries, distorting a variety of business production decisions, including those regarding goods produced, the capital/labor mix and the extent of vertical integration. Moreover, these distortionary effects may be quite large since a relatively low sales tax rate can translate into a significant increase in the effective tax rate applied to business income.

Furthermore, note that the current franchise tax system is in an important sense even worse than a conventional income tax system, as the former has both an income-based component and a wealth-based component. As a result, profitable firms typically pay the income-based component of the tax, but unprofitable businesses must still pay the wealth-based component of the tax. Such asymmetric tax treatment is quite harsh on businesses and is, for at least some firms, likely to discourage risk-taking since firms must pay tax regardless of whether or not they are profitable. Thus, another efficiency argument for an income tax system in Texas is that the more symmetric treatment of the returns to risky investment under a true income tax system would be less of a disincentive to such investment.

On the other hand, a state corporate tax based on the federal corporate tax only exacerbates the distortions of the latter tax described above. Moreover, recall that the apportionment formula in Texas includes only sales. Thus, for large multistate firms, the income-based component of the corporate franchise tax acts largely as a kind of sales tax. However, this "sales" tax includes a very large fraction of business purchases; indeed, this fraction is much higher than under the retail sales tax, since all transactions, even those involving goods sold for resale or used in the production of other goods, are included in the measure of sales. The state corporate tax thus results in a significant tax burden on capital and is also highly distortionary across business assets and sectors and creates tax incentives for business mergers.[35]

Another feature of the corporate franchise tax in Texas is also problematical. Specifically, compensation paid to officers and directors is generally not deductible under the income-based component of the franchise tax, effectively assessing an indirect personal income tax on such compensation. Given widespread concerns about structuring the state tax system to encourage economic development, this provision is especially peculiar, since it singles out for a special implicit tax those individuals who are likely to be among the most influential in making business location decisions. More generally, this provision imposes a differentially large tax burden in a capricious way on many relatively mobile high-income individuals.

Thus, in the absence of an explicit analysis of all of these distortions in the context of a general equilibrium model of the Texas economy, it is difficult to construct a strong argument for either a state income tax or the state sales tax on efficiency grounds in terms of their relative effects on business decision making.

By comparison, the efficiency case for a personal income tax over the consumer portion of the state sales tax is fairly clear. Due to differential taxation of various commodities, the sales tax is considerably more distortionary of individual consumption decisions. Although an income tax is more likely to create incentives for high-income individuals to move out of the state (or not move in), this effect is limited if the income tax is at most moderately progressive—as is generally recommended—and is mitigated by the deductibility of the income tax against individual federal tax liability. On balance, the sales tax is likely to be more distortionary of individual decisions than is a flat rate or a moderately progressive income tax.

Finally, the relative desirability of the two taxes in terms of their effects on the efficiency of government decision making probably favors the income tax to a fairly small extent. Both taxes include a significant business component and are thus undesirable in the sense that they include an important "hidden tax" component. This argument favors the income tax to the extent that the total business tax burden is higher under the combination of the sales tax and corporate franchise tax. In addition, the personal income tax is arguably more visible than is the sales tax on consumer purchases.

Equity Considerations

The tool most commonly used by economists to evaluate the fairness of a tax system is the estimation of taxes paid, relative to income, by households in various groups characterized by annual income. Such studies typically conclude that an income tax is preferable to a state sales tax because the former results in a more progressive distribution of the tax burden (although the question of the optimal degree of progressivity of a state tax system is obviously a contentious one, with notions of fairness varying widely across different observers).

Such an analysis of the incidence of the Texas state tax system in 1984 has been conducted by Fritz (1989).[36] He assumes first that excise taxes and general sales taxes on consumption commodities are borne by consumers in proportion to their consumption levels of the taxed commodities, as estimated from data obtained from the Consumer Expenditure Survey.[37] He then notes that the incidence of taxes on businesses (primarily sales taxes on business purchases, the corporate franchise tax, severance taxes, and nonresidential property taxes) is unclear from a theoretical perspective, as such taxes may be shifted forward to consumers in the form of higher prices, shifted backward to the owners of capital or the suppliers of labor, or some combination of these effects. In light of this uncertainty, Fritz reports incidence results under the following four possible scenarios: (1) full forward shifting to consumers, (2) full backward shifting of all business taxes to business owners, (3) an equal split of business taxes between consumers and owners, and (4) an equal split of business taxes among consumers, owners, and employees. The first scenario is the most regressive, since the ratio of consumption to annual income declines with income. The second scenario is the most progressive, as capital income is earned disproportionately by high-income families. The final two cases are intermediate to the first two. In addition, assumptions about tax exporting affect the estimates of tax burden. In case one (full forward shifting), Fritz draws on Phares (1980) to assume that 3.2 percent of the consumer tax burden is exported to out-of-state residents, which is not an unreasonable estimate. However, in the other cases, Fritz assumes that as much as 80 percent of the business tax burden is exported, which (as discussed in chapter 3) is a highly implausible assumption.

As noted by Fritz, choosing between the alternative tax shifting scenarios is difficult. In general, incidence is determined by relative elasticities of supply and demand, that is, by the extent to which supply and demand are responsive to price. The general rule is that taxes tend to be borne by factors of production or consumers that are relatively immobile. Thus, incidence is determined by the structure of the market in which a tax is imposed. For taxes imposed at the state level, the key distinction is whether the commodity that is being taxed (either directly or indirectly) is sold primarily in a "state" market (one in which virtually all sales are made within the state and there are few out-of-state exports) or in a "national" market (one in which much of the output of state firms is exported and firms compete on a national or an international scale).[38] In the former case, local consumers are likely to bear most of the burden of the tax, especially to the extent that markets are competitive and production is characterized by "constant returns to scale"—that is, unit production costs are independent of the level of operations. In contrast, in the latter case, forward shifting is difficult or impossible since prices are determined in a national or an international market, and backward shifting to in-state factors of production is the likely outcome. Moreover, since capital owners are relatively "mobile" in the sense that they are free to invest in any state (or, indeed, in any country), most of the tax burden is likely to fall on relatively immobile owners of labor and land.

For the assumptions noted above, Fritz estimates that the overall Texas state tax system is quite regressive at low-income levels (0–$15,000) and either mildly regressive or mildly progressive (depending on the incidence assumptions) at the middle- and upper-income levels. In the most regressive case (full forward shifting), families in the 0–$10,000 income class pay 9 percent of their income in taxes, while the remaining families bear a burden in the range of 3.5 to 5.5 percent of income. A similar incidence pattern is reported in the GTFR report, with families in the 0–$10,000 income class paying somewhat under 8 percent of their income in taxes, while the remaining families bear a burden in the range of 4.7 to 5.7 percent of income. As suggested above, these calculations form the basis for one of the criticisms most often voiced of the tax system in Texas—it is a regressive system that bears disproportionately on the poor.

However, to repeat the arguments presented in chapter 4, such criticisms can be exaggerated. Specifically, if one is willing to think about tax incidence in terms of periods longer than a single year—and indeed, as long as an individual's lifetime—then equity arguments should take into account differences in the relationship between consumption and income over the life cycle (as consumption typically exceeds income during youth and old age and income typically exceeds consumption during the prime earning years) as well as the effects of transitory income fluctuations. The implications of taking these considerations into account in the Texas context are basically the same as those stressed in chapter 4. Specifically, (1) at least some—and probably a significant portion—of the measured regressivity of the state sales tax is due to the use of annual income as a measure of ability to pay, (2) alternative measures that attempt to capture lifetime income, including annual consumption, are a preferable measure of ability to pay, (3) the state sales tax is probably roughly proportional with respect to lifetime income, except for the highest income classes where some regressivity is likely to obtain, and (4) progressive income taxes are in fact less progressive than they appear when their incidence is evaluated from a lifetime perspective.

This analysis suggests that the equity issue in evaluating the Texas tax structure should be rephrased. Specifically, the primary issue is whether it is desirable to structure the state tax system in such a way that low-income individuals are entirely exempt from tax, or whether such individuals should bear a tax burden that is roughly proportional to consumption or lifetime income. If one's views regarding equity are consistent with the former approach, an income tax is the more desirable option. In contrast, if the latter view of equity is seen as more reasonable (e.g., because everyone should contribute to the provision of public services), the sales tax is the preferred option.

In addition, it must be emphasized that the achievement of equity goals under the state sales tax in Texas has a rather high cost. Specifically, excluding various items from the tax base on the grounds that they are consumed disproportionately by the poor does reduce the regressivity of the tax, but only at the cost of dramatically reducing the size of the tax base. As a result, the tax rate required to achieve any given level of revenue is relatively high. In contrast, under a personal income tax system, a given level of consumption can be excluded through the use of personal exemptions and a standard deduction. Such an approach is more targeted than sales tax exemptions, which apply to all purchases of the exempt items whether they are made by the poor or reflect the relatively high consumption levels of the rich. As a result, the tax rate under the income tax can be lower, which reduces the distortions associated with achieving any particular equity goal.

At the same time, recall that two additional arguments favor the use of the sales tax over the income tax on equity grounds. Specifically, only the sales tax is effective in taxing the elderly who are wealthy but have relatively little current taxable income, and only the sales tax is likely to result in at least some tax burden on tourists and business travelers, who are also consumers of public services and thus, according to the benefit principle, should pay at least some tax.

Revenue Stability

The differences between the sales tax and income tax options in terms of the criterion of revenue stability over the business cycle are not great and can be moderated by adequate funding of the state's "rainy day" revenue stabilization fund.

An often-mentioned problem with the state tax system in Texas is that the sales tax base grows less than proportionately with the state economy, which can result in chronic revenue shortages. This problem arises because the sales tax base excludes various items, especially some services and government expenditures, that have in recent years accounted for an increasing fraction of the state economy. This problem would not arise under a broad-based income tax that would tend to grow proportionately (or more than proportionately if it were moderately progressive) with the state economy. Many observers, however, reasonably argue that, at least in the case of a progressive tax, an income tax is undesirable because it results in an increasing ratio of revenues to income in the presence of economic growth, and thus it tends to lead to a higher level of services than would occur in the absence of such an easy source of revenue.

A separate issue is whether an income tax or the current state tax structure would result in more stable revenues in the face of cyclical fluctuations. Unfortunately, no one has conducted an optimal state tax portfolio analysis of the state revenue structure under the assumption that a state income tax could be included in the tax mix.[39] Thus, it is difficult to compare the income and sales tax options in terms of the criterion of revenue stability. In general, one would expect a consumption-based tax, like the sales tax, to be more stable than a taxed based on income. However, note that a significant fraction of necessities—the consumption of which is very stable over the business cycle—is excluded from the consumer portion of the sales tax base. As a result, consumer durables—of which purchases tend to fluctuate significantly with the business cycle—are an important part of the consumer goods tax base. In addition, the base of the sales tax includes many business purchases, which also tend to fluctuate with the business cycle. Thus, much of the inherent stability of a tax on consumption is lost under the current state sales tax. Hamilton (1989d, p. 78) characterizes the sales tax in Texas as having only "medium" or average stability in the sense that the growth rate of revenues was within 2 percent of the average overall state growth rate in only 25 to 50 percent of the years between 1947–87.

Cyclical considerations also suggest that a tax based on a business firm's assets, such as the wealth component of the corporate franchise tax, will be more stable than a tax based on corporate income, which fluctuates significantly over the business cycle. This, however, has not been the case with corporate franchise tax revenues in Texas, which have been rather unstable over the years. Hamilton (1989b) attributes this instability to the legal challenges (discussed above) that have altered the legal base of the tax. The component of the sales tax assessed on sales to businesses is probably also more stable than a tax on income, but this distinction may be quite small.

The net effect of these factors is impossible to ascertain without a detailed "optimal state tax portfolio" analysis of the current tax structure and an alternative system that would potentially include a personal income tax. Although one might expect that the current sales tax/franchise tax combination would exhibit somewhat lower revenue growth and greater stability than an income tax alternative, the results presented in the two studies by Gentry and Ladd (1994) and Harmon and Mallick (1994) cited above demonstrate that this is not necessarily the case. Instead, it is quite possible that an income tax would provide both higher revenue growth and more revenue stability in Texas than does the current sales tax, given the exemptions granted under the state sales tax base and the fact that any personal income tax in the state is not likely to be very progressive. Thus, the main difference between an income tax and a sales tax is that tax revenues would increase more uniformly with growth of the state economy under the income tax. It would otherwise appear that the differences between the sales and income tax options in terms of the criterion of revenue stability are not great.

Administrative and Compliance Costs

The analysis above indicates that a state income tax closely related to the federal personal and corporate taxes would be relatively simple in terms of compliance, administration, and enforcement. However, any significant reductions in lowering state compliance, administration, and enforcement costs would occur only if the state sales tax were replaced entirely with an income tax. Given the level of political opposition to an income tax system in the state of Texas, this, to say the least, would appear to be a rather unlikely proposition.

As a result, the introduction of a new state income tax system would result in additional compliance and administration costs, especially at the individual level. These costs could be minimized by having the state income tax system be closely related to the federal income tax system, although this obviously implies that the state tax system would then be characterized by all the problems that plague the current federal income tax.

The Bottom Line in the Case of Texas Taxes

To sum up, in the case of Texas taxes, the main argument for a comprehensive income tax system is that the state in effect already has a system that has many of the negative features commonly associated with income taxation but, without the explicit adoption of such a tax, forgoes some of its benefits. In particular, since taxes on business purchases form an important part of the sales tax base and the vast majority of corporate franchise tax revenues are raised with the corporate income component of that tax, the tax burdens on businesses and capital income under the current system are broadly similar to those that would occur under an income tax on corporate and personal incomes. Indeed, since the current effective corporate income tax rate assessed through the combination of the franchise tax and the sales tax on business purchases is already fairly high, a move to an income tax might very well shift some of the current tax burden to individuals. The discussion earlier in this book of the taxation of business in a small open economy implies that such a shift would be desirable. In addition, the asymmetry of the existing tax treatment of businesses under the corporate franchise tax—with taxation of successful firms under the income-based component coupled with taxation of unsuccessful firms under the wealth-based component—creates tax disincentives to risk-taking for some firms. Moreover, the capricious tax burden on businesses under the current sales tax is also problematical, although it is unclear whether a move to an income tax, given the distortions it would create, would improve matters on this score or make them worse. It does appear, however, that an income tax would be less distortionary of individual consumption decisions than the current tax system, although such a tax should be at most moderately progressive to avoid creating large incentives for the emigration of high-income individuals. The implicit taxation of compensation paid to officers and directors of businesses under the corporate franchise tax is also rather problematical and does not appear to be conducive to economic development.

In addition, explicit adoption of a personal income tax is clearly desirable in the sense that it increases the extent to which the state tax burden can be exported to out-of-state taxpayers through the mechanism of deductibility against federal tax liability. Some rough calculations imply that on average the marginal cost of government services to Texas taxpayers could be lowered by something in the neighborhood of 10 percent by using an individual income tax rather than the sales tax. Federal deductibility also reduces the impact of any progressivity that might be built into the state income tax structure and presumably weakens the resistance of high-income taxpayers to the provision of services to lower-income residents.

On equity grounds, an argument that is often made in support of an income tax is that it is less regressive than a sales tax. (Of course, views about the optimal degree of progressivity of a state tax system vary widely.) Although this is true in the context of annual measure of tax incidence, the analysis above argues that it is much less of a concern if incidence is measured in a lifetime context. Nevertheless, a sales tax will typically still impose a smaller tax burden on the very wealthy than an income tax does, even under a lifetime measure of tax incidence.

Another equity-based argument for an income tax is that it is desirable if public sentiment in Texas supports the ideas that low-income individuals should face minimal taxes and that some modest degree of progressivity is desirable. Although these goals can also be achieved under a sales tax, the various exemptions used in an attempt to reduce the tax burden of the poor imply that tax rates (and the associated distortions of consumption decisions, including those involving out-of-state purchases) must be relatively high. Such equity goals can be achieved much more directly through the use of personal exemptions, standard deductions, and rate progressivity under the income tax. In addition, the use of an income tax, especially if it is moderately progressive, facilitates increased utilization of user fees for government services (by making such charges less objectionable on equity grounds), which is desirable in terms of both efficiency and equity. On the other hand, if Texans believe that all individuals should contribute to the financing of public services roughly in proportion to their consumption levels, a general sales tax (or a flat-rate income tax with no deductions or exemptions) is the more desirable option on equity grounds.

Moreover, the enactment of a moderately progressive state income tax would alleviate the problem of a tax base that increases less than proportionately with the economy. This consideration is a potentially important one because none of the three main options for increasing sales tax revenues in response to a revenue shortfall attributable to a slowly growing tax base is very appealing. Specifically, (1) increasing sales tax rates would exacerbate current economic distortions, (2) further broadening of the sales tax base to include services, although desirable to the extent that it applied to consumer services, would also be likely to apply to some extent to business services and thus increase the business tax burden in an undesirable and capricious way (while adding some administrative costs), and (3) broadening the consumer tax base by eliminating current sales tax exemptions is undesirable on equity grounds. This argument is of course especially relevant if the state wishes (or is forced by court order) to raise additional revenues to provide additional funds to local governments to finance public education.

In addition to the various arguments against an income tax noted above, several other factors argue against its adoption. First, since both the individual and corporate state income taxes would presumably be based on the analogous federal taxes, a state income tax would in general exacerbate all the problems associated with the current federal income tax system, including distortions of business investment, financing and organizational decisions, and individual saving decisions. Second, the income tax may have negative effects on the state's ability to attract and keep high-income individuals. Third, the income tax is less effective than the sales tax in assessing tax on the elderly and on tourists and business travelers.[40] Fourth, the introduction of an income tax, in conjunction with continued use of the sales tax, would involve additional administrative and compliance costs, especially for individuals.

Weighing these various factors is not easy and, in the absence of detailed data on many of the issues discussed above, such a weighing is an inevitably subjective exercise. Nevertheless, in my view, it appears on balance that the introduction of a state income tax system would be preferable to the expansion of the current system of sales and corporate franchise taxes. Such a reform would allow the state to gain several of the benefits associated with such a system, while most of the negative aspects of income taxation already plague the current sales/corporate franchise tax system. At a minimum, a clear implication of this book is that from an economic perspective it is unreasonable simply to preclude discussion of the state income tax alternative as an inherently undesirable or infeasible policy option for the state of Texas.

ALTERNATIVE REFORMS OF THE TEXAS TAX SYSTEM

This section focuses on potential reforms of the Texas state tax system—although most of the reforms discussed could be implemented in other states as well. In the context of the Texas tax system, the discussion above suggests that the current state tax structure is sufficiently flawed that it would be preferable to use a new personal/corporate income tax system to finance any significant reductions in local property taxes or increases in state expenditures, relative to increasing reliance on the existing tax structure. The underlying analysis has assumed, however, that the sole alternative to an income tax is the existing state tax system. By comparison, this section focuses on a very different tax reform question—what types of fundamental changes might be implemented to improve the existing tax system. This issue is relevant for at least two reasons. First, as suggested above, political constraints suggest that the income tax reform option may simply be infeasible, regardless of whether or not one is persuaded by the economic arguments in favor of such a tax. Second, as noted at length previously, the essence of the argument for a state income tax is not that income-based taxation is inherently superior to consumption-based taxation; indeed, it is arguably the case that the reverse is true. Rather the primary motivation for consideration of an income tax in the Texas context is that the current tax system is so seriously flawed, especially if its goal is to tax consumption comprehensively. Accordingly, a natural question is whether the current system could be reformed to approximate more closely a tax on consumption and thus obviate many of the arguments that favor the income tax option over the current tax system. Additional questions of interest are whether increased reliance on user taxes or even the sole use of a truly consumption-based sales tax are feasible alternative revenue options. The following section briefly discusses such reforms.

Reforms of the Existing Tax System

The discussion in this chapter has indicated a number of rather serious problems with the existing tax structure in Texas.[41] Accordingly, it will be useful to consider briefly the nature of some potential major reforms that would significantly improve the current tax system. Specifically, Texas state policymakers should consider reforms in the following five areas: (1) reducing sales taxation of business purchases, (2) increasing sales taxation of consumer purchases of services, (3) replacing the current system of commodity sales tax exemptions with a tax rebate system, (4) eliminating the wealth-based component of the corporate franchise tax, and (5) eliminating the disallowance of a deduction for salaries paid to the officers and directors of large corporations. Alternatively, the state could elect to move to a true consumption-based system by implementing the first three reforms to the sales tax noted above and then simply eliminating the corporate franchise tax.

REDUCING SALES TAXATION OF BUSINESS PURCHASES

As stressed throughout this study, the retail sales tax, as administered in Texas (and to varying degrees in all other states that utilize the tax), cannot be characterized as a true consumption tax since a significant fraction of the tax base, on the order of 40 percent, consists of business purchases. As a result, the tax does not achieve the benefits of taxation on the basis of consumption rather than income and is probably best characterized as a haphazard income tax rather than a true consumption-based tax. A clear implication of the analysis in this book—and a standard prescription of sales tax experts—is that a movement toward reduced sales taxation of business purchases would be desirable.[42]

This might be achieved in one of two ways. First, greater efforts could be devoted within the context of the current system to ensure that business purchases are made tax-exempt. This would involve broadening the extent to which firms can make exempt purchases of production inputs, coupled with greater efforts devoted to ensure that such purchases were in fact used for business purposes. As noted above, the primary problem areas are business purchases of office furniture, computers and other office equipment, some services, fuels, various intermediate goods, certain types of machines and tools, certain raw materials, and structures (which are implicitly taxed since sales taxes are paid on the purchases of many of the components of business structures and are thus incorporated in their prices).

Alternatively, another approach, which is sometimes discussed in the context of a national retail sales tax, might be employed. Under this approach, goods that are used exclusively as business inputs would simply be made exempt from the retail sales tax. Thus, transactions involving such goods would have no implications for tax purposes. At the same time, all goods that might be used for personal consumption would be made subject to tax, and business firms would then have to file for rebates of tax on the purchases of such goods to the extent that they could document that the goods were used for business purchases. This approach has two important advantages. First, it requires the purchasing firm, rather than the seller, to establish whether a good is used for business or personal purposes. This is highly desirable, since the purchaser obviously has better information on how a product will be used, and the seller has no incentive to determine how a product is to be used (and indeed may wish to assume business use in questionable cases in order to stimulate sales). Second, such treatment seems likely to improve compliance, since it requires the purchasing firm to file with the tax authorities for a rebate, rather than simply asserting to the seller that a purchase is for business purposes. Mikesell (1996) argues that purchasers are more willing to make false statements to another firm than to the tax authorities, so the rebate approach should reduce fraudulent claims of business use of goods that are actually used for personal consumption.

However, this approach is not without its problems. It is clear that the categorization of certain goods as purely business inputs and others as goods with both business and personal uses would inevitably involve serious definitional problems. In addition, a considerable amount of administrative and compliance resources would be used in collecting taxes only to refund them later. A related point is that the prospect of having a large number of firms in the tax system, likely including many out-of-state firms, solely for the purpose of receiving refunds is not appealing from a political perspective. Finally, the prospect of obtaining sales tax refunds could lead to widespread efforts to defraud the system, including fraudulent attempts to classify personal consumption as business purchases by firms formed solely or primarily for that purpose.

Nevertheless, such an approach seems likely to increase considerably the extent to which legitimate business purchases would be excluded from the base of the retail sales tax. As a result, a retail sales tax operated under these principles would in fact be much closer to a tax system that is truly based on consumption than the current system. Accordingly, this approach is worthy of serious consideration in the state sales tax context.[43]

INCREASING SALES TAXATION OF CONSUMER PURCHASES OF SERVICES

Another potential reform is further expansion of the tax base to include consumer services. Although Texas has made strides in increasing the extent to which consumer services are taxed, further expansions of the tax base in this area are feasible.[44] Nevertheless, the potential for a desirable expansion of the tax base in this area should not be exaggerated. In particular, such an effort should not include services purchased by businesses, as this would only exacerbate the problem of subjecting business inputs to sales taxation that plagues the current system.[45] In addition, political considerations would likely play an undesirably large role in determining which services were included in the tax base and which were excluded.

IMPLEMENTING A TAX REBATE SYSTEM

As discussed in chapter 4, the current practice in Texas of reducing the relative sales tax burden on low-income households by exempting certain commodities consumed disproportionately by such households suffers from several problems. The administrative difficulties involved in identifying which goods qualify for exemption can be considerable. More important, exemption is a very poorly targeted means of achieving distributional goals, since all consumers benefit from exemption, and the size of the benefit—and the associated revenue losses—increase, although less than proportionately, with the level of consumption. This in turn implies that the tax system is characterized by relatively high tax rates, which cause large inefficiencies and increased incentives for tax evasion and tax avoidance.

One way (which is used in several states and is also often mentioned in discussions of federal consumption-based tax reforms such as a national retail sales tax or a value-added tax) to avoid these problems is the use of a rebate or refund that would be paid to qualifying individuals.[46] Such a rebate could simply be paid to all residents of the state, in which case it would still be somewhat untargeted, although at least the amount of the rebate would not increase with consumption. Alternatively, the rebate could be means-tested, which would increase administrative costs but would reduce the revenue cost of relieving the sales tax burden on the poor. Either approach would result in a lower overall tax rate than the commodity exemption approach and also would not be characterized by either its definitional problems or its distortions of consumer expenditure decisions.[47]

The primary problem with the rebate approach is its administrative costs, which could be relatively high given the difficulty of identifying and transferring funds to low-income individuals without falling prey to fraudulent submissions for rebates. This would be especially true for a means-tested program. Moreover, the complexity of filing requirements under a means-tested rebate would be imposed on the poor, who generally would be least able, due to less education and experience, to cope with even fairly simple filing requirements. An administrative advantage of means-tested rebates is that there would be no need for high-income individuals to file for the rebates. In addition, considerable effort might have to be devoted to ensure that the poor are aware of the rebate program and file for its benefits.

ELIMINATING THE WEALTH-BASED COMPONENT
OF THE FRANCHISE TAX

As discussed above, the corporate franchise tax system in Texas is particularly harsh on businesses in that it includes both an income-based component and a wealth-based component, with businesses required to pay the larger of the tax liabilities calculated under the two components of the tax. Such asymmetric tax treatment creates a particularly strong disincentive for risk-taking, as profitable firms typically pay the income-based component of the tax, while unprofitable firms still must pay the wealth-based component.

This situation could best be remedied simply by eliminating the wealth-based component of the corporate franchise tax, which would result in symmetric tax treatment of profitable firms and those with net losses and would eliminate the tendency to discourage risk-taking that characterizes the current tax system.[48] The primary problem with this reform would be the associated reduction in revenues.

ALLOWING A DEDUCTION FOR SALARIES PAID TO
OFFICERS AND DIRECTORS

As noted above, the current practice under the income-based component of the corporate franchise tax of disallowing a deduction for compensation paid to officers and directors effectively imposes an indirect personal income tax on such compensation. Such treatment is inequitable because it singles out only a small subset of the population for income taxation. Moreover, given widespread concerns about structuring the state tax system to encourage economic development, this provision is especially peculiar, since it singles out for a special implicit tax those individuals who are likely to be among the most influential in making business location decisions.

This situation would best be remedied simply by allowing all compensation to be deductible under the income-based component of the corporate franchise tax. Again, the primary problem with this reform would be the associated reduction in revenues.

Increased Utilization of User Charges

Yet another alternative revenue source is increased utilization of user charges. As stressed in chapter 6, user charges are viewed by many public finance experts as a particularly desirable form of finance at the state level, as they have both efficiency and equity advantages over alternative taxes. Accordingly, in-

TABLE 7.8. USER CHARGES AS A PERCENTAGE OF TOTAL STATE
AND LOCAL EXPENDITURES, BY CATEGORY, 1992

Service	U.S.	Texas
Higher Education	38.0	32.7
Hospitals	64.2	56.5
Highways	7.1	3.6
Airports	72.3	56.5
Parking Facilities	112.1	179.6
Water Transport	87.3	73.6
Natural Resources	14.0	5.8
Parks and Recreation	24.2	19.7
Housing and Community Development	17.4	16.1
Sewerage	75.0	93.2
Solid Waste Management	52.6	67.2

Source: U.S. Bureau of the Census (1994a, pp. 1, 45).

creased reliance on user charges is a revenue option that is worthy of consideration in Texas—and indeed in any other state.

It appears that Texas is fairly average in the extent to which it relies on user charges. Nevertheless, data on the relative utilization of user charges suggest some potential for increasing the extent to which the state relies on user charges, if such a change were deemed desirable for the reasons noted above. In 1990, the ratio of user charges to total state and local own-source revenue in the state was 0.295; Texas ranked seventeenth out of the fifty states and Washington D.C. in this category. By comparison, the state with the highest ratio is Tennessee (0.486).[49] Thus, if Texas were to raise its utilization rate to that of Tennessee, total user charges would rise by roughly 65 percent. In 1989, this would have implied an increase in total user-charge revenue from $13.6 billion to $22.4 billion, a revenue increase that would have allowed a reduction in tax revenues of $8.8 billion, holding total state revenues constant. Although this calculation is obviously a very rough one that ignores a variety of factors, including especially differences across states in expenditure mix, it does suggest that it would be worthwhile to investigate the extent to which reliance on user charges by the state government—as well as by local governments, which provide many of the services most amenable to the implementation of user charges—could increase.[50] Some more detailed information is presented in table 7.8, which provides data on the percentages of total state and local expenditures financed by user charges, by function, in Texas and in the United States. While these data suggest that Texas is near or above the national average in its utilization of user charges in several areas, they also indicate that it may be particularly useful to investigate the potential for increased user-charge finance in those areas in which Texas utilizes user charges to a smaller extent than the national average—higher education, hospitals, highways, airports, water transport, natural resources, parks and recreation, and housing and community development.[51] Note also that environmental fees provide another source of revenue that could be characterized as a user fee, although state governments typically do not rely on environmental taxes and fees to any large extent. Cordes (1992) reports that in 1989 Texas raised $10.6 million from this source, ranking thirteenth among the states in total revenues raised from environmental taxes and fees.

Finally, some observers have argued that the nature of the distribution of service responsibilities between state and local governments typically implies that the feasibility of user fees is considerably greater at the local level.[52] In this case, the implication for the state tax structure is an indirect one. Specifically, one could argue that it is desirable to utilize a personal income tax at the state level in order to reduce equity concerns about the increased utilization of user charges at the local level. That is, if the state tax structure includes personal exemptions and a standard deduction and is modestly progressive, there should be far fewer objections to the implementation of user charges at the local level than when the primary source of state revenue from individuals is the state sales tax. Indeed, state adoption of a personal income tax could be accompanied by the creation of incentives for the utilization of user fees at the local level.[53]

Moving to a True Consumption-Based State Tax System

Finally, a rather radical but potentially attractive reform package would be to move to a true consumption-based state tax system. This would require effective implementation of all of the first three reforms noted above—eliminating sales taxation of business purchases, taxing all consumer purchases of services, and replacing the current system of commodity sales tax exemptions with an effective tax rebate system—coupled with complete elimination of the corporate franchise tax. (As suggested in chapter 6, such a reform package should be accompanied by increases in the utilization of user charges to the maximum extent possible.)

Adoption of such a reform package would achieve all of the gains of taxation on the basis of consumption rather than income, and the rebate system would achieve the equity goal of relieving the poor from bearing any tax burden. The system would result in a proportional tax on all consumption in excess of the tax-free amount implied by the rebate. It would thus be roughly similar in its effects to a flat rate SAT.[54] If it could be implemented effectively, it would, in my view, be considerably superior to either the current tax system or a state income tax.[55]

DIRECTIONS FOR FUTURE RESEARCH

There are a number of areas in which additional information would be very helpful in evaluating options for reform of the Texas tax structure. In particular, further research on the following seven topics would illuminate the ongoing debate on tax reform in Texas. More generally, the same information, cast in the appropriate state context, would be highly relevant in most states contemplating reforms of their tax systems.

First, the estimate of the benefits of federal deductibility of a state personal income tax made above was obviously a rather rough approximation. A much more accurate estimate could be obtained from an analysis of a large sample of representative individual federal income tax returns, which could more clearly identify the current and future costs of using nondeductible general sales taxes to finance state services rather than deductible personal income taxes.

Second, the analysis of the relative efficiency properties of the current tax system and the income tax option was necessarily descriptive. Thus, it identified the nature of the many distortions attributable to either system, but did not calculate the net efficiency effects of the two options. A complete analysis would require the construction of a comprehensive computable general equilibrium model of the state, which would include all major tax structure provisions. Such a model could then be used to analyze quantitatively the effects of various individual tax distortions as well as the net efficiency effects of the alternative tax reform options on the welfare of the citizens of the state. In addition, such an analysis could be used to simulate the distributional effects of alternative reforms across individuals, classified by income or other characteristics. This approach would be especially useful in comparing the differential effects of a new income tax with the current tax system, which, as described above, already has many of the elements of an income tax system.

A third issue relates to the extent to which some of the burden of the state sales tax or other taxes, especially those assessed on businesses, might be exported to residents of other states. The analysis above has generally assumed that the potential for tax exportation is rather limited. Although such an assumption seems reasonable, it would certainly be more convincing if it were supported by a systematic analysis of the extent to which any market power is exercised by state exporters.

Fourth, current estimates that roughly 40 percent of the state sales tax base consists of business purchases have played a large role in the analysis in this text. However, as noted previously, this estimate is a fairly rough one in that the fraction of business purchases in the sales tax base is calculated simply as the residual after consumer purchases are estimated. In particular, this estimate does not correct for purchases by tourists, nonprofit organizations, and government agencies. Accordingly, further research refining this estimate would be extremely useful, including especially an explicit analysis of the nature of sales to businesses that are subject to sales taxation and what changes in tax administration would be most effective in reducing the fraction of business sales that are subject to tax.

Fifth, the analysis in the text argues that both equity and efficiency considerations imply that user charges are an excellent revenue source for state and local governments. The discussion also notes that rough comparisons with other states suggest that Texas could increase the extent to which it relies on such charges. However, this conclusion is rather tentative. Accordingly, it would be very worthwhile to examine this possibility more systematically by identifying at a highly disaggregated level those individual functions for which cross-state comparisons suggest the potential for increased utilization of user charges.

Sixth, chapter 6 examined briefly the case for the use of a progressive consumption-based tax—the Simplified Alternative Tax—as a state tax. Unfortunately, as noted in that discussion, there is very little in the way of academic research evaluating this particular policy option as a tax instrument at the state level. However, many of the properties of the SAT are highly desirable, especially in comparison to state use of either the income or sales tax option. Accordingly, a comprehensive analysis of the advantages and disadvantages of the SAT as a state tax, including the problem areas described above (especially the treatment of interstate transactions and multistate firms) would be extremely useful.

Finally, the most plausible tax reform scenario in Texas presumably involves neither the implementation of a state income tax nor a state SAT, but rather reforms of the existing tax system. The tax changes described in the first part of this chapter would represent a big step toward fundamental reform of the existing tax system. However, several of them would involve significant changes relative to current practice in Texas (and in other states). Moreover, it is clear that this discussion was only suggestive of the relative advantages and disadvantages of these reforms, including especially the final option considered (complete reform of the state sales tax coupled with elimination of the state corporate franchise tax). Accordingly, further research on the desirability of these potential reforms would be very useful and would include the considerable side benefit of shedding additional light on current discussions of reform proposals involving the replacement of the federal income tax structure with a national retail sales tax.

APPENDIX

Expenditures in Texas and Other States

Although the focus of this book is on alternative state tax structures, tax and expenditure policies are obviously linked. In particular, as noted in chapter 7, one of the arguments most often offered in support of an income tax in Texas is that the state needs (or may be required) to increase expenditures in a number of critical areas, and that revenues from the current tax system cannot easily be increased to support such an expansion of services. In light of the prevalence of such arguments, it may be useful to present some data on expenditure levels in Texas and to compare the levels of public services in Texas to those in other states. This appendix presents data for the following seven major expenditure categories: (1) primary/secondary education, (2) higher education, (3) public welfare, (4) health and hospitals, (5) highways, (6) police and corrections, and (7) all other direct general expenditures. Comparisons are drawn between the expenditure levels in Texas and those in all fifty states and the District of Columbia, in the ten most populous states, and in the Southern states.[1] The data presented can of course be used to draw similar comparisons for other states.

The first portion of this appendix simply compares per capita expenditures by category, adjusted for cost differentials, across all states. Such comparisons are incomplete, however, because they do not take into account differences in the levels of expenditures that would be required to attain any given level of services. For example, a state with a high population density would be expected to spend less per capita on highways to provide a given level of capacity for automobile transportation than would a state with a low population density. Similarly, a state with a population that is disproportionately young would be expected to require higher than average expenditures on primary/secondary education in order to achieve a given level of educational attainment. Accordingly, this appendix also includes a comparison across states of the actual level of state expenditures relative to the expenditure levels that would be required to finance a "representative" expenditure package. This comparison utilizes the methodology and data presented in U.S. Advisory Commission on Intergovernmental Relations (ACIR) (1990).[2]

ACTUAL (COST-ADJUSTED) EXPENDITURES

This section compares expenditure levels in Texas to those in other states without introducing any corrections for differences in relative needs across the states. However, the figures presented are adjusted for differences in the costs of inputs used in the production of public-sector goods, following the approach used in U.S. Advisory Commission on Intergovernmental Relations (1990).[3] In all cases, expenditure levels are expressed as percentages of national per capita average expenditures and reflect combined state and local expenditures.[4]

Cost-adjusted state and local government expenditures for all fifty states and the District of Columbia are presented in table A.1. These data indicate that expenditure levels vary considerably, ranging from 71.0 percent of the per capita national average in Arkansas to 370.7 percent of the average expenditure in Alaska. Since the condition of the public sector in Alaska is so unique, with expenditure levels much greater than those in any other state, Alaskan data will not be included in discussions of the ranges of expenditures in the remainder of the analysis. In this case, the state with the next highest level of total expenditures is Wyoming, with expenditures equal to 164.7 percent of the national average. The differences in the individual spending categories are also very pronounced; for example, Alabama spends only 47.8 percent of the national average on public welfare, while per capita spending on police and corrections is 445.1 percent of the national average in the District of Columbia.

Per capita total spending in Texas is 13.5 percent below the national average, and the state ranks thirty-ninth in total spending. This ranking masks significant differences in spending on the various expenditure categories. In particular, Texas' spending on both primary/secondary education and on higher education slightly exceeds the national average, and the state ranks eighteenth and twenty-seventh, respectively, in these two categories. Similarly, spending on highways in Texas exceeds the national average by 12.2 percent, and Texas ranks twenty-sixth in this category. In marked contrast, Texas spends less than half

State	Total	Primary and Secondary Education	Higher Education	Public Welfare	Health and Hospitals	Highways	Police and Corrections	All Other Expenditures
Alabama	77.3	65.3	104.5	47.8	138.8	81.2	61.8	78.6
Alaska	370.7	283.8	174.1	168.6	104.5	518.3	226.8	665.7
Arizona	104.4	108.3	137.8	65.2	53.8	169.5	134.1	77.4
Arkansas	71.0	82.9	81.1	69.1	74.0	99.7	47.4	48.5
California	113.9	99.8	122.0	124.1	114.9	65.8	149.4	139.1
Colorado	105.6	112.9	112.3	85.1	88.3	116.0	103.9	82.8
Connecticut	108.9	105.7	63.9	112.3	88.2	118.3	91.8	153.1
Delaware	111.3	102.6	161.1	65.6	63.0	127.1	103.5	99.2
D. of Columbia	192.3	120.1	55.7	272.7	207.4	87.2	445.1	205.1
Florida	87.6	89.0	54.5	52.0	103.5	81.6	116.6	91.0
Georgia	89.3	96.7	76.7	63.6	184.6	92.6	82.2	68.7
Hawaii	105.4	73.8	108.9	86.6	79.1	63.7	106.1	163.7
Idaho	77.5	77.8	114.2	51.7	83.3	117.2	61.3	63.8
Illinois	93.8	90.9	92.0	102.5	67.3	102.6	93.6	103.2
Indiana	80.5	89.2	115.6	77.5	90.8	82.2	57.1	69.8
Iowa	93.6	90.9	150.0	91.9	107.0	146.7	62.5	57.6
Kansas	92.8	98.9	122.6	65.0	85.1	146.2	67.3	72.4
Kentucky	77.7	68.7	89.9	82.1	55.5	115.9	58.4	69.9

State	Total	Primary and Secondary Education	Higher Education	Public Welfare	Health and Hospitals	Highways	Police and Corrections	All Other Expenditures
Louisiana	91.9	80.0	84.1	71.8	125.2	106.2	85.2	81.1
Maine	92.2	96.5	82.5	129.8	49.9	112.4	60.8	83.9
Maryland	102.9	97.9	106.9	94.2	48.4	120.3	124.6	112.0
Massachusetts	111.5	98.6	71.2	155.0	118.8	77.5	97.4	144.3
Michigan	107.9	113.9	130.3	140.3	122.7	82.5	108.1	95.0
Minnesota	122.2	116.5	135.5	145.7	110.4	146.9	77.0	102.8
Mississippi	75.5	73.6	91.2	64.4	138.4	98.1	49.2	53.7
Missouri	77.0	84.6	90.0	66.0	93.7	88.2	75.3	56.8
Montana	107.3	122.2	92.1	92.9	63.2	177.0	62.9	93.2
Nebraska	92.3	100.1	125.7	79.1	113.2	132.5	61.3	69.5
Nevada	104.6	89.8	79.8	49.3	82.2	130.0	150.0	139.7
New Hampshire	83.3	93.7	72.2	77.8	52.4	121.8	67.0	72.4
New Jersey	113.0	117.4	83.7	106.5	74.6	111.0	116.3	140.5
New Mexico	100.3	105.2	120.1	66.7	86.6	148.4	97.1	74.1
New York	145.2	133.6	87.1	194.8	168.7	99.7	163.6	173.6
N. Carolina	77.4	88.8	119.2	59.9	86.7	75.3	80.0	63.4

TABLE A.1. CONTINUED

State	Total	Primary and Secondary Education	Higher Education	Public Welfare	Health and Hospitals	Highways	Police and Corrections	All Other Expenditures
N. Dakota	107.9	101.5	157.9	106.8	70.7	156.8	45.2	135.1
Ohio	90.7	97.7	98.5	118.9	87.8	82.2	88.6	67.1
Oklahoma	82.5	90.5	94.6	78.7	89.1	94.0	64.8	57.1
Oregon	104.6	113.6	122.9	64.6	75.2	107.1	87.9	112.2
Pennsylvania	87.5	98.3	52.7	112.7	55.3	100.8	72.2	93.5
Rhode Island	103.8	92.5	82.7	151.6	84.1	77.3	82.6	123.3
S. Carolina	79.0	88.1	108.0	55.1	125.8	62.3	75.2	66.2
S. Dakota	94.7	87.9	95.0	66.3	51.8	161.8	57.6	155.8
Tennessee	77.4	67.1	84.4	76.1	113.4	89.4	67.7	77.4
Texas	**86.5**	**103.3**	**103.9**	**48.2**	**80.4**	**112.2**	**77.6**	**59.2**
Utah	94.8	100.1	153.1	71.0	74.5	100.1	83.8	73.4
Vermont	102.4	110.3	131.6	105.3	41.9	158.1	56.5	106.3
Virginia	89.4	98.4	109.6	57.2	94.3	118.0	90.6	63.1
Washington	103.4	105.7	120.1	95.5	83.7	116.2	92.2	108.0
West Virginia	84.7	96.0	76.0	81.9	61.8	124.6	37.9	89.1
Wisconsin	105.9	107.8	134.1	148.0	73.4	121.4	87.0	77.1
Wyoming	164.7	183.5	162.0	70.5	225.5	306.7	105.7	113.7

Source: U.S. Advisory Commission on Intergovernmental Relations (1990, p. 20).

the national average on public welfare, spending more than only one other state (Alabama). Texas expenditure levels in the other categories also fall below national averages, although the shortfall is not as great as in the case of public welfare spending. Specifically, Texas' spending levels on health and hospitals and on police and corrections are roughly 20 percent below the national average, and spending categorized as "all other expenditures" is roughly 40 percent below the national average.[5]

One might argue that since Texas is the third most populous state in the nation, its relative needs for government spending are likely to be more comparable to those in the other highly populated states. Accordingly, a comparison of Texas spending levels to those in the ten most populous states in the United States is presented in table A.2.[6] Total spending in Texas exceeds only that of North Carolina among the ten most populous states, and state expenditure levels on welfare and on "all other expenditures" are the lowest of those ten states. In contrast, Texas ranks first among the ten most populous states in spending on highways, and ranks fourth in spending on both primary/secondary and higher education. Texas ranks seventh in spending on health and hospitals and ninth in expenditures on police and corrections.

On the other hand, one might argue that for cultural and historical reasons, public service levels tend to be low in the Southern states, and that the level of Texas expenditures should be compared to the states in this region. The data presented in table A.3 indicate that in fact government expenditures are relatively low in the South, as total per capita expenditures in twelve of the fourteen Southern states are below the national average.

Texas ranks sixth in the level of total expenditures among the fourteen Southern states. Its spending level of 86.5 percent of the national average is roughly two percentage points greater than the average for the Southern states (84.1 percent). Within this group, Texas ranks high in spending on highways and on primary/secondary and higher education, is near the average for spending on police and corrections, and ranks relatively low in spending on welfare, health and hospitals, and "all other expenditures."

REPRESENTATIVE (COST-ADJUSTED) EXPENDITURES

As noted above, the comparisons made in the previous section are of questionable value because they make no allowances for differences in the levels of expenditures that would be required to attain any given level of public services. In an attempt to provide more informative comparisons of expenditure levels and of the extent to which states are meeting their public service needs, the

TABLE A.2. EXPENDITURES BY CATEGORY FOR TEN MOST POPULOUS STATES, 1986–87 (AS PERCENTAGE OF AVERAGE NATIONAL PER CAPITA EXPENDITURES, ADJUSTED FOR INPUT COST DIFFERENCES)

State	Total	Primary and Secondary Education	Higher Education	Public Welfare	Health and Hospitals	Highways	Police and Corrections	All Other Expenditures
1. California	113.9	99.8	122.0	124.1	114.9	65.8	149.4	139.1
2. New York	145.2	133.6	87.1	194.8	168.7	99.7	163.6	173.6
3. Texas	86.5	103.3	103.9	48.2	80.4	112.2	77.6	59.2
4. Florida	87.6	89.0	54.5	52.0	103.5	81.6	116.6	91.0
5. Pennsylvania	87.5	98.3	52.7	112.7	55.3	100.8	72.2	93.5
6. Illinois	93.8	90.9	92.0	102.5	67.3	102.6	93.6	103.2
7. Ohio	90.7	97.7	98.5	118.9	87.8	82.2	88.6	67.1
8. Michigan	107.9	113.9	130.3	140.3	122.7	82.5	108.1	95.0
9. New Jersey	113.0	117.4	83.7	106.5	74.6	111.0	116.3	140.5
10. N. Carolina	77.4	88.8	119.2	59.9	86.7	75.3	80.0	63.4
Sample Average	100.4	103.27	94.39	105.99	96.19	91.37	106.6	102.56
Texas' Rank	9th	4th	4th	10th	7th	1st	9th	10th

Source: U.S. Advisory Commission on Intergovernmental Relations (1990, p. 20).

TABLE A.3. EXPENDITURES BY CATEGORY FOR SOUTHERN STATES, 1986–87 (AS PERCENTAGE OF AVERAGE NATIONAL PER CAPITA EXPENDITURES, ADJUSTED FOR INPUT COST DIFFERENCES)

State	Total	Primary and Secondary Education	Higher Education	Public Welfare	Health and Hospitals	Highways	Police and Corrections	All Other Expenditures
Alabama	77.3	65.3	104.5	47.8	138.8	81.2	61.8	78.6
Arizona	104.4	108.3	137.8	65.2	53.8	169.5	134.1	77.4
Arkansas	71.0	82.9	81.1	69.1	74.0	99.7	47.4	48.5
Florida	87.6	89.0	54.5	52.0	103.5	81.6	116.6	91.0
Georgia	89.3	96.7	76.7	63.6	184.6	92.6	82.2	68.7
Kentucky	77.7	68.7	89.9	82.1	55.5	115.9	58.4	69.9
Louisiana	91.9	80.0	84.1	71.8	125.2	106.2	85.2	81.1
Mississippi	75.5	73.6	91.2	64.4	138.4	98.1	49.2	53.7
New Mexico	100.3	105.2	120.1	66.7	86.6	148.4	97.1	74.1
N. Carolina	77.4	88.8	119.2	59.9	86.7	75.3	80.0	63.4
S. Carolina	79.0	88.1	108.0	55.1	125.8	62.3	75.2	66.2
Oklahoma	82.5	90.5	94.6	78.7	89.1	94.0	64.8	57.1
Tennessee	77.4	67.1	84.4	76.1	113.4	89.4	67.7	77.4
Texas	**86.5**	**103.3**	**103.9**	**48.2**	**80.4**	**112.2**	**77.6**	**59.2**
Sample Average	84.1	86.3	96.4	64.3	104.0	101.9	78.4	69.0
Texas' Rank	6th	3rd	6th	13th	11th	4th	7th	11th

Source: U.S. Advisory Commission on Intergovernmental Relations (1990, p. 20).

ACIR has constructed an alternative framework for comparing state expenditure levels—the "representative expenditure approach."[7]

The Representative Expenditure Approach

The calculations underlying the representative expenditure approach (REA) proceed in three steps. First, the "representative expenditure functions" are defined; in the ACIR analysis, these correspond to the seven categories listed in the previous section. Second, a "workload factor," which provides a measure of the state's relative cost in supplying a given level of any particular public service to all of its citizens, is defined. In most other analyses, including the one in the previous section, the workload factor is implicitly assumed to simply be the population; that is, public expenditures are compared in per capita terms rather than using absolute dollars. However, as suggested above, population is a poor measure of relative need in many cases. Accordingly, the REA arrives at an alternative measure, which consists of other measurable factors that are (sometimes) weighted and then aggregated to arrive at the workload factor.[8] Third, for each of the seven expenditure functions and their respective workload measures, the representative expenditure per unit of workload for each function is calculated as the ratio of total state and local expenditures in that category in the United States to the national total for the workload measure. Given this average cost per unit of workload factor, the "representative expenditure" for a state is calculated by multiplying the state's workload measure for a function by the national average expenditure per unit of workload.

This procedure can be illustrated by considering the case of public welfare (described in more detail below). Rather than total population, the workload factor for this function is the number of people living in households with incomes below the official poverty line. The representative expenditure per unit of workload equals total state and local expenditures on public welfare in the United States divided by the total population living in poverty in the nation. The "representative expenditure" for Texas then equals the product of this representative expenditure per unit of workload and the size of the population living in poverty in the state (the Texas public welfare workload factor).

The Workload Factors

Since identifying the workload factors for each expenditure function is the critical step in the construction of the REA, this section explains briefly how each of the seven measures is calculated. Additional details, including more complete justifications for the particular measures used, can be found in U.S. Advisory Commission on Intergovernmental Relations (1990, pp. 9–16).

PRIMARY AND SECONDARY EDUCATION

The workload factor is the weighted sum of three population groups: (1) children of elementary school age (5–13) net of enrollment in private elementary schools, (2) youth of secondary school age (14–17) net of private secondary school enrollment, and (3) the population under 18 living in households with incomes below the poverty line. The respective weights are 0.6, 1.0, and 0.25, which adjust for the lower cost per student for students of elementary school age relative to secondary school age, and the higher cost of compensatory and remedial programs for pupils from impoverished households relative to other households.

HIGHER EDUCATION

The workload factor is the weighted sum of the population in the age groups 14–17, 18–24, 25–34, and 35 and older. The age distribution takes into account the recent shift in the age mix of students obtaining higher education. Each weight (0.0132, 0.2244, 0.0416, and 0.0083, respectively) reflects the number of full-time students relative to the total population within the age group.

PUBLIC WELFARE

The workload factor is the population living in households with incomes below the poverty line. It should be noted that the data for this measure are fairly rough approximations (they are based on 1979 census data, updated to 1987) for each state using an extrapolation method that assumes that the change in each state's poverty rate equals the change that occurred in the major census region in which the state is located. Since there are only four such census regions, this extrapolation is unlikely to be very accurate.

HEALTH AND HOSPITALS

The workload factor is the equally weighted sum of (1) persons in the age range 16–64 with work disabilities, (2) the population living in households with incomes below 150 percent of the poverty line, and (3) the total population. The work disability variable attempts to represent the extent to which a state's economy is associated with injuries or illnesses that may increase the demands on public health and hospital programs. The poverty variable accounts for the greater probability that such individuals will qualify for and rely on publicly supported health and hospital programs than those with higher incomes.

HIGHWAYS

The workload factor is the weighted sum of (1) vehicle miles traveled, and (2) lane miles of streets and roads other than those on federally controlled land; the weights are 0.825 and 0.175, respectively, reflecting relative contributions to highway deterioration over time.

The workload factor is the equally weighted sum of (1) the size of the population with ages between 18–24, (2) the number of murders committed, and (3) the total population. The size of the population aged between 18–24 is frequently used as an indicator of an area's potential for serious crimes.

ALL OTHER DIRECT GENERAL EXPENDITURES

The workload factor is simply total population.

Estimates of Representative Expenditures

The ACIR estimates of representative state expenditures, which (as described above) indicate the per capita cost to the state of providing the national average level of public services, as adjusted by the ACIR workload factors, are presented in table A.4. As in the previous analysis, these data are expressed as a percentage of the average per capita cost in the nation and are adjusted for input cost differences. It must be emphasized that these figures do not reflect actual expenditure levels but rather the expenditures that would be required to provide the average level of expenditures in the nation, taking into account differences in expenditure needs as captured by the ACIR workload factors. Thus, a high level of per capita representative expenditures implies high expenditure needs, relative to the rest of the nation, which are attributable to relatively high values of the various workload factors described above.

In contrast to the wide range of actual state expenditures, the representative expenditure estimates range from 85.4 to 113.3 percent of the national average. Note that Texas ranks fifth in the nation in total representative expenditures, 9.7 percent above the national average expenditure; by comparison, recall that Texas ranked thirty-ninth in total actual expenditures, 13.5 percent below the national average actual expenditure. In addition, Texas is the only state for which representative spending is greater than the national average in each of the seven expenditure functions considered in the analysis. Thus, in comparison to the other states, the cost of providing a representative expenditure package in Texas is rather high, and indeed is higher in only four other states— Alaska, Louisiana, Mississippi, and New Mexico. Finally, note that the highest relative representative expenditure level in the state is in the category of primary and secondary education. This provides one explanation for the extent to which education finance, including property tax relief and state financing of primary and secondary education, is perpetually an issue in Texas politics.

Table A.5 provides representative expenditures for the ten most populous states. The estimated total representative expenditure estimate for Texas— 109.7 percent of the national average—is the largest in this group. In addition, representative expenditures in each category are generally rather high. Thus,

State	Total	Primary and Secondary Education	Higher Education	Public Welfare	Health and Hospitals	Highways	Police and Corrections	All Other Expenditures
Alabama	108.8	107.9	94.9	145.5	115.5	117.5	97.4	97.7
Alaska	121.3	150.2	130.3	92.8	104.6	113.8	140.9	109.1
Arizona	102.6	103.0	97.2	110.6	104.9	112.3	94.3	99.3
Arkansas	106.0	105.2	88.4	144.8	117.7	111.4	86.2	96.4
California	101.3	101.1	103.6	96.0	102.8	93.7	113.7	101.6
Colorado	98.1	101.1	102.2	84.6	92.1	110.1	90.0	100.1
Connecticut	91.7	89.7	105.1	59.3	83.5	97.0	92.2	102.4
Delaware	96.1	87.1	105.1	91.7	95.5	109.1	89.9	100.2
D. of Columbia	102.9	73.0	98.7	140.7	117.4	58.4	204.8	99.0
Florida	92.6	79.1	86.5	103.9	99.3	89.1	101.3	97.7
Georgia	108.6	109.9	99.9	127.9	112.4	119.1	110.9	98.5
Hawaii	89.6	85.5	102.2	81.1	83.5	73.4	85.8	99.1
Idaho	100.1	113.0	86.4	104.3	93.5	119.1	68.7	96.3
Illinois	102.4	105.8	106.4	100.7	101.6	84.4	108.3	102.7
Indiana	99.3	106.6	101.6	86.9	94.3	102.8	90.1	100.2
Iowa	95.8	97.0	94.5	90.1	88.2	120.3	71.0	98.7
Kansas	98.4	96.2	94.4	89.9	89.9	145.7	79.9	98.7

TABLE A.4. CONTINUED

State	Total	Primary and Secondary Education	Higher Education	Public Welfare	Health and Hospitals	Highways	Police and Corrections	All Other Expenditures
Kentucky	108.3	108.5	101.0	135.7	120.4	105.8	96.5	99.4
Louisiana	110.4	110.1	105.6	145.2	119.1	87.5	115.9	100.7
Maine	89.0	83.4	85.8	91.4	88.7	108.5	63.7	94.3
Maryland	97.0	94.8	108.2	77.0	94.5	93.2	112.5	101.6
Massachusetts	87.3	81.4	101.6	69.3	84.1	81.4	77.6	99.0
Michigan	108.3	115.2	111.0	95.8	109.7	104.6	128.8	103.2
Minnesota	98.0	99.0	101.8	85.2	90.7	122.9	78.6	100.7
Mississippi	113.3	112.9	91.8	181.7	124.2	106.7	96.2	95.9
Missouri	100.2	985.0	95.1	108.8	102.8	114.4	96.0	99.0
Montana	102.0	100.0	86.7	100.9	91.1	186.7	71.9	96.3
Nebraska	96.2	90.6	91.5	94.8	86.3	146.8	73.1	97.3
Nevada	95.9	95.3	97.6	73.5	89.6	122.0	97.3	99.5
New Hampshire	85.4	82.1	93.8	60.4	77.2	102.3	71.3	96.5
New Jersey	93.1	92.3	104.1	71.1	89.2	85.2	90.5	102.2
New Mexico	110.6	112.1	93.1	146.4	108.5	137.7	98.6	97.2
New York	95.3	89.6	100.2	98.5	97.8	65.1	113.3	100.3
N. Carolina	98.6	96.6	94.9	111.8	100.6	101.7	90.6	96.7
N. Dakota	105.2	96.6	91.6	110.3	88.4	223.9	65.0	96.6
Ohio	99.9	105.0	101.5	93.6	101.8	90.1	92.8	101.1
Oklahoma	103.8	106.2	95.0	102.9	104.7	137.9	92.0	98.6

TABLE A.4. CONTINUED

State	Total	Primary and Secondary Education	Higher Education	Public Welfare	Health and Hospitals	Highways	Police and Corrections	All Other Expenditures
Oregon	97.9	99.2	94.0	89.2	101.8	111.4	85.1	99.6
Pennsylvania	90.4	85.6	97.8	76.6	92.3	80.2	87.4	100.1
Rhode Island	85.8	77.9	97.7	73.8	88.4	69.4	77.4	98.2
S. Carolina	103.3	102.9	97.0	125.5	104.7	109.6	96.1	96.7
S. Dakota	104.7	91.4	83.3	146.3	96.8	193.0	60.3	94.2
Tennessee	103.5	100.6	94.8	126.4	110.3	108.1	97.0	98.0
Texas	**109.7**	**120.8**	**102.6**	**114.3**	**101.6**	**115.6**	**116.4**	**100.7**
Utah	104.9	140.7	97.4	86.4	87.1	100.3	77.9	98.8
Vermont	89.1	82.5	90.6	84.5	84.2	118.2	66.6	94.7
Virginia	98.6	96.1	105.2	90.8	96.5	109.6	97.9	99.5
Washington	98.6	101.6	100.9	82.5	98.8	108.1	90.4	100.9
West Virginia	102.7	109.1	94.2	116.2	114.5	94.5	81.5	98.4
Wisconsin	94.2	93.7	100.0	77.9	85.3	113.1	80.4	99.7
Wyoming	102.2	113.5	93.3	65.9	78.1	197.4	71.7	99.1

Source: U.S. Advisory Commission on Intergovernmental Relations (1990, p. 22)

State	Total	Primary and Secondary Education	Higher Education	Public Welfare	Health and Hospitals	Highways	Police and Corrections	All Other Expenditures
California	101.3	101.1	103.6	96.0	102.8	93.7	113.7	101.6
New York	95.3	89.6	100.2	98.5	97.8	65.1	113.3	100.3
Texas	109.7	120.8	102.6	114.3	101.6	115.6	116.4	100.7
Florida	92.6	79.1	86.5	103.9	99.3	89.1	101.3	97.7
Pennsylvania	90.4	85.6	97.8	76.6	92.3	80.2	87.4	100.1
Illinois	108.3	108.5	101.0	135.7	120.4	105.8	96.5	99.4
Ohio	99.9	105.0	101.5	93.6	101.8	90.1	92.8	101.1
Michigan	108.3	115.2	111.0	95.8	109.7	104.6	128.8	103.2
New Jersey	93.1	92.3	104.1	71.1	89.2	85.2	90.5	102.2
N. Carolina	98.6	96.6	94.9	111.8	100.6	101.7	90.6	96.7
Sample Average	99.8	99.4	100.3	99.7	101.6	93.1	103.1	100.3
Texas' Rank	1st	1st	4th	2nd	5th	1st	2nd	5th

Source: U.S. Advisory Commission on Intergovernmental Relations (1990, p. 22).

when compared to other highly populated states rather than to all states, the cost of providing a representative level of expenditures is still relatively high in Texas.

Table A.6 presents representative expenditures for the Southern states. The Southern states have the highest regional representative expenditures.[9] In fact, eight of the ten states with the highest representative expenditures are in the South. Texas ranks fourth among the fourteen Southern states in total representative expenditures and has the highest representative expenditures for primary/secondary education, police and corrections, and "all other expenditures." The estimate of representative expenditures in Texas for higher education is the second highest among the Southern states, and Texas ranks fifth in highways, tenth in public welfare, and twelfth in health and hospitals.

Comparing Actual and Representative Expenditures

A comparison of actual and representative state expenditures in 1986–87 is provided in table A.7. These figures provide the best data for comparing expenditure levels across states, in that they correct for both (1) differences in the ACIR workload factors, which attempt to measure the differences in expenditures across states required to attain any given level of government services, and (2) differences in input costs across states.

Actual total expenditures in Texas equal 78.9 percent of representative expenditures, and Texas ranks forty-third among the fifty states and the District of Columbia in terms of this measure of expenditures. Actual expenditures on higher education and on highways in Texas are quite close to representative expenditures. However, in all other categories, actual expenditures fall short of representative expenditures. Actual expenditures are fairly near representative expenditures for primary/secondary education (85.6 percent) and for health and hospitals (79.1 percent), with somewhat larger shortfalls for police and corrections (66.6 percent), and for "all other expenditures" (58.8 percent). The most dramatic difference between actual and representative expenditures arises for public welfare, where Texas' actual outlay of 42.2 percent of representative expenditures exceeds only that of Alabama (32.8 percent) and Mississippi (35.4 percent).

A comparison of actual expenditures as a percentage of representative expenditures in the ten most populous states is provided in table A.8. Texas ranks ninth in total expenditures in this grouping (above only North Carolina). Within the individual spending categories, Texas is last among the ten most populous states in four of the seven functions—primary/secondary education, public welfare, police and corrections, and "all other expenditures"—and

State	Total	Primary and Secondary Education	Higher Education	Public Welfare	Health and Hospital	Highways	Police and Corrections	All Other Expenditures
Alabama	108.8	107.9	94.9	145.5	115.5	117.5	97.4	97.7
Arizona	102.6	103.0	97.2	110.6	104.9	112.3	94.3	99.3
Arkansas	106.0	105.2	88.4	144.8	117.7	111.4	86.2	96.4
Florida	92.6	79.1	86.5	103.9	99.3	89.1	101.3	97.7
Georgia	108.6	109.9	99.9	127.9	112.4	119.1	110.9	98.5
Kentucky	108.3	108.5	101.0	135.7	120.4	105.8	96.5	99.4
Louisiana	110.4	110.1	105.6	145.2	119.1	87.5	115.9	100.7
Mississippi	113.3	112.9	91.8	181.7	124.2	106.7	96.2	95.9
New Mexico	110.6	112.1	93.1	146.4	108.5	137.7	98.6	97.2
N. Carolina	98.6	96.6	94.9	111.8	100.6	101.7	90.6	96.7
S. Carolina	103.3	102.9	97.0	125.5	104.7	109.6	96.1	96.7
Oklahoma	103.8	106.2	95.0	102.9	104.7	137.9	92.0	98.6
Tennessee	103.5	100.6	94.8	126.4	110.3	108.1	97.0	98.0
Texas	**109.7**	**120.8**	**102.6**	**114.3**	**101.6**	**115.6**	**116.4**	**100.7**
Sample Average	105.7	105.4	95.9	130.2	110.3	111.4	99.2	98.1
Texas' Rank	4th	1st	2nd	10th	12th	5th	1st	1st

Source: U.S. Advisory Commission on Intergovernmental Relations (1990, p. 22).

TABLE A.7. ACTUAL EXPENDITURES AS A PERCENTAGE OF REPRESENTATIVE EXPENDITURES,
BY FUNCTION, 1986–87 (ADJUSTED FOR INPUT COST DIFFERENCES)

State	Total	Primary and Secondary Education	Higher Education	Public Welfare	Health and Hospitals	Highways	Police and Corrections	All Other Expenditures
Alabama	71.0	60.5	110.1	32.8	120.2	69.1	63.5	80.4
Alaska	305.7	188.9	133.6	181.6	99.9	455.6	160.9	610.4
Arizona	101.8	105.2	141.7	59.0	51.3	151.0	142.2	77.9
Arkansas	67.0	78.8	91.8	47.7	62.9	89.5	55.0	50.3
California	112.4	98.7	117.7	129.3	111.8	70.2	131.3	137.0
Colorado	107.6	111.6	114.8	100.6	95.9	105.4	115.4	82.8
Connecticut	118.8	117.9	60.8	189.4	105.6	121.9	99.5	149.6
Delaware	115.8	117.9	153.2	71.5	66.0	116.5	115.1	98.9
D. of Columbia	186.9	164.4	56.5	193.8	176.6	149.4	217.3	207.1
Florida	94.6	112.6	63.0	50.1	104.2	91.5	115.1	93.1
Georgia	82.2	87.9	76.8	49.8	164.2	77.8	74.1	69.7
Hawaii	117.6	86.3	106.5	106.8	94.7	86.8	123.7	165.2
Idaho	77.5	68.8	132.2	49.6	89.1	98.3	89.2	66.2
Illinois	91.6	85.9	86.5	101.7	66.2	121.5	86.4	100.6
Indiana	81.1	83.7	113.7	89.2	96.3	80.0	63.3	69.7
Iowa	97.7	93.7	158.6	102.0	121.2	122.0	88.0	58.3
Kansas	94.3	102.7	129.8	72.3	94.7	100.3	84.1	73.4
Kentucky	71.7	63.4	89.0	60.5	46.1	109.6	60.6	70.3
Louisiana	83.3	72.7	79.7	49.4	105.1	121.3	73.5	80.6
Maine	103.5	115.6	96.2	142.0	56.2	103.6	95.4	89.0
Maryland	106.0	103.2	98.8	122.4	51.2	129.0	110.8	110.2
Massachusetts	127.7	121.1	70.0	223.6	141.3	95.2	125.5	145.7
Michigan	99.6	98.9	117.3	146.4	111.8	78.9	83.9	92.0

TABLE A.7. CONTINUED

State	Total	Primary and Secondary Education	Higher Education	Public Welfare	Health and Hospitals	Highways	Police and Corrections	All Other Expenditures
Minnesota	124.7	117.8	133.2	171.0	121.8	119.6	97.9	102.2
Mississippi	66.6	65.2	99.3	35.4	111.4	91.9	51.1	56.0
Missouri	76.8	89.0	94.6	60.7	91.2	77.0	78.4	57.3
Montana	105.2	122.2	106.3	92.0	69.3	94.8	87.5	96.7
Nebraska	95.9	110.5	137.4	83.5	131.1	90.2	83.8	71.4
Nevada	109.1	94.2	81.7	67.1	91.8	106.5	154.1	140.3
New Hampshire	97.5	114.2	77.0	128.8	67.8	119.0	93.9	75.0
New Jersey	121.4	127.1	80.4	149.9	83.6	130.3	128.5	137.4
New Mexico	90.7	93.8	129.0	45.5	79.8	107.8	98.5	76.3
New York	152.4	149.2	87.0	197.8	172.5	153.1	144.4	173.0
N. Carolina	78.5	91.9	125.6	53.6	86.2	74.1	88.3	65.6
N. Dakota	102.6	105.0	172.5	96.9	80.0	70.0	69.6	139.8
Ohio	90.8	93.1	97.0	127.0	86.2	91.2	95.5	66.3
Oklahoma	79.5	85.2	99.6	76.5	85.1	68.2	70.5	57.9
Oregon	106.9	114.5	130.8	72.5	73.9	96.1	103.4	112.7
Pennsylvania	96.8	114.9	53.9	147.1	59.9	125.7	82.5	93.5
Rhode Island	121.1	118.8	84.6	205.3	95.1	111.4	106.7	125.5
S. Carolina	76.4	85.6	111.4	43.9	120.2	56.9	78.3	68.5
S. Dakota	90.5	96.1	114.1	45.3	53.5	839.0	95.6	165.4
Tennessee	74.7	66.7	89.0	60.2	102.8	82.7	69.8	79.0

TABLE A.7. CONTINUED

State	Total	Primary and Secondary Education	Higher Education	Public Welfare	Health and Hospitals	Highways	Police and Corrections	All Other Expenditures
Texas	**78.9**	**85.6**	**101.3**	**42.2**	**79.1**	**97.0**	**66.6**	**58.8**
Utah	90.3	71.1	157.1	82.2	85.5	99.8	107.6	74.3
Vermont	114.9	133.6	145.3	124.6	49.8	133.8	84.7	112.2
Virginia	90.7	102.4	104.2	63.0	97.8	107.7	92.6	63.4
Washington	104.9	104.0	119.0	115.8	84.7	107.4	102.0	107.0
West Virginia	82.4	88.0	80.7	70.5	54.0	131.8	46.5	90.5
Wisconsin	112.4	115.1	134.1	189.9	86.1	107.3	108.2	77.3
Wyoming	161.2	161.7	173.6	107.0	288.5	155.3	147.4	114.8

Source: U.S. Advisory Commission on Intergovernmental Relations (1990, p. 24).

State	Total	Primary and Secondary Education	Higher Education	Public Welfare	Health and Hospitals	Highways	Police and Corrections	All Other Expenditures
1. California	112.4	98.7	117.7	129.3	111.8	70.2	131.3	137.0
2. New York	152.4	149.2	87.0	197.8	172.5	153.1	144.4	173.0
3. Texas	78.9	85.6	101.3	42.2	79.1	97.0	66.6	58.8
4. Florida	94.6	112.6	63.0	50.1	104.2	91.5	115.1	93.1
5. Pennsylvania	96.8	114.9	53.9	147.1	59.9	125.7	82.5	93.5
6. Illinois	91.6	85.9	86.5	101.7	66.2	121.5	86.4	100.6
7. Ohio	90.8	93.1	97.0	127.0	86.2	91.2	95.5	66.3
8. Michigan	99.6	98.9	117.3	146.4	111.8	78.9	83.9	92.0
9. New Jersey	121.4	127.1	80.4	149.9	83.6	130.3	128.5	137.4
10. N. Carolina	78.5	91.9	125.6	53.6	86.2	74.1	88.3	65.6
Sample Average	101.7	105.8	93.0	114.5	96.2	103.4	102.3	101.7
Texas' Rank	9th	10th	4th	10th	8th	5th	10th	10th

Source: U.S. Advisory Commission on Intergovernmental Relations (1990, p. 24).

ranks fourth in higher education, fifth in highways, and eighth in health and hospitals.

Finally, table A.9 presents actual expenditures as a percentage of representative expenditures for the fourteen Southern states; these data indicate that Texas ranks seventh in total spending. Among the individual spending categories, Texas ranks in the upper middle of the group for actual relative to representative expenditures on primary/secondary education, higher education and highways, and near the bottom of the group for actual relative to representative expenditures on health and hospitals, public welfare, and "all other expenditures."

SUMMARY

The analysis in this appendix suggests that the pattern of expenditures in Texas, relative to those in other states, can be summarized as follows. In terms of actual per capita total expenditure levels, adjusted only for differences in input costs, Texas ranks thirty-ninth out of the fifty states and the District of Columbia. Its expenditures on primary/secondary education, higher education, and highways exceed national averages by between 3 and 12 percent, while its expenditures for health and hospitals and police and corrections fall roughly between 20 and 25 percent below the national average, and expenditures for public welfare and "all other expenditures" fall roughly between 40 and 50 percent below national averages. When compared to the ten most populous states, Texas total expenditures per capita are quite low (exceeding only North Carolina). Texas ranks first in spending on highways, in the middle of the group for spending on education and health and hospitals, next to last in expenditures on police and corrections, and last in expenditures on public welfare and "all other expenditures." When compared to the Southern states, which tend to have low expenditure levels in comparison to the rest of the nation, Texas ranks near the middle in total expenditures. Within the various spending categories, Texas ranks high in spending on highways and on primary/secondary and higher education, is near average for spending on police and corrections, and ranks relatively low in spending on welfare, health and hospitals, and "all other expenditures."

The next part of the analysis attempted to correct for differences in state characteristics that would result in differences across states in the levels of expenditures required to attain any given level of services by using the representative expenditure approach constructed by the U.S. Advisory Commission on Intergovernmental Relations (1990). This method estimates the per capita cost to the state of providing the national average level of public services, given

TABLE A.9. ACTUAL EXPENDITURES AS A PERCENTAGE OF REPRESENTATIVE EXPENDITURES FOR THE SOUTHERN STATES, BY FUNCTION, 1986–87 (ADJUSTED FOR INPUT COST DIFFERENCES)

State	Total	Primary and Secondary Education	Higher Education	Public Welfare	Health and Hospitals	Highways	Police and Corrections	All Other Expenditures
Alabama	71.0	60.5	110.1	32.8	120.2	69.1	63.5	80.4
Arizona	101.8	105.2	141.7	59.0	51.3	151.0	142.2	77.9
Arkansas	67.0	78.8	91.8	47.7	62.9	89.5	55.0	50.3
Florida	94.6	112.6	63.0	50.1	104.2	91.5	115.1	93.1
Georgia	82.2	87.9	76.8	49.8	164.2	77.8	74.1	69.7
Kentucky	71.7	63.4	89.0	60.5	46.1	109.6	60.6	70.3
Louisiana	83.3	72.7	79.7	49.4	105.1	121.3	73.5	80.6
Mississippi	66.6	65.2	99.3	35.4	111.4	91.9	51.1	56.0
New Mexico	90.7	93.8	129.0	45.5	79.8	107.8	98.5	76.3
N. Carolina	78.5	91.9	125.6	53.6	86.2	74.1	88.3	65.6
S. Carolina	76.4	85.6	111.4	43.9	120.2	56.9	78.3	68.5
Oklahoma	79.5	85.2	99.6	76.5	85.1	68.2	70.5	57.9
Tennessee	74.7	66.7	89.0	60.2	102.8	82.7	69.8	79.0
Texas	78.9	85.6	101.3	42.2	79.1	97.0	66.6	58.8
Sample Average	79.8	82.5	100.5	50.5	94.2	92.0	79.1	70.3
Texas' Rank	7th	6th	6th	12th	11th	4th	10th	11th

Source: U.S. Advisory Commission on Intergovernmental Relations (1990, p. 24).

differences in workload factors, which provide measures of the state's relative costs of providing given service levels to all its citizens. In general, representative expenditures in Texas were high relative to those of other states when compared to all states or to the ten most populous states. Among the fourteen Southern states, the results are more mixed. Texas ranks fourth in total representative expenditures; relatively high in representative expenditures for primary/secondary education, higher education, police and corrections, highways, and "all other expenditures"; and relatively low in representative expenditures for public welfare and for health and hospitals.

The last set of results compared actual expenditures as a percentage of representative expenditures across states. In this comparison, Texas ranks forty-third among the fifty states and the District of Columbia in total expenditures. Actual expenditures on higher education and on highways in Texas are quite close to representative expenditures. Actual expenditures are roughly 15 to 20 percent short of representative expenditures for primary/secondary education and for health and hospitals and roughly 35 to 40 percent short of representative expenditures for police and corrections and for "all other expenditures." The most dramatic difference between actual and representative expenditures arises for public welfare, where Texas' actual outlay of 42.2 percent of representative expenditures exceeds that of only two other states. Among the ten most populous states, Texas ranks ninth in total expenditures and is near or at the bottom for all service categories except higher education and highways, where its expenditure levels are in the middle of the group. Among the fourteen Southern states, Texas ranks seventh in total spending; in the upper middle of the group for actual relative to representative expenditures on primary/secondary education, higher education, and highways; and near the bottom of the group for actual relative to representative expenditures on health and hospitals, police and corrections, public welfare, and "all other expenditures."

In general, these results suggest that public expenditures in Texas are rather low in comparison to the rest of the states in the union, and relatively low only in certain categories when compared to the states in the South. This result does not necessarily imply that Texas public service levels are "low" in an absolute sense. In particular, recall that the estimated representative expenditures calculated by the ACIR and presented above do not necessarily reflect the "correct" needs of the states. Rather, they only indicate the level of expenditure associated with providing the national average service level for each function. Thus, the differences in expenditure levels presented above may simply reflect differences in tastes. Indeed, the primary advantage of a system of fiscal federalism is that it allows states (and local governments) to tailor their tax-expenditure packages to the tastes of their citizens. On the other hand, the fact that Texas expenditures are often significantly below those in other states (including the Southern states in certain expenditure categories) suggests that it is difficult to argue that government spending in Texas is somehow wildly out of hand.

In addition, several important caveats to the above analysis should be noted. First, the figures implicitly assume that all of the states provide public services with the same degree of efficiency; thus, they do not consider the possibility that a state such as Texas, which has an apparently low level of expenditures, may simply be relatively efficient in meeting the public-service needs of its citizens.

Second, the workload factors used in the calculation of each state's representative expenditures are only rough approximations of the factors that lead to differences across states in the levels of expenditures required to attain any given level of service quality. Thus, the estimates of representative expenditures are fairly rough approximations as well.

Third, note that one potential explanation of Texas' relatively low ranking in terms of actual relative to representative expenditures is simply that the state has relatively low demands for public services because it has a low "ability to pay" state and local taxes. However, the taxpaying capacity of the state appears to be near the national average. Specifically, in its calculations of taxpaying capacity using the representative tax system approach noted above, the ACIR estimates that Texas ranked twenty-second among the fifty states and the District of Columbia in 1991. In particular, the revenue that would have been raised in Texas in that year if the state were to adopt the representative tax system fell only 3 percent below the national average.[10]

Finally, it must be noted that the data presented above are for 1986–87, the last year for which data on representative expenditures across states are available. Since these figures are rather dated, changes in expenditure patterns in the intervening time period may have changed Texas' relative position. Some idea of how per capita expenditures (but not representative expenditures) have been changing over the intervening period can be obtained from table A.10, which provides a comparison of per capita expenditures in the United States and in Texas in 1986–87 and 1991–92.[11] These data indicate that the rate of increase in the overall level of per capita state and local expenditures over this three year period was greater on average in the United States (29.6 percent) than in Texas (26.1 percent); thus, it seems unlikely that Texas' ranking in terms of overall expenditures has increased over that period.

In the various spending categories, the largest increase for all states was for expenditures on public welfare, which increased 45.6 percent. This increase was even more pronounced in Texas, where spending on public welfare rose

	Total	Primary and Secondary Education	Higher Education	Public Welfare	Health and Hospitals	Highways	All Other Expenditures
US 1991–92	3811	897	331	605	319	261	1398
US 1986–87	2685	644	247	329	234	214	846
% Change	29.55	28.21	25.38	45.62	26.65	18.01	39.48
TX 1991–92	3146	884	324	416	293	222	1006
TX 1986–87	2324	666	257	159	188	241	683
% Change	26.13	24.66	20.68	61.78	35.84	−8.56	32.11
Difference in % Changes	3.42	3.54	4.70	−16.16	−9.19	26.57	7.38

Sources: U.S. Advisory Commission on Intergovernmental Relations (1990, p. 70) and (1994, pp. 124–25).

by 61.8 percent. In contrast, spending on highways in Texas declined by 8.6 percent, while for all states, spending on highways increased by only 18.0 percent, considerably below the increase in total expenditures. Texas increased spending on health and hospitals at a rate of 35.8 percent, relative to the national average of 26.7 percent. In the other spending categories (primary/secondary education, higher education, and "all other expenditures"), Texas experienced increases roughly similar, although somewhat smaller, to those in other states.[12] These results generally suggest that some narrowing of the differences (both positive and negative) in expenditures across categories between Texas and the other states has occurred in recent years.

NOTES

PREFACE

1. See also McLure, Mutti, Thuronyi, and Zodrow (1990), McLure and Zodrow (1990, 1996b), Zodrow and McLure (1991), and Zodrow (forthcoming). The case for such a tax at the state level is analyzed in chapter 6 of this book.
2. Of course, this is a benefit as seen from the perspective of the residents of the taxing state rather than from the perspective of the nation as a whole. Note also that some discussions of state tax policy focus on the potential for exporting tax burdens through higher commodity prices to out-of-state residents or lower returns to out-of-state factor owners. The analysis in chapter 3 argues that the potential for such tax exportation is rather limited and is not a critical factor in choosing between a state sales or income tax.
3. See Bradford (1986) and McLure and Zodrow (1990).
4. See Ring (1989), which is discussed in more detail in chapter 7.
5. The most commonly discussed direct consumption tax plans are the "flat tax" proposed by House Majority Leader Richard Armey (1996), which is based on the plan constructed by Hall and Rabushka (1985, 1995), and the Unlimited Savings Allowance (USA) tax proposed by Senators Nunn and Domenici (see "Unlimited Savings Allowance [USA] Tax System," 1995 and Weidenbaum, 1996). For further discussion of direct consumption taxation, see U.S. Department of the Treasury (1977), Mieszkowski (1977, 1980), Aaron and Galper (1985), Bradford (1986), Zodrow and McLure (1991), and McLure and Zodrow (1996a).

   Of course, proposals for a national retail sales tax (see Archer 1996 and Moore 1996 for discussions) or a national value-added tax (see Metcalf 1996 for a discussion) are important exceptions to this characterization.
6. A few states utilize personal sales tax rebates, sometimes in the form of credits against a state income tax; see Due and Mikesell (1995, pp. 80–84). These will be discussed further in chapter 7.
7. A state corporate tax still exacerbates the distortions of the federal corporate tax, but it does so in the sense of slightly increasing the overall corporate tax burden on all of the activities of the corporation nationwide, rather than just its in-state activities. See McLure (1980, 1981) and Mieszkowski and Zodrow (1985).
8. See Gordon and Wilson (1986) for an extended discussion of these distortions.
9. The experience during the debate surrounding the passage of the Tax Reform Act of 1986 suggests that the elimination of deductibility for all state and local taxes is unlikely; see McLure and Zodrow (1987) for a discussion of the initial Treasury I proposal, which called for the elimination of deductibility for all state and local taxes, and the final law, which eliminated deductibility only for state sales taxes.
10. A progressive (regressive) tax system is usually defined as one in which the ratio

of total tax burden to the tax base increases (decreases) as the tax base increases. In contrast, a progressive rate structure is defined as one in which the marginal tax rate (the tax rate applied to an incremental increase in the tax base) increases as the tax base increases.

CHAPTER 2

1. Most economists typically would not include exportability as a separate criterion to be used in evaluating a tax system. Instead, exportability would enter indirectly in evaluations of the efficiency and equity properties of the tax system in the context of an analysis that assumes state policy is set to maximize the well-being of state residents and takes into account the nature of the various interactions between the state and the rest of the national and world economies. However, given the importance that state policymakers often attach to exportability, as well as the fact that the analysis of exportability sets the stage for much of the subsequent discussion of the desirable features of a state tax system, exportability is treated as a separate criterion in this book.

2. In marked contrast, the ability of states to export part of their tax burdens is generally perceived as undesirable from a national standpoint, since states are likely to overconsume public services to the extent that the costs of such services can be shifted (or are perceived to be shifted) to nonresidents. This point will be ignored in the analysis in this book, which assumes that tax exporting is desirable from the viewpoint of the policymakers of the individual state (especially since other states are very likely to be engaged in similar attempts to export their tax burdens).

3. The elimination of federal deductibility for all state and local taxes—rather than for only one type of state and local tax—was recommended in the initial reform proposals made by the U.S. Treasury Department; see McLure and Zodrow (1987). Property taxes are also deductible under TRA86.

4. Note that this discussion assumes that revenues are held constant and thus should not be interpreted as implying that efficiency requires no taxation. More generally, the efficiency implications of government policies should consider the net efficiency effects of both government expenditures and the taxes used to finance them. Exceptions to this general rule are discussed later.

5. Note that efficiency issues cannot be resolved simply by "counting distortions." For example, an income tax distorts both the savings and labor/leisure choices while a general consumption tax distorts only the labor/leisure choice. Nevertheless, one cannot simply assert that a general sales tax is preferable to an income tax since, for any given level of revenue, the tax rate under the consumption tax is larger (and thus more distorting of the labor/leisure choice) than under the income tax.

6. As discussed later, benefit taxes are also desirable on equity grounds. These points are discussed in detail in chapter 6.

7. One should note a counterargument—to the extent one believes that public services are systematically underfunded (for whatever reason), a tax with low "visibility" could be viewed as desirable in that it facilitates expansion of the public sector. This argument does not appear to be a compelling one.

8. It is often argued that a common perception of the pre-1986 federal tax code as being fundamentally unfair was one of the driving forces behind passage of the Tax Reform Act of 1986; see Birnbaum and Murray (1987).

9. Note that even a highly regressive tax system—one in which the tax burden rises with income, but much less than proportionately—could be viewed as consistent with vertical equity.

10. For example, see Cline and Shannon (1986) and Shannon (1987).

CHAPTER 3

1. Perceptions about potential exportability may have important implications for the tax structure in a state. For example, Ebel (1990) notes that virtually all of the states without income taxes derive significant amounts of revenue from taxes on tourism or from severance taxes—taxes for which exporting is (or at one time was believed to be) possible. This suggests that one explanation for the absence of income taxes in such states is the desire to export the tax burden through alternative tax instruments.

2. See Pollock (1991).

3. However, the extent to which federal deductibility implies that business taxes can be shifted to out-of-state taxpayers is open to question. This issue is addressed later.

4. More recently, between 1991 and 1994, six states increased their sales tax rate, while three states decreased it. Also, during this period four states increased rates on their personal income tax, while five states lowered their rates. There were four states that both increased rates for some income brackets and lowered rates for other income brackets. See U.S. Advisory Commission on Intergovernmental Relations (1992a, pp. 68–72 and 1995, pp. 65–69, 93–94).

5. Another potential opportunity for tax exporting, which is presumably of relatively minor significance in the aggregate, is on sales to cross-border shoppers, especially those from Mexico and Canada.

6. In addition, a few states have attempted to export state taxes internationally by making worldwide income subject to state apportionment. This approach has proved very unpopular and all of the states that have attempted to use it have either eliminated it or allow a "water's edge" option (that is, a base that includes only domestic income) for most companies.

7. Indeed, many economists argue that the market for capital is an international one, and that capital is quite mobile across countries. However, the less restrictive assumption of perfect mobility across states is sufficient for the analysis in the text.

8. For a clear exposition of this open economy argument, see Slemrod (1988). Similar points are made in the context of a state economy by Henderson (1990). Note that this analysis makes the reasonable assumption that labor is significantly less mobile than capital.

9. This figure includes shifting of 3 percent of the sales tax burden to tourists. However, even Pollock notes that a state may "end up 'exporting' jobs and economic development rather than its taxes" (1991, p. 300).

10. Pollock (1991) also notes that the amount of sales tax paid by firms is small rela-

tive to gross sales. Presumably, the implication is that forward shifting of the tax would not have noticeable effects on price. Note, however, that a relatively small price increase may still have significant effects on profits and thus should not necessarily be viewed as too "small" to be significant. See McLure, Mutti, Thuronyi, and Zodrow (1990) for an analysis of the effects of sales taxes on business purchases on the marginal effective tax rates applied to capital income.

11. Pollock (1991) also notes that the scenario of full backward shifting of business sales taxes is a plausible one. He then argues that a mechanism for tax exporting exists in this case as well because lower wages imply lower federal income taxes. This avenue of exportation, however, is more modest, as he estimates that full backward shifting implies that 11 percent of the Connecticut state tax burden is exported to federal taxpayers. In any case, the same effect would occur under a personal state income tax, so that this potential avenue for tax exporting has little bearing on the choice between a sales tax and a personal income tax.

12. Similarly, Brown notes that "in the long run, incidence of taxes is likely to remain in-state to a far greater extent than is generally appreciated" (1992, p. 100).

13. Note that the same analysis applies to the potential for shifting the burden of a corporate income tax to out-of-state residents.

14. For further elaboration on many of the points made in this section, see Oakland (1992). This section is relatively technical as it discusses a wide variety of efficiency issues raised by the choice between state income and sales taxes. Readers who are not interested in these technical details may simply review the summary of these results provided in chapter 1 and skip to the following chapter on equity considerations.

15. An elasticity is defined as the ratio of percentage changes of two variables. For example, an own-price demand elasticity of -0.5 implies that a commodity price increase of 10 percent will result in a 5 percent reduction in demand for that commodity. Elasticities that are large in absolute value imply large behavioral responses.

16. Note that this is not necessarily the case, as the burden of a national tax on capital income, such as the federal corporate income tax, may be shifted at least partially; for example, this would occur if individuals save less in response to reductions in the after-tax real rate of return or if capital can move abroad to avoid increased domestic taxation.

17. See Rosen (1995, p. 325).

18. Before proceeding further, it may be useful to provide definitions of a few terms that appear frequently in discussions of state and local taxes. One important distinction is that between residence-based and source-based taxes. Residence-based taxes are assessed on the basis of residence, independent of the jurisdiction in which the base of the tax originated. Income taxes, estate taxes, and head taxes are good examples. In addition, benefit taxes can be interpreted as residence-based taxes to the extent that local public services can be consumed only by local residents. Source-based taxes are assessed in the jurisdiction in which the base of the tax originated, regardless of the jurisdiction of residence of the owner of the item being taxed. They are often justified on the grounds that states are entitled to tax the income attributable to production within their jurisdiction. Produc-

tion taxes, including corporate income and franchise taxes, and property taxes are the most common examples. A similar distinction is drawn for a consumption-type value-added tax (VAT) or a sales tax. A destination-based VAT—the most common form—is assessed in the jurisdiction in which the consumption occurs. Accordingly, imports are taxed and exports are relieved of tax. In contrast, an origin-based VAT is assessed in the jurisdiction in which the production occurs. Accordingly, imports are tax exempt and exports are not relieved of tax.

19. This analysis thus makes the reasonable assumption that labor is significantly less mobile than capital.

20. For a clear exposition of this argument, see Slemrod (1988). Diamond and Mirrlees (1971) and Gordon (1986) make the same point in more complicated models.

21. See Burgess (1988).

22. See Gordon and Varian (1989).

23. For a recent discussion of this justification for corporate taxation in a small open economy, see Gordon and MacKie-Mason (1994).

24. Thus, even consumption-based (rather than income-based) tax systems typically include a business tax designed to capture in the tax base business expenditures that represent personal consumption; see Zodrow and McLure (1991).

25. However, the conditions required for this result to hold are fairly stringent; for example, Bird and Oldman review these conditions in the international context and conclude that any effects of taxation on investment are "unlikely to be much dampened by the interaction of different national income tax systems" (1990, p. 166).

26. See Oakland (1992) for further discussion.

27. There is, however, an element of truth to this view. As described at length in the text, the local effects of a tax on capital in a small open economy are generally borne by local factors of production and/or local consumers. However, if the national capital stock is fixed, an increase in capital income taxation by a small jurisdiction in the nation is fully reflected in a slight decline in the national return to capital and in total national capital income, which is borne by all capital owners; see Bradford (1978) and Mieszkowski and Zodrow (1985). Note also that this implies that if the fraction of the national capital stock owned by the residents of a state is smaller than the fraction of the national capital stock utilized in the state, a state tax on capital or capital income is to a small extent "exported" to out-of-state capital owners.

28. Note however that this rationale may be misleading. The tax shifting arguments made above require only enough capital outflow to equalize the after-tax rate of return to capital. All capital need not be mobile to achieve this result.

29. See Bartik (1991) for a discussion of two other less common types of studies— evaluations of specific state or local development programs (such as enterprise zones) and case studies of how state or local policies affected particular investment decisions.

30. Note, however, that other factors that are also under the control of policymakers, including rules regulating labor contracts, workmen's compensation policies, and price regulation of intrastate transportation, may be as or more important than tax policy.

31. In addition, Calzonetti and Walker (1991) note that it may be difficult to get a comprehensive sample of firms and to contact the "correct" individual decision makers, that response rates may be quite low, that responses may be colored by the passage of time, and that surveys are quite expensive.

32. See Calzonetti and Walker (1991) for a review article of the industrial survey literature.

33. See Blair and Premus (1987) and Bartik (1991).

34. In addition, Premus (1982) notes that 67 percent of the high-technology firms in his sample reported that taxes were a significant factor in decisions regarding plant locations, and more than 85 percent reported that taxes were important in intraregional location decisions.

35. In addition, nearly half of the firms that opened new branches did so because space limitations precluded expansion at existing sites.

36. This point is stressed by Wasylenko (1991). Such a policy can also be justified on the grounds that highly targeted incentives create uncertainty regarding tax policy, which can also be harmful to economic development; see Hamilton and Linehan (1989).

37. Note that these personal reasons might include high individual income tax rates.

38. This discussion follows Bartik (1991), which should be consulted for additional details on the difficulties encountered in econometric analyses of industrial location decisions.

39. This point will be discussed further later in this chapter.

40. See Bartik (1991, pp. 33–34).

41. An econometric technique called instrumental variables estimation is usually used to deal with this "endogeneity" problem; see Maddala (1992, chap. 9).

42. This survey is necessarily selective. For a recent comprehensive survey, see Bartik (1991).

43. For a review of some of this early literature, see Due (1961).

44. For further discussion of the differences between average and marginal effective tax rates, see Bradford and Fullerton (1981). For details of the construction of marginal effective tax rates, see King and Fullerton (1984).

45. Benson and Johnson (1986) also find that taxes have negative effects on investment. Their analysis focuses on the dynamics of the investment response.

46. See Bartik (1991, p. 222) for a survey of the tax elasticities obtained in the literature.

47. Ondrich and Wasylenko (1993) also find that foreign direct investment is sensitive to taxes, especially corporate taxes and user charges. They also note that such investment is sensitive to expenditures on higher education. In addition, similar but weaker results are obtained by Coughlin, Terza, and Arromdee (1991).

48. Vedder (1982) also concludes that relatively high-tax states tended to have lower employment growth in the 1970s.

49. This point is stressed by McDonald (1989).

50. Recall that several of the studies discussed above suggest that the responsiveness of business activity to taxes is likely to vary significantly across industries (even within manufacturing, which is generally expected to be more responsive to taxes than other industries). In addition, Bartik notes that the research of New-

man (1983) and Gyourko (1987) suggests that, as implied by the small open economy assumption, capital-intensive firms are more sensitive to taxes on business capital than are other industries. Similarly, Bartik concludes that "the elasticity of a local community's business activity with respect to lower taxes is around −2.0" (1994, p. 853), although this relatively high elasticity reflects intrametropolitan reallocation as well as movements of capital across states and metropolitan areas.

51. Similarly, Hamilton and Linehan note that although early studies "concluded that taxes had at best only a limited impact on business decisions . . . Recent studies have shown that taxes do have an impact on many business decisions, and this role is becoming more prominent" (1989, p. 207).

52. Indeed, as described above, the research of Helms (1985) suggests that a tax increase used to finance expenditures other than expanded welfare spending has a positive effect on state personal income. Similarly, Bartik (1989) estimates that tax increases used to finance increased fire protection and education increase business start-ups, and Munnell (1990) argues that increased levels of public capital or infrastructure expenditures increase employment. However, results presented by Holtz-Eakin (1992) indicate that public sector investment has no effect on private sector productivity. He argues that the contrary results obtained by Munnell (1990) and others are flawed because they do not control appropriately for unobserved state-specific characteristics.

53. Note that such expenditures might include those on education, if the availability of a large skilled labor pool lowers a firm's labor costs.

54. It should be noted, however, that even if business tax cuts are effective in attracting new investment and new jobs, it does not necessarily follow that they are desirable in the sense that they increase the welfare of a state's residents. For example, the revenue cost of such a program may be too large relative to the employment gains obtained, or most of the benefits may go to workers who migrate to the area. For an extended discussion of this point, see Courant (1994).

55. Recall that under the formula apportionment approach used in the United States, the tax base for a state is determined as a fraction of the firm's total national profits, where that fraction is a weighted average of the fractions of the firm's total national property, payroll, and sales that are located in the state. McLure (1980, 1981) stresses that for large multistate firms, formula apportionment tends to convert a state corporate tax into a tax on the factors in the formula.

56. Note that the extent of taxation of capital goods attributable to the sales factor in the apportionment formula can be quite large, as all sales are included in the calculation, with no exemptions, even for items such as goods for resale or goods used in the production of other goods. Thus, the business share of sales in the sales component of the typical state corporate tax is larger than the business share of goods taxed under the typical state sales tax.

57. For a general discussion of such models, see Whalley (1988).

58. Recall that it is this inefficiency that underlies the conclusion of the small open economy analysis that capital income taxes should be avoided. Capital outflows

not only shift the burden of a capital tax to consumers or other factors, but they also reduce the productivity of the factors remaining in the state, thus causing an excess burden or efficiency loss.

59. Note, however, that Gordon (1985) challenges the assumption that the government can absorb risk more easily than the private sector and concludes that the effects of the corporate income tax on investment are very small.

60. Note that these results assume a fixed level of wealth. Income taxation may also affect risk-taking primarily by reducing the total amount of saving available. The effect of income taxes on saving is discussed later in this chapter.

61. See Atkinson and Stiglitz (1980, pp. 108–109).

62. The Gravelle and Kotlikoff estimate is larger primarily because it considers substitution of production between corporate and noncorporate producers of similar goods in response to the corporate tax.

63. Note that efficiency does not necessarily imply that uniform or neutral taxation of capital income is optimal. This is especially true if, as is the case in the United States, capital invested in owner-occupied housing is untaxed; see Feldstein (1990). In addition, differential taxation of capital income may be desirable if monopoly rents are earned in some industries or if it is deemed desirable on efficiency or equity grounds to tax certain commodities differentially and it is impossible to do so directly. Nevertheless, a uniform capital income tax structure may be as close to an efficient system as is likely to be achieved in practice.

64. For example, see Fullerton (1987), Fullerton, Gillette, and Mackie (1987), Fullerton, Henderson, and Mackie (1987), and Gravelle (1994).

65. For example, Fullerton and Lyon (1988) conclude that including intangible assets in a model that examines the improvements in resource allocation attributable to the Tax Reform Act of 1986 reduces by one-third the efficiency gain attributable to repealing the investment tax credit.

66. For firms whose operations are mostly or fully within the taxing state, a state corporate tax would simply exacerbate the distortions of the federal corporate tax. For a large multistate corporation, formula apportionment implies that this increased distortionary effect would occur for all the national operations of the corporation, as the state tax adds to the total tax burden on national profits, but the effect on a corporation's operations within a state would be relatively small; see Mieszkowski and Zodrow (1985). However, formula apportionment also creates its own set of distortions across assets and sectors, depending on the specific formula used, as well as other distortions of firm behavior; see Gordon and Wilson (1986).

67. In addition, in-state firms are put at a competitive disadvantage relative to firms in states that are more successful in eliminating business purchases from the sales tax base.

68. The importance of this point depends on an issue that has not been fully resolved in the public finance literature—the extent to which taxation of dividends at the individual level results in double taxation of equity-financed investments; see Zodrow (1991).

69. In addition, it would reduce the distortion of savings decisions that characterizes the income tax.

70. See Poterba (1987).

71. For example, see Rosen (1995, pp. 329–33).
72. Note that some of these efficiency costs are borne by the poor, thus offsetting some of the redistributive effects of exemption of necessities under the sales tax.
73. Although one would normally expect the income tax base to be considerably more comprehensive than the sales tax base, this conclusion must be qualified because (1) the sales tax base includes a large volume of business purchases, and (2) the income base—assuming that it would be based on the U.S. income tax— is not as comprehensive as it should be to reflect real economic income accurately. In particular, the federal income tax favors the consumption of owner-occupied housing and certain employer-provided fringe benefits. Note also that the sales tax base does not include government services, while the income tax does include the incomes of government employees.
74. For example, Due and Fairchild (1988) survey several empirical articles on cross-border purchases that estimate that a sales tax differential of 1 percent results in a reduction in sales that generally falls in the range of 3 to 7 percent in the relatively high-tax jurisdiction.
75. That is, savings (S) equals investment (I) in a closed economy, and, ignoring the government sector, total income (Y) must be spent on either consumption (C) or saving, which implies $Y = C + S = C + I$, so that the base of a comprehensive income tax is identical to the base of a comprehensive sales tax on consumption and investment goods. Alternatively, since, $Y - S = C$, the base of an income tax that allows a deduction for saving is identical to the base of a sales tax that applies only to consumption goods. For further discussion, see McDonald (1989).
76. See Triest (1993) for a recent discussion of the empirical evidence on labor supply.
77. See Hausman (1985).
78. Although there is no consensus on the effects of taxes on labor supply, most estimates of the aggregate elasticity of labor supply with respect to changes in the net wage are rather small. For example, Killingsworth (1988) reports that twelve of the fifteen empirical studies he surveys estimate that the (uncompensated) labor supply elasticity is actually negative, ranging from −0.07 and −0.33; the estimates in the other three studies vary from 0.17 to 0.88.
79. That is, human capital investment financed with foregone earnings is accorded "cash flow" treatment, which, as discussed in detail in chapter 6, implies tax exemption of the normal returns to such investment.
80. See also Trostel (1993).
81. See Mueller (1989).
82. A related argument is that the taxes that are characterized as visible are also desirable because their incidence is generally much clearer than the incidence of hidden taxes. To the extent that there is general agreement on the incidence of alternative taxes, it is much easier to determine (and debate) their relative merits.
83. For a recent exposition of these "public choice" arguments relating the tax structure and the level of expenditures, see Cullis and Jones (1992). The most prominent work in this area is by Brennan and Buchanan (1977, 1980).
84. See Zodrow and Mieszkowski (1986) for a formal model of this argument.

CHAPTER 4

1. See Rosen (1995, pp. 61–63) for a discussion of these characteristics of a public good.
2. Note also that, as discussed above, such a wage increase for high-skilled workers may have a negative effect on firm location decisions.
3. See Wildasin (1992, 1993), who shows that in this case, the only effect of the income redistribution policy is to reduce the returns to immobile factors in the jurisdiction (e.g., land and perhaps low-skilled labor).
4. These points are reinforced by empirical evidence that suggests that low-income families (especially welfare recipients) are more mobile than the general population and tend to migrate to high-benefit states. See, for example, Peterson and Rom (1990), who also note that relatively high welfare benefits may induce low-income families to remain in a state they would otherwise leave.
5. In addition, Oakland (1983) notes that differences in living costs and in amenities might encourage states to use ability-to-pay taxes to modify the pattern of redistributions implicit in the federal tax and transfer system.
6. See Slemrod (1986), Goodspeed (1991), and Oates (1991) for further discussion of these issues.
7. In addition, as will be discussed below, lifetime incidence analysis has suggested that the incidence of income taxes with increasing marginal rates is less progressive when measured with respect to lifetime rather than annual income.
8. Note that this effect will be accentuated if taxed goods tend to be consumed disproportionately by either the young or the old.

   In one typical state incidence analysis, Fritz notes that for the lowest income category in his sample "over 61 percent of households are either elderly or under 25 (a fair number of whom are probably college students drawing some measure of parental support)" (1989, p. 28). This suggests that life-cycle considerations are important in the results he obtains regarding the regressivity of the sales tax.
9. More generally, proportionality holds only if inheritances are included in lifetime income and bequests are treated as consumption. Such treatment is consistent with the "lifetime endowment" view of equity, which holds that the individual tax base should reflect all the resources available to the individual over the lifetime. Alternatively, the "dynastic" view of equity adopts a multigenerational approach; specifically, it holds that individuals should be taxed only on what they consume, which implies that inheritances should be included in the tax base but deductions should be allowed for bequests. (Thus, inheritances are taxed only if consumed.) For further discussion, see Zodrow and McLure (1991). From an empirical standpoint, Menchik and David (1982) indicate that bequests as a function of lifetime income decline until the eightieth percentile of the income distribution and then increase for the very wealthy. This implies that under the lifetime endowment view of equity, lifetime incidence analyses that ignore bequests and inheritances understate progressivity over most of the lifetime income distribution, but overstate progressivity at the upper end of the distribution.
10. For further discussion, see McLure and Zodrow (1987).

11. It is interesting to note that Joseph Pechman, the most prominent analyst in the incidence field, explicitly recognizes that incidence estimates based on annual income are likely to overstate the regressivity of sales taxes; specifically, Pechman notes that, "Whether the regressivity of these taxes with respect to income would remain for accounting periods longer than one year is not known. It seems clear, however, that the regressivity shown in the lowest income levels on the basis of annual figures would be moderated, if not completely eliminated, over the longer period" (1985, pp. 50–51).

   Note, however, that several problems are common to all such monetary indicators of ability to pay. Specifically, none makes any allowances for differences in leisure time, differences in amenities or disamenities in the work environment, or differences in the level of well-being or "utility" different individuals get from consumption. It is impossible to measure such factors accurately enough to include them in a widely acceptable measure of ability to pay.

12. Some observers have argued that the empirical evidence indicates that consumption tracks income more closely than would be implied by the life-cycle hypothesis, and that individuals, especially when young, cannot borrow as freely as implied by this theory; see Thaler (1990) and Viard (1993) and the references cited therein. Note, however, that these arguments do not invalidate the view that consumption is a better measure of ability to pay than is income. They do, however, suggest that income may not be as poor an approximation to consumption as is usually assumed in discussions of permanent and lifetime income.

   For some general discussions of the argument that annual consumption is a better measure of ability to pay than is income, see Pechman (1980).

13. This approach generally estimates lifetime income using data from the Panel Study of Income Dynamics (PSID), a survey that began in 1968 and provides details on the economic characteristics of 5,000 families.

14. As will be discussed later, these studies indicate that the lifetime incidence of certain taxes can be quite different from their annual incidence. Interestingly, however, studies that have examined the overall effect of tax systems have found relatively little difference between the lifetime and annual incidence approaches, as the changes in the incidence of individual taxes as calculated under the two approaches tend to cancel; see Davies, St-Hilaire, and Whalley (1984) and Fullerton and Rogers (1993).

15. The U.S. Congressional Budget Office (1990) and Poterba (1991) reached similar conclusions. For example, using annual consumption as a proxy for permanent or lifetime income, the former study found that taxes on motor fuels were roughly proportional, taxes on alcohol were moderately progressive, and taxes on tobacco were regressive but less so than if annual income were used as the measure of ability to pay.

16. Drawing on the study by Menchik and David (1982), Metcalf argues that this pattern implies that his analysis understates tax progressivity.

17. In addition, their model considers efficiency costs (or excess burdens) in measuring the costs of taxes, including distortions of the labor/leisure choice.

18. Fullerton and Rogers (1993) tend to find that sales taxes are somewhat regressive rather than proportional primarily because untaxed leisure comprises a relatively

large fraction of the total budget of the upper lifetime income categories. For the case in which the specification of their utility function is altered so that a uniform minimum purchase of leisure is not specified, they obtain rough proportionality.

19. For example, see Barthold (1993).

20. Note that the exception to this rule is a state sales tax system that provides for rebates of sales taxes paid by low-income households.

21. Note that similar arguments are sometimes applied to business taxes. For example, application of the benefit principle to firms implies that they should pay tax irrespective of income. This suggests that wealth-based or production-based taxes are superior to an income tax. Conversely, application of the ability-to-pay principle to firms implies that an income-based tax is desirable. Note that the latter approach is rather tenuous, since a firm with a low income may be owned by wealthy individuals and vice versa. For a discussion of these points, see Thrash and Kennedy (1989).

22. Note, however, that the withdrawal of saving that takes a tax-deferred form— e.g., savings in IRAs or 401 (k) plans—is subject to income taxation.

23. Note that if the income brackets under the income tax are not indexed for inflation, automatic growth in the ratio of revenues to income will occur even with purely inflationary nominal growth. There is general agreement that such revenue increases are undesirable and should be eliminated by inflation-indexing the income brackets under the income tax.

24. Dye and McGuire obtain this result for recreation services (primarily admissions to sporting and entertainment events).

25. See also White (1983) and Misiolek and Perdue (1987).

26. This point reinforces the argument, made in chapter 2, that state governments should not necessarily strive for "balance" in their revenue structures in the sense of roughly equal reliance on state sales, income, and property taxes; rather, the optimal tax mix should be determined by evaluating alternative tax structures in terms of the other criteria discussed in that chapter.

27. However, as noted above, some argue that pressure on state revenues is desirable as it causes periodic reevaluation of the need for government expenditures.

28. In addition, McDonald (1989) suggests that the stabilizing effect of the income tax is likely to reduce government outlays on unemployment insurance and welfare and may reduce crime.

29. See U.S. Advisory Commission on Intergovernmental Relations (1995, pp. 50–51).

30. Ibid., pp. 78–87.

31. See Fox and Murray (1988) and the articles in Fox (1992a).

32. For elaboration of this argument, see Bradford (1986).

33. Interestingly, supporters of a European-style, invoice-credit method value-added tax often note its positive effects in reducing tax evasion. Specifically, they argue that since firms in the later stages of a production process receive credits for taxes paid by firms in the earlier stages only if they can provide invoices documenting the tax payments, the VAT encourages compliance. In addition, the existence of the credit "paper trail" also encourages compliance and facilitates the audit process.

CHAPTER 5

1. In addition, taxpayers with taxable income in excess of $250,000 are subject to a 10 percent surtax, which implies a marginal tax rate of 39.6 percent and a tax price of 60.4 cents on the dollar. Note also that some taxpayers in certain income ranges are subject to higher effective marginal tax rates (and thus lower tax prices for state and local services financed with income or property taxes) due to provisions such as the phasing out of personal exemptions and limitations on itemized deductions. See U.S. House of Representatives (1993).

2. As noted above, the primary exception is sales taxes borne by tourists or business travelers. However, this form of tax exportation, if deemed to be sufficiently important, can be achieved by specific excise taxes on hotel/motel occupancy, car rentals, and perhaps entertainment and admissions to amusements.

3. For a discussion of the incentive effects of formula-apportioned state corporate income taxes, see Gordon and Wilson (1986).

4. Also, some argue that firms organized as corporations receive special "benefits," especially limited liability of shareholders. It seems unlikely, however, that a firm's tax liability under a state corporate income tax is related to such benefits.

5. Indeed, it is possible to "phase out" personal exemptions and standard deductions so that wealthy individuals receive none of the benefits of these provisions. This was done under TRA86; see Rosen (1995).

6. Note, however, that the regressivity of the sales tax can also be addressed by providing refundable tax credits to poor families (who must apply to receive the credit). The primary problems with this approach are that (1) the application process creates complexity for low-income individuals who may have difficulty coping with the filing process, (2) some of the poor—perhaps a large fraction—may not be aware of the program or may not apply for the credit for other reasons, and (3) an end-of-year credit may create cash flow problems for the poor during the year. For a discussion of such programs, see Gold (1992).

7. Note that the same argument can be made with respect to the use of the lottery to raise state revenues. The use of an income tax would mitigate the equity problems that are often raised by the regressive incidence of the lottery.

CHAPTER 6

1. This discussion draws heavily on U.S. Advisory Commission on Intergovernmental Relations (1987), Downing (1991), and U.S. Congressional Budget Office (1993).

2. In particular, one can argue that user charges are most appropriate when a differentially high level of services is provided to a particular subset of the population; see Brazer (1984).

3. Downing (1991) notes that the external benefits of providing local public services to relatively poor individuals may be larger than average, implying that the fraction of the service financed with user fees should be lower for such individuals.

4. Note, however, that if state or local services generate positive external effects, efficiency requires that these be paid for by the nonresidents who enjoy the exter-

nal benefits. Local user charges should cover only local benefits. Recall that this rationale implies that taxes that can be exported are undesirable from the perspective of (national) efficiency because they encourage an overexpansion of public services.

5. This factor is particularly important when the price elasticity of demand for a public service is fairly high, so that the utilization of user charges has a significant effect on demand and thus on the efficiency of resource allocation.

6. Note that the Tiebout (1956) model, which provides the classic theoretical efficiency rationale for expenditure decentralization, assumes the existence of lump sum taxes, which in the context of the model are equivalent to benefit taxes. For a collection of papers that evaluate the Tiebout model, see Zodrow (1983).

7. This possibility is discussed by Zodrow and Miewzkowski (1986). For a brief review of this "tax competition" literature, see Wildasin and Wilson (1991).

8. For an excellent discussion of these issues, see Wildasin (1986).

9. For a survey of this evidence, see Romer and Rosenthal (1979); see also Hamilton (1983).

10. For example, see Rosen (1995, pp. 66–69).

11. See Musgrave and Musgrave (1976, p. 213).

12. See Mieszkowski and Zodrow (1989) for a discussion of this and related results.

13. Ibid.

14. Note, however, that if the United States were to adopt a national consumption-based tax system such as the "flat tax" proposed by Representative Armey, then state adoption of the similar option considered in this section would not be at all far-fetched.

15. See Zodrow and McLure (1991) and McLure, Mutti, Thuronyi, and Zodrow (1990). The name was chosen to emphasize the simplicity advantages of this tax structure relative to the income tax. For similar proposals, see Bradford (1986), Hall and Rabushka (1985, 1995), and the "tax prepayment" consumption tax option discussed in U.S. Treasury (1977). Note that in contrast to the Hall-Rabushka "flat tax" proposal, which forms the basis of the reform proposed by Representative Armey, the SAT would follow Bradford (1986) in allowing a (modestly) progressive marginal rate structure.

16. The discussion assumes that a state would adopt the SAT in isolation and does not address the many issues raised by adoption of such a tax by all states simultaneously. See McLure (1992) for a discussion of these issues in an international context.

17. The rationale underlying this characterization, which is strictly valid only in a closed economy, is described below.

18. Using the terminology of the Institute for Fiscal Studies (1978), the business tax has an "R-base" which includes real transactions but ignores financial transactions. Under the alternative "R + F" or "real plus financial" base, the proceeds of loans are included in the tax base and both interest expense and the repayment of principal are deductible. This is equivalent in present value terms to ignoring loans, but is clearly much more complicated. See McLure and Zodrow (1990) for a discussion of this equivalence result and a comparison of the two approaches in terms of the criterion of tax simplicity.

19. See McLure (1987) for a discussion of alternative means of implementing a VAT.

20. For example, McLure (1992) argues that such an approach is the appropriate one for the SAT.

21. Under the alternative "destination" principle (which is used in the case of European VATs), exports are relieved of tax and imports are subject to tax. In the context of the SAT, application of the destination principle would imply that exports would not be included in the tax base and imported inputs would not be deductible. The former treatment might be interpreted as too generous to in-state exporters; the latter treatment would be perceived as extremely harsh by out-of-state producers and might be interpreted as unconstitutional state taxation of imports. Accordingly, the following discussion considers only an origin-based state SAT. The feasibility and desirability of a destination-based state SAT are, however, worthy of further consideration and are discussed briefly by Carlson and McLure (1985). Note also that the retail sales tax is in principle levied on a destination basis, as traded consumer goods are not subject to tax in the exporting state, and importing states often attempt to assess sales tax on imported consumer goods by applying use taxes to such imports. Such attempts are, however, typically not very successful.

    It is also interesting to note that some analysts have argued that an origin-based tax on businesses can be justified as an approximation to a benefit tax; see Cline (1988).

22. Note that the prescribed treatment of pensions is roughly equivalent to simply making pension contributions deductible to the firm and then taxing them currently at the individual level, with subsequent earnings tax-free. However, the suggested treatment is more consistent with current treatment (which approximates consumption-based taxation) and results in tax-base averaging over the life cycle.

23. More accurately, under both types of tax systems, ordinary returns to capital are exempt from tax, while above normal returns, including economic rents and returns to risk-taking, are subject to tax (at the business level in the case of the SAT). See Bradford (1996) and Gentry and Hubbard (1995) for discussions of this important point.

24. Note, however, that this would not be the case for an origin-based state VAT, since imported consumer goods would not be subject to tax.

25. The explanation for this result is analogous to that for the individual cash flow tax. Specifically, the larger value of the initial deduction for expensing (rather than for depreciation) offsets the subsequent taxation of the returns to the investment, resulting in a marginal effective tax rate of zero. See Zodrow and McLure (1991) for further discussion and some numerical examples.

26. By allowing expensing (rather than deductions for depreciation) and then taxing the returns to the investment, the government is effectively a silent partner in the investment. Private returns are unaffected, but the government obtains positive revenue because, like the firm, it earns above-normal returns on its share of the investment. See Zodrow and McLure (1991) for a discussion of this issue, and Zodrow (1995) for a discussion of saving behavior under the alternative forms of consumption taxation.

27. These returns can be viewed, however, simply as compensation for the riskiness of the revenue stream under the business cash flow approach; see Kaplow (1994).

28. Such treatment is administratively much simpler than attributing such expenses to individuals and including them in the individual tax base; note, however, that the definition of the personal component of such expenses is often extremely difficult.

29. Alternatively, economic rents and the returns to risk-taking are subject to "source-based" taxation. However, as will be discussed further in this chapter, individuals are taxed on their wage income in the state of their residence.

30. Note that a state VAT would presumably not be deductible either.

31. Note that forward shifting of the portion of the SAT that applies to the economic rents earned by the businesses in a state may be possible if the state's firms are part of an oligopolistic market structure that responds to taxes by raising prices; see Katz and Rosen (1985).

32. Note that this would also be one of the main advantages of a state VAT.

33. Recall from the discussion in chapter 3 that under certain circumstances, the base of a sales tax that applies to both consumption and investment goods is equivalent to the base of a comprehensive income tax.

34. As noted previously, a consumption-based tax is an efficient tax under certain circumstances in the sense of minimizing the excess burdens associated with attaining a given level of revenue. This result depends, however, on the nature of the assumptions made regarding individual preferences.

35. Note, however, that the introduction of a SAT could result in serious transitional equity problems, since the consumption of the elderly out of nonpension savings is entirely untaxed. This does not occur with expansion of the sales tax or, to a much lesser extent, with increased usage of an income tax. The replacement of a state corporate income tax with the business tax portion of the SAT would also result in a host of difficult transitional issues. For general discussions of these transitional problems, see Sarkar and Zodrow (1993) and Bradford (1996).

36. See Gentry and Hubbard (1995) for further elaboration of this point.

37. However, as will be discussed later, banking services are an exception to this general rule.

38. Since the tax base of the SAT is only indirectly related to consumption, the fact that consumption is more stable than income is not directly relevant.

39. Of course, some might argue that application of the SAT to exports is desirable in that it provides an opportunity to export the tax burden to out-of-state residents. The discussion in chapter 3 suggests that such opportunities for tax exporting are rather limited.

40. On the other hand, if the destination principle were applied (imported inputs not deductible), out-of-state producers of production inputs would be placed at a significant tax disadvantage relative to in-state firms. Application of the destination principle would also require finding a constitutional way of subjecting imports of consumer goods to tax, as is currently done very incompletely through the application of use taxes under state sales tax regimes.

Yet another alternative treatment would be to use a hybrid approach, similar to that proposed by Francis (1993) for a state VAT. Specifically, the SAT could nominally be based on the origin principle, but the destination principle could effectively be applied to imports of business inputs by using an "invoice-credit" approach to calculating the SAT. Under such an approach, tax would be applied to receipts less expenditures on labor costs, with a credit for taxes on inputs that were paid previously (and thus recorded on the firm's invoices). Under this approach, imports of out-of-state production inputs would still be deductible, as specified under the origin principle. However, when the production good that used the input was sold, the input would effectively be taxed in full since there would be no SAT credit for taxes paid. As a result, such a "hybrid" SAT would favor the purchase of in-state over out-of-state production inputs. Such a tax would of course be subject to the criticisms that it attempts to tax both imports and exports.

41. Note that one important advantage of the destination principle is that these valuation issues disappear, since imports are not deductible and exports are not included in the tax base.

42. See McLure (1992) for a discussion of this issue.

43. See McLure (1980, 1992) and Gordon and Wilson (1986).

44. The following discussion summarizes several problems with the SAT; for complete discussions, see Zodrow and McLure (1991) and McLure, Mutti, Thuronyi, and Zodrow (1990). McLure and Zodrow (1996a, b) propose a modified version of a national SAT that is explicitly designed to deal with these problems and might also be considered in the state context.

45. Insurance companies obtain the same result by paying low rates of interest on the cash value of insurance policies while charging relatively low premiums.

46. For further discussions of these tax avoidance issues, see Zodrow and McLure (1991).

47. Note, however, that this is not necessarily the case if the state tax system includes significant modifications to the federal tax.

CHAPTER 7

1. One issue of interest in the state is whether government spending has been increasing at an unwarranted rate in recent years; see Moore (1994). The Governor's Task Force on Revenue report argues that much of the recent increase has been in reaction to, or in anticipation of, court actions or federal mandates; see also Hobby (1994).

2. See Hamilton (1989d, Vol. 1, p. 2); the two volumes issued by the Select Committee on Tax Equity will hereafter be referred to as the SCOTE report. Similarly, the subsequent report of the Governor's Task Force on Revenue (1991) will be referred to as the GTFR report. This chapter draws frequently on these two reports, especially the contribution by McDonald (1989) to the SCOTE report. In addition to these two studies of the Texas tax structure, a number of excellent recent analyses of the tax systems in other states are useful references on most of the issues discussed in this book, including Tannenwald (1990) on the tax system in Massachusetts; Ebel (1990) on Nevada; Dearborn and Ladin (1990) on Maryland; McGuire (1989) on Arizona; Wasylenko and Yinger (1988) on Nebraska; and Coe, Coleman, and Bradford (1988) on New Jersey. Earlier academic studies of the question of the desirability of a state income tax in Texas have also come to opposing conclusions; see Greenhut (1986) and Holt (1993).

3. The primary exceptions appear to be former Lieutenant Governor William P.

Hobby and, temporarily, Lieutenant Governor Bob Bullock, whose support of the state income tax option was extremely short-lived. See Hailey (1991), Robison (1991, 1993), and Hobby (1993).

4. See Texas Comptroller of Public Accounts (1995a, p. 12).

5. See U.S. Advisory Commission on Intergovernmental Relations (1995, pp. 93–94).

6. This information was obtained from the office of the Texas Comptroller of Public Accounts. This is an upper-bound figure on the business share of the sales tax base, since the estimation methodology, which is similar to that used by Ring (1989), calculates the consumer share of the tax base and then assumes that the remainder is attributable to businesses. In particular, no attempt is made to reduce the estimate of the business share for sales to tourists, nonprofit organizations, and government agencies. Although corrections for these factors would lower the fraction of the sales tax base attributable to business purchases, it seems clear that remaining fraction would still be quite large.

For details of the exemption from the sales tax base of equipment used in manufacturing, processing or fabrication, see Texas Comptroller of Public Accounts (1992b, pp. 1–5).

The approximation mentioned here is based on an estimate by the Texas Comptroller of Public Accounts (1993c, p. 5) that the full exemption would exclude about $550 million annually from sales tax receipts.

7. See Ring (1989, p. 171). This implies a relatively high business share of somewhat less than 54 percent (by comparison to the 49 percent figure noted above). Note that neither of these estimates make any correction for the amount of sales attributable to tourists, nonprofit organizations, or government agencies. Again, this share has been reduced by the recently enacted exemption of equipment purchases from the state sales tax.

8. See Fox (1992b) for a general discussion of sales taxation of services, and Hellerstein (1988), Fox and Murray (1988), and Fox (1992a) for a discussions of efforts to expand sales taxation to services in other states.

9. See Craymer (1989, p. 139) and Texas Comptroller of Public Accounts (1995c).

10. See Craymer (1989, p. 149), who discusses the methodology used to measure comprehensiveness.

11. See Hamilton (1989b) for a detailed discussion of the corporate franchise tax.

12. This estimate was provided by the office of the Texas Comptroller of Public Accounts.

13. See U.S. Advisory Commission on Intergovernmental Relations (1995, pp. 74–76).

14. For further details, see Hamilton (1989b, pp. 184–86).

15. For a general discussion of the use of severance taxes in Texas, see Merjanian (1989).

16. For detailed information on excise tax rates, see Texas Comptroller of Public Accounts (1995a, pp. 17–18).

17. See U.S. Advisory Commission on Intergovernmental Relations (1994, p. 85, 118). Combined state and local sales taxes are the second largest source of revenue for state and local governments, raising 32 percent of total state and local tax revenue.

18. County education districts have been ruled unconstitutional by the Texas Supreme Court.
19. See U.S. Advisory Commission on Intergovernmental Relations (1994, p. 111).
20. Ibid., p. 187.
21. Ibid., pp. 104–105.
22. See U.S. Advisory Commission on Intergovernmental Relations (1995, pp. 74–76).
23. Ibid., p. 32.
24. In addition, only two states—Nevada and New Hampshire—had a higher degree of reliance upon selective sales taxes, and only Nevada has a greater reliance on combined sales and excise taxes than does Texas. See U.S. Bureau of the Census (1994b, p. 6).
25. See also Brooks, Tannenwald, Sale, and Puri (1993).
26. See Tannenwald (1993, Table 3). Note that a high ranking implies a relatively low tax burden and thus suggests that a state is relatively competitive in attracting business.
27. See Tannenwald (1993, Table 8). Indeed, this ranking probably understates the fraction of taxes in Texas with an initial impact on business because Tannenwald simply assumes that the business share of general sales taxes is 20 percent. As noted above, the business share of sales taxes in Texas is more likely to be roughly 40 percent.
28. See Tannenwald (1993, Table 12).The combined state and local tax burden on a family of four with a 1991 income of $75,000 ($100,000) was estimated to be $5,005 ($6,324).
29. This approach is described in more detail in the discussion of the work of Papke (1987, 1991a, b) in chapter 3.
30. However, recall from chapter 3 that, contrary to popular opinion, this incentive was not increased under the Tax Reform Act of 1986. For an analysis of this point in the Texas context, see Kenyon (1989), who argues that, roughly speaking, the differential advantage of personal income taxes over sales taxes due to deductibility against federal tax liability was unchanged by the 1986 reform.
31. The 25 percent figure is the weighted average difference between the fraction of itemizers in Texas and the fraction of itemizers in the United States, by income group; the weights are the fractions of all state and local income taxes deducted in the United States by each income group. See U.S. Internal Revenue Service (1995a, b) for the relevant data.
32. An accurate estimate of the gain from switching to a deductible state income tax from the nondeductible sales tax could be obtained by analyzing a representative sample of federal income tax returns for residents of the state. For any specific state income tax proposal, which presumably would be based on the federal tax, the distribution of the tax burdens across itemizers and nonitemizers could be determined, as could the benefits of additional tax deductions for the itemizers. Aggregating these benefits would yield the net gain to the state. As noted above, the estimate of the aggregate gain should include the gains to those nonitemizers who become itemizers due to the additional deductions for the state income tax.
33. Note that this estimate corresponds to the figure obtained by Brown (1989).
34. In the Texas case, the petrochemical industry and the export-import business are

probably the best examples of industries that might be able to export some of their tax burden. Texas exports approximately 26 percent of its production output. The most important export industries are petroleum refining (17.5 percent of total business exports), oil, gas, and mining (14.3 percent), chemicals (12.7 percent), wholesale trade (7.2 percent), electronic machinery (7.2 percent), finance, insurance, and real estate (6.2 percent), and food and kindred products (5.4 percent). These estimates are calculated from data presented in Texas Comptroller of Public Accounts (1989b).

Phares estimates that for the nation as a whole the average amount of tax exporting of the general sales tax (due to higher prices for out-of-state consumers) is 6.0 percent (1980, p. 67).

35. Recall that with such sales taxation of business purchases, multiple taxation of goods at various stages in the production process is quite possible, and that this "cascading" of the tax can result in effective tax rates that are considerably higher than the statutory rate and thus quite distortionary.

36. Fritz also provides incidence estimates of the combined state and local tax burden, on the assumption that residential property taxes are borne by homeowners and renters. The inclusion of local property taxes tends to reduce the regressivity of the tax system, as the ratio of housing consumption to annual income rises modestly with income. (That is, the data presented by Fritz suggest that the income elasticity of the demand for housing is somewhat greater than one.)

37. Fritz argues that this is the only possible scenario. This is incorrect, as taxes on consumption goods can in principle be shifted to suppliers (unless supply is perfectly elastic) as consumers substitute away from taxed goods into untaxed goods or leisure, thus driving down the net price received by producers. Nevertheless, the assumption that consumers bear the final burden of taxes on consumption goods is a standard one in tax incidence analyses.

The Consumer Expenditure Survey is conducted annually by the Bureau of Labor Statistics of the U.S. Department of Labor and includes estimates of consumption expenditures as a function of estimated income (as reported by the participants in the survey).

38. Note that Fritz incorrectly argues that a key distinction is whether a tax is imposed on consumers or producers. In fact, a standard result in tax incidence theory in competitive markets is that it is irrelevant whether a tax is imposed on consumers or producers, as incidence is determined solely by market conditions as described by supply and demand elasticities; for example, see Rosen (1995, pp. 281–82).

39. Such an analysis would of course have to specify the details of the state income tax being considered as a reform alternative. Perdue and Weed (1991) provide an optimal state tax portfolio analysis for the Texas revenue structure as of 1985. They conclude that the volatility of state revenues could be reduced dramatically (by nearly two-thirds) without reducing the growth rate of revenues. Although this result is achieved by a complex change in the mix of the forty-three different taxes they include in their study, the primary change is an increase of somewhat more than 50 percent in the share of revenues provided by the general sales tax, which is relatively more stable than most of the other taxes considered in their analysis.

40. This concern about the elderly might be addressed through the increased utilization of user charges and/or with a reduction or elimination of preferential treatment of the elderly under the local property tax.

41. Note, however, that most of these issues are by no means unique to Texas, as similar problems plague many other state tax systems. In particular, a number of these issues are quite typical of state retail sales tax systems.

42. For example, see Due and Mikesell (1995).

43. See Gillis, Mieszkowski, and Zodrow (forthcoming) for further discussion.

44. Due and Mikesell (1995) cite Hawaii, New Mexico, and South Dakota as the states that have the most comprehensive sales taxation of services. These states could serve as models for further expansion of the sales taxation of services in Texas. As noted above, Due and Mikesell characterize the taxation of services in Texas as "relatively extensive."

45. For example, Thrash (1989b) notes that Texas businesses accounted for 53 percent of total service purchases in 1979. This percentage varied widely according to the type of service, suggesting that certain services (e.g., advertising and indeed most professional services other than medical services) should be excluded from an expansion of the sales tax base in order to reduce its impact on businesses.

46. For a list of the states that use a rebate or refund, see Due and Mikesell (1995, pp. 80–84). For a discussion of individual rebates in the context of a value-added tax, see Brashares, Speyrer, and Carlson (1988). See Gillis, Mieszkowski, and Zodrow (forthcoming) for further discussion of this approach.

47. In addition, Case and Ebel (1989) note that a rebate does not apply to nonresidents, thus increasing the extent to which the tax burden can be exported to tourists (who pay the tax but do not get refunds).

48. In addition, consideration should be given to changing the single-factor (sales) formula used for the formula apportionment of the corporate tax in Texas. As discussed above, this formula results in a significant and highly distortionary tax burden on capital. Including a payroll factor would, for large multistate firms, reallocate some of the burden of the tax from capital to labor; the discussion in chapter 3 suggests that such a change would be desirable. Alternatively, if a tax on capital were deemed desirable, including a property factor would at least make this tax more uniform across assets and business sectors, and avoid the multiple taxation or cascading of tax implied by the sales factor (which applies to all business sales) in the current formula.

49. See Netzer (1992, p. 504). In this calculation, user charge revenue is defined fairly broadly as the sum of current charges, utility revenue, and revenue from motor fuel and motor vehicle license taxes, and own-source revenue is defined as total own-source general revenue plus utility revenue.

At the municipal level, sixteen of the twenty-nine Texas cities with a population in excess of 75,000 utilized user charges to a greater extent than the national average. See U.S. Bureau of the Census (1993).

50. A similar picture emerges at the local level. The U.S. Advisory Commission on Intergovernmental Relations (1987) reports that the ratio of local user charges per dollar of local taxes was 0.37 in Texas. By comparison, the national average is 0.35, although seven states had ratios of 0.70 or more. Also, the growth of local

user charges per dollar of local taxes has been relatively slow in Texas, as it increased by only 0.9 percent per year between 1972–85. By comparison, the average rate of growth in the nation was 3.6 percent, and four states had growth rates in excess of 6 percent.

51. For a detailed discussion of the application of user charges in various functions, see U.S. Advisory Commission on Intergovernmental Relations (1987); see also Downing (1991). For a similar list of areas with a potential for increased user charge finance, see Brown (1989).

52. For example, see U.S. Advisory Commission on Intergovernmental Relations (1987).

53. The most obvious way to create such incentives would be to make state grants a function of the level of utilization of user charges at the local level. However, in Texas, use of this approach would apparently require a constitutional amendment since the constitution precludes most forms of state aid to municipalities and counties (although there is an exception for transfers to local governments that are used for state purposes). State transfer payments for education are made directly to local school districts. For a discussion of this issue, see Thrash (1989a).

54. The primary difference would be that such a comprehensive retail sales tax would apply to consumption out of existing assets, while such consumption would be tax free under the SAT.

55. Another consumption-based option would be the implementation of a state value-added tax (VAT). This option is discussed in the GTFR report and by Wieferman (1989). Michigan is the only state in the union that utilizes a VAT.

APPENDIX

1. The Southern states include ten in the Southeast—Alabama, Arkansas, Florida, Georgia, Kentucky, Louisiana, Mississippi, North Carolina, South Carolina, Tennessee—and four in the Southwest—Arizona, New Mexico, Oklahoma, Texas. This classification is taken from U.S. Advisory Commission on Intergovernmental Relations (1990, p. 27).

2. These results are clearly somewhat dated, but represent the latest adjusted expenditure data published by the U.S. Advisory Commission on Intergovernmental Relations.

3. It should be noted that the ACIR approach is fairly crude, as it assumes that all the variation in public-sector input costs comes either from variations in labor costs across states or from variations in the fraction of input costs accounted for by labor; that is, differences in the costs of nonlabor inputs are assumed to cancel across states. For a description of this methodology, see U.S. Advisory Commission on Intergovernmental Relations (1990, Appendix C).

4. Since the division of responsibilities between state and local governments varies considerably across states, combined figures are a better indicator of public service levels than either expenditures at only the state or only the local level.

5. The "all other expenditures" category includes expenditures on sewerage and sanitation, housing and community development, parks and recreation, natural resources, agriculture, fire protection, "other" educational expenditures, interest

and administrative expenses. For more detail, see U.S. Advisory Commission on Intergovernmental Relations (1990, p. 16).

6. Note that the figures still express state and local spending as a percentage of average national spending per capita (rather than relative to average spending for the ten most populous states).

7. The representative expenditure approach is related to an analogous tax concept, the "representative tax system" (also developed by the ACIR), that measures the potential of a state to raise revenues from own sources. Specifically, this potential is measured as the revenue that would be raised if the state were to adopt the specific taxes and tax rates that reflect, on average, the actual policies enacted across the country.

8. The workload factors are chosen to be independent of government policies in any particular state.

9. Note that these high costs should not be attributed to differences in inputs costs, since all the data presented in this appendix are adjusted for such differences.

10. See U.S. Advisory Commission on Intergovernmental Relations (1994, p. 182).

11. Note that these figures are not adjusted for differences in input costs.

12. Note that expenditures for "police and corrections" have been included with "all other expenditures" in table A.10. For all states, expenditures in this category had a relatively large percentage increase (39.5 percent), approximately 10 percentage points greater than the increase in overall expenditures.

BIBLIOGRAPHY

Aaron, Henry J., and Harvey Galper. 1985. *Assessing Tax Reform*. Washington, D.C.: Brookings Institution.

Archer, Bill. 1996. "Goals of Fundamental Tax Reform." In *Frontiers of Tax Reform*, edited by Michael Boskin. Palo Alto, Calif.: Hoover Institution Press.

Armey, Dick. 1996. *The Flat Tax: A Citizens' Guide to the Facts on What It Will Do for You, Your Country, and Your Pocketbook*. New York: Fawcett Columbine.

Atkinson, Anthony B., and Joseph E. Stiglitz. 1980. *Lectures On Public Economics*. New York: McGraw-Hill.

Auerbach, Alan J.; Jagadeesh Gokhale; and Laurence J. Kotlikoff. 1991. "Generational Accounts: A Meaningful Alternative to Deficit Accounting." In *Tax Policy and the Economy*, edited by David Bradford. Vol. 5. Cambridge: MIT Press.

Auerbach, Alan J., and Laurence J. Kotlikoff. 1987. *Dynamic Fiscal Policy*. Cambridge: Cambridge University Press.

Barthold, Thomas A. 1993. "How Should We Measure Distribution?" *National Tax Journal* 46:291–300.

Bartik, Timothy J. 1985. "Business Location Decisions in the United States: Estimates of the Effects of Unionization, Taxes, and Other Characteristics of States." *Journal of Business and Economic Statistics* 3:14–22.

———. 1989. "Small Business Start-Ups in the United States: Estimates of the Effects of Characteristics of States." *Southern Economic Journal* 55:1004–18.

———. 1991. *Who Benefits from State and Local Economic Development Policies?* Kalamazoo, Mich.: W. E. Upjohn Institute for Employment Research.

———. 1994. "Jobs, Productivity, and Local Economic Development: What Implications Does Economic Research Have for the Role of Government?" *National Tax Journal* 47:847–61.

Benson, Bruce L., and Ronald N. Johnson. 1986. "The Lagged Impact of State and Local Taxes on Economic Activity and Political Behavior." *Economic Inquiry* 24:389–401.

Bird, Richard M., and Oliver Oldman, eds. 1990. *Taxation in Developing Countries*. London: Johns Hopkins University Press.

Birnbaum, Jeffrey H., and Alan S. Murray. 1987. *Showdown at Gucci Gulch*. New York: Random House.

Blair, John P., and Robert Premus. 1987. "Major Factors in Industrial Location: A Review." *Economic Development Quarterly* 1:72–85.

Blomquist, N. S. 1981. "A Comparison of Distributions of Annual and Lifetime Income: Sweden Around 1970." *Review of Income and Wealth* 27:243–64.

Bradford, David F. 1978. "Factor Prices May Be Constant, But Factor Returns Are Not." *Economics Letters* 1:199–203.

Bradford, David F. 1986. *Untangling the Income Tax*. London: Harvard University Press.

———. 1996. "Consumption Taxes: Some Fundamental Transition Issues." In *Frontiers of Tax Reform*, edited by Michael Boskin. Palo Alto, Calif.: Hoover Institution Press.

Bradford, David F., and Don Fullerton. 1981. "Pitfalls in the Construction and Use of Effective Tax Rates." In *Depreciation, Inflation and the Taxation of Income from Capital*, edited by Charles R. Hulten. Washington, D.C.: The Urban Institute.

Brashares, Edith; Janet Furman Speyrer; and George M. Carlson. 1988. "Pros and Cons of Alternative Approaches to the Taxation of Consumption." *National Tax Journal* 41:155–73.

Brazer, Harvey E. 1984. "User Charges in an Environment of Fiscal Limitation." In *Proceedings of the Seventy-Sixth Annual Conference on Taxation 1983*, edited by Stanley J. Bowers. Columbus, Ohio: National Tax Association–Tax Institute of America.

Break, G. 1980. *Financing Government in a Federal System*. Washington D.C.: Brookings Institution.

Brennan, Geoffrey, and James J. Buchanan. 1977. "Towards a Tax Constitution for Leviathan." *Journal of Public Economics* 8:255–73.

———. 1980. *The Power to Tax: Analytical Foundations of a Fiscal Constitution*. Cambridge: Cambridge University Press.

Brooks, Stephen. 1993. "Report to the Massachusetts Special Commission on Tax Policy." March 30.

Brooks, Stephen; Robert Tannenwald; Hillary Sale; and Sandeep Puri. 1990. "The Competitiveness of the Massachusetts Tax System." In *Research of the Massachusetts Special Commission on Tax Reform*, edited by Robert Tannenwald. Boston: Massachusetts Special Commission on Tax Reform.

Brown, Stephen P. 1989. "Tax Policy and Texas Economic Development." In *Rethinking Texas Taxes: Final Report of the Select Committee on Tax Equity*, edited by Billy C. Hamilton. Austin: Reproduction Division of the Texas House of Representatives.

Brown, William R. 1992. "Techniques of State Tax Exporting." In *State Taxation of Business*, edited by Thomas F. Pogue. London: Praeger.

Burgess, David F. 1988. "On the Relevance of Export Demand Conditions for Capital Income Taxation in Open Economies." *Canadian Journal of Economics* 21:285–311.

Calzonetti, F. J., and Robert T. Walker. 1991. "Factors Affecting Industrial Location Decisions: A Survey Approach." In *Industry Location and Public Policy*, edited by Henry Herzog and Alan Schlottmann. Knoxville: University of Tennessee Press.

Carlson, George N., and Charles E. McLure, Jr. 1985. "Pros and Cons of Alternative Approaches to the Taxation of Consumption." In *Proceedings of the Seventy-Seventh Annual Conference 1984*, edited by Stanley J. Bowers. Columbus, Ohio: National Tax Association–Tax Institute of America.

Carlton, Dennis W. 1979. "Why Do New Firms Locate Where They Do? An Econometric Model." In *Interregional Movements and Regional Growth*, edited by William C. Wheaton. Washington, D.C.: The Urban Institute.

———. 1983. "The Location and Employment Choices of New Firms: An Econometric Model with Discrete and Continuous Endogenous Variables." *The Review of Economics and Statistics* 65:440–49.

Carroll, Robert, and Michael Wasylenko. 1989. "The Importance of Structural Changes Over Time for Measuring the Impact of Policy Variables on State Business Climates." Manuscript, Syracuse University, Syracuse N.Y.

————. 1990. "The Shifting Fate of Fiscal Variables and Their Effect on Economic Development." In *Proceedings of the Eighty-Second Annual Conference 1989,* edited by Frederick D. Stocker. Columbus, Ohio: National Tax Association–Tax Institute of America.

————. 1994. "Do State Business Climates Still Matter?—Evidence of a Structural Change." *National Tax Journal* 47:19–37.

Case, Bradford, and Robert Ebel. 1989. "Using State Consumer Tax Credits for Achieving Equity." *National Tax Journal* 42:323–37.

Casperson, Erik, and Gilbert Metcalf. 1994. "Is a Value Added Tax Progressive? Annual versus Lifetime Incidence Measures." *National Tax Journal* 47:731–46.

Chernick, Howard. 1996. "Tax Progressivity and Economic Performance." Manuscript, Hunter College, New York, N.Y.

Citizens for Tax Justice. 1991. *A Far Cry from Fair.* Washington, D.C.: Citizens for Tax Justice.

Cline, Robert J. 1988. "Should States Adopt a Value-Added Tax?" In *The Unfinished Agenda for State Tax Reform,* edited by Steven D. Gold. Denver: National Conference of State Legislatures.

Cline, Robert J., and John Shannon. 1986. "Characteristics of a Balanced and Moderate State-Local Revenue System." In *Reforming State Tax Systems,* edited by Steven D. Gold. Denver: National Conference of State Legislatures.

Coe, Bruce G.; Henry A. Coleman; and David F. Bradford. 1988. *New Jersey State and Local Expenditure Revenue Policy Commission, Final Report.* Trenton, N.J.: State and Local Expenditure Revenue Policy Commission.

Cordes, Joseph J. 1992. "State Environmental Taxes and Fees." In *State Taxation of Business,* edited by Thomas F. Pogue. London: Praeger.

Coughlin, Cletus C.; Joseph V. Terza; and Vachira Arromdee. 1991. "State Characteristics and the Location of Foreign Direct Investment Within the United States." *The Review of Economics and Statistics* 73:675–83.

Courant, Paul N. 1994. "How Would You Know a Good Economic Policy if You Tripped Over One? Hint: Don't Just Count Jobs." *National Tax Journal* 47:863–81.

Craymer, Dale K. 1989. "The Texas Sales and Use Tax." In *Rethinking Texas Taxes: Final Report of the Select Committee on Tax Equity,* edited by Billy C. Hamilton. Austin: Reproduction Division of the Texas House of Representatives.

Cullis, John, and Philip Jones. 1992. *Public Finance and Public Choice: Analytical Perspectives.* London: McGraw-Hill.

Davies, James B.; France St-Hilaire; and John Whalley. 1984. "Some Calculations of Lifetime Tax Incidence." *American Economic Review* 74:633–49.

Davies, James B., and John Whalley. 1991. "Taxes and Capital Formation: How Important Is Human Capital?" In *National Saving and Economic Performance,* edited by Douglas B. Bernheim and John B. Shoven. Chicago: University of Chicago Press.

Dearborn, Philip M., and Jay Ladin. 1990. *Report of the Maryland Commission on State Taxes and Tax Structure.* Annapolis, Md.: Commission on State Taxes and Tax Structure.

Deich, Michael. 1990. "State Taxes and Manufacturing Plant Location." In *Proceedings of the Eighty-Second Annual Conference 1989,* edited by Frederick D. Stocker. Columbus, Ohio: National Tax Association–Tax Institute of America.

Diamond, Peter A., and James A. Mirrlees. 1971. "Optimal Taxation and Public Production I: Production Efficiency" and "II: Tax Rules." *American Economic Review* 61:8–27 and 261–78.

Diewert, W. Erwin. 1987. "Comments." In *The Impact of Taxation on Business Activity,* edited by Jack M. Mintz and Douglas D. Purvis. Ontario: John Deutsch Institute for the Study of Economic Policy.

Downing, Paul B. 1991. "Efficient Local User Charges in a Tiebout World." Florida State University Department of Economics Working Paper Series No. 91–11-4.

———. 1992. "The Revenue Potential of User Charges in Municipal Finance." *Public Finance Quarterly* 20:512–27.

Driffill, E. John, and Harvey S. Rosen. 1983. "Taxation and Excess Burden: A Life Cycle Perspective." *International Economic Review* 24:671–83.

Due, John F. 1961. "Studies of State-Local Tax Influences on Location of Industry." *National Tax Journal* 14:50–60.

Due, John F., and Loretta Fairchild. 1988. "The Nebraska State and Local Sales and Use Taxes." In *Final Report, Nebraska Comprehensive Study,* edited by Michael Wasylenko and John Yinger. Syracuse, N.Y.: Maxwell School, Syracuse University.

Due, John F., and John L. Mikesell. 1995. *Sales Taxation.* Washington, D.C.: Urban Institute Press.

Dye, Richard F., and Therese J. McGuire. 1991. "Growth and Variability of State Individual Income and General Sales Taxes." *National Tax Journal* 44:55–66.

Ebel, Robert D., ed. 1990. *A Fiscal Agenda for Nevada.* Reno: University of Nevada Press.

Feldstein, Martin. 1990. "The Second Best Theory of Differential Capital Taxation." *Oxford Economic Papers* 42:25–69.

Feldstein, Martin, and Marian Vaillant. 1994. "Can State Taxes Redistribute Income?" National Bureau of Economic Research Working Paper No. 4785.

Fox, William F., ed. 1992a. *Sales Taxation: Critical Issues in Policy and Administration.* Westport, Conn.: Praeger.

———, ed. 1992b. "Sales Taxation of Services: Has Its Time Come?" In *Sales Taxation: Critical Issues in Policy and Administration,* edited by William F. Fox. Westport, Conn.: Praeger.

Fox, William F., and Matthew Murray. 1988. "Economic Aspects of Taxing Services." *National Tax Journal* 41:19–36.

Francis, James. 1993. "A Close Look at a State Credit Invoice VAT." In *Proceedings of the Eighty-Fifth Annual Conference on Taxation,* edited by Frederick D. Stocker. Columbus, Ohio: National Tax Association–Tax Institute of America.

Friedman, Milton. 1957. *A Theory of the Consumption Function.* Princeton, N.J.: Princeton University Press.

Fritz, Randy. 1989. "Who Pays Texas Taxes." In *Rethinking Texas Taxes: Final Report of the Select Committee on Tax Equity,* edited by Billy C. Hamilton. Austin: Reproduction Division of the Texas House of Representatives.

Fullerton, Don. 1987. "The Indexation of Interest, Depreciation and Capital Gains and Tax Reform in the U.S." *Journal of Public Economics* 32:25–51.

Fullerton, Don; Robert Gillette; and James Mackie. 1987. "Investment Incentives Under the Tax Reform Act of 1986." In *Office of Tax Analysis, Compendium of Tax Research 1987.* Washington, D.C.: GPO.

Fullerton, Don; Yolanda K. Henderson; and James Mackie. 1987. "Investment Allocation and Growth Under the Tax Reform Act of 1986." In *Office of Tax Analysis, Compendium of Tax Research 1987*. Washington, D.C.: GPO.

Fullerton, Don, and Andrew B. Lyon. 1988. "Tax Neutrality and Intangible Capital." In *Tax Policy and the Economy 2*, edited by Lawrence H. Summers. Cambridge: MIT Press.

Fullerton, Don, and Diane Lim Rogers. 1991. "Lifetime versus Annual Perspectives on Tax Incidence." *National Tax Journal* 44:277–87.

———. 1993. *Who Bears the Lifetime Tax Burden?* Washington, D.C.: Brookings Institution.

———. 1994. "Distributional Effects on a Lifetime Basis." National Bureau of Economic Research Working Paper No. 4682.

Gentry, William M., and R. Glenn Hubbard. 1995. "Distributional Implications of Introducing a Broad-Based Consumption Tax." Manuscript, Columbia University, New York, N.Y.

Gentry, William M., and Helen F. Ladd. 1994. "State Tax Structure and Multiple Policy Objectives." *National Tax Journal* 47:747–72.

Gillis, Malcolm; Peter Mieszkowski; and George R. Zodrow. forthcoming. "Indirect Consumption Taxes: Common Issues and Differences Among the Alternative Approaches." *Tax Law Review*.

Gold, Stephen D. 1992. "Simplifying the Sales Tax: Credits or Exemptions?" In *Sales Taxation: Critical Issues in Policy and Administration*, edited by William F. Fox. Westport, Conn.: Praeger.

Goodspeed, Timothy J. 1989. "A Re-examination of the Use of Ability to Pay Taxes by Local Governments." *Journal of Public Economics* 38:319–42.

———. 1991. "The Assignment of Ability to Pay Taxes in the OECD Countries." In *Public Finance with Several Levels of Government*, edited by Remy Prud'homme. The Hague: Foundation Journal Public Finance.

Gordon, Roger H. 1985. "Taxation of Corporate Capital Income: Tax Revenues versus Tax Distortions." *Quarterly Journal of Economics* 50:1–27.

———. 1986. "Taxation of Investment and Savings in a World Economy." *American Economic Review* 76:1086–1102.

Gordon, Roger H., and Jeffrey K. MacKie-Mason. 1994. "Why Is there Corporate Taxation in a Small Open Economy? The Role of Transfer Pricing and Income Shifting." National Bureau of Economic Research Working Paper No. 4690.

Gordon, Roger H., and Burton G. Malkiel. 1981. "Corporation Finance." In *How Taxes Affect Economic Behavior*, edited by Henry J. Aaron and Joseph A. Pechman. Washington, D.C.: Brookings Institution.

Gordon, Roger H., and Hal R. Varian. 1989. "Taxation of Asset Income in the Presence of a World Securities Market." *Journal of International Economics* 26:205–26.

Gordon, Roger H., and John Wilson. 1986. "An Examination of Multijurisdictional Corporate Income Taxation under Formula Apportionment." *Econometrica* 54:1357–73.

Governor's Task Force on Revenue. 1991. *Charting a Course for Texas' Future: Toward a More Equitable System of Taxation*. Austin, Tex.: Governor's Task Force on Revenue.

Gravelle, Jane G. 1994. *The Economic Effects of Taxing Capital Income*. Cambridge: MIT Press.

Gravelle, Jane G., and Laurence J. Kotlikoff. 1993. "Corporate Tax Incidence and Inefficiency When Corporate and Noncorporate Goods Are Close Substitutes." *Economic Inquiry* 31:501–16.

Greenhut, Melvin L. 1986. "Report on an Income Tax in Texas." Center for Education and Research in Free Enterprise, Series on Public Issues No. 21.

Gyourko, Joseph. 1987. "Effects of Local Tax Structures on the Factor Intensity Composition of Manufacturing Activities Across Cities." *Journal of Urban Economics* 22:151–64.

Hailey, Mike. 1991. "Bullock Drops Bombshell, Supports State Income Tax." *Houston Post*, (March 7).

Haliassos, Michael, and Andrew B. Lyon. 1993. "Progressivity of Capital Gains Taxation With Optimal Portfolio Selection." National Bureau of Economic Research Working Paper No. 4253.

Hall, Robert E. 1988. "Intertemporal Substitution in Consumption." *Journal of Political Economy* 96:339–57.

Hall, Robert E., and Frederic S. Mishkin. 1982. "The Sensitivity of Consumption to Transitory Income: Estimates from Panel Data on Households." *Econometrica* 50:461–81.

Hall, Robert E., and Alvin Rabushka. 1985. *The Flat Tax.* Stanford, Calif.: Hoover Institution Press.

———. 1995. *The Flat Tax.* 2d ed. Stanford, Calif.: Hoover Institution Press.

Hamilton, Billy C. 1989a. "The Past and Future of Texas State Finances." In *Rethinking Texas Taxes: Final Report of the Select Committee on Tax Equity,* edited by Billy C. Hamilton. Austin: Reproduction Division of the Texas House of Representatives.

———. 1989b. "Texas Business Tax Policy." In *Rethinking Texas Taxes: Final Report of the Select Committee on Tax Equity,* edited by Billy C. Hamilton. Austin: Reproduction Division of the Texas House of Representatives.

———. 1989c. "What Is a 'Good' Tax System?" In *Rethinking Texas Taxes: Final Report of the Select Committee on Tax Equity,* edited by Billy C. Hamilton. Austin: Reproduction Division of the Texas House of Representatives.

———, ed. 1989d. *Rethinking Texas Taxes: Final Report of the Select Committee on Tax Equity.* Austin: Reproduction Division of the Texas House of Representatives.

Hamilton, Billy, and Tom Linehan. 1989. "Taxes and the Economy." In *Rethinking Texas Taxes: Final Report of the Select Committee on Tax Equity,* edited by Billy C. Hamilton. Austin: Reproduction Division of the Texas House of Representatives.

Hamilton, Bruce W. 1975. "Zoning and Property Taxation in a System of Local Governments." *Urban Studies* 12:205–11.

———. 1983. "A Review: Is the Property Tax a Benefit Tax?" In *Local Provision of Public Services: The Tiebout Model after Twenty-Five Years,* edited by George R. Zodrow. New York: Academic Press.

Hamilton, Jonathan H. 1987. "Taxation, Savings, and Portfolio Choice in a Continuous Time Model." *Public Finance* 42:264–82.

Harmon, Oskar, and Rajiv Mallick. 1994. "The State Tax Portfolio and Implications for State Tax Reform." University of Connecticut Department of Economics Working Papers Series No. 94–112.

Hausman, Jerry A. 1981. "Labor Supply." In *How Taxes Affect Economic Behavior,* edited by Henry J. Aaron and Joseph A. Pechman. Washington, D.C.: Brookings Institution.

———. 1985. "Taxes and Labor Supply." In *Handbook of Public Economics*, edited by Alan J. Auerbach and Martin Feldstein. Vol. 1. New York and Oxford: North Holland.

Helms, L. Jay. 1985. "The Effect of State and Local Taxes on Economic Growth: A Time Series Cross Section Approach." *The Review of Economics and Statistics* 67:574–82.

Hellerstein, Walter. 1988. "Florida's Sales Tax on Services." *National Tax Journal* 41:1–18.

Henderson, Yolanda K. 1990. "The Massachusetts Corporations Excise Tax." In *Research of the Massachusetts Special Commission on Tax Reform*, edited by Robert Tannenwald. Boston: Massachusetts Special Commission on Tax Reform.

Hines, James R., Jr. 1993. "Altered States: Taxes and the Location of Foreign Direct Investment in America." National Bureau of Economic Research Working Paper No. 4397.

Hobby, Bill. 1993. "State Can't Continue Handicapped by Its Outdated Tax System." *Houston Chronicle* (June 6).

———. 1994. "Feds Have Forced It on Us." *Houston Chronicle* (June 12).

Holt, Charles C. 1993. "Texas Taxes in Perspective: Pain, Gain and the Need for Reform." Manuscript, Graduate School of Business, University of Texas at Austin.

Holtz-Eakin, Douglas. 1992. "Public-Sector Capital and the Productivity Puzzle." National Bureau of Economic Research Working Paper No. 4122.

Institute for Fiscal Studies. 1978. *The Structure and Reform of Direct Taxation.* Report of a Committee chaired by Professor J. E. Meade. London: Allen and Unwin.

Jorgenson, Dale W., and Kun-Young Yun. 1991. "The Excess Burden of Taxation in the United States." *Journal of Accounting, Auditing and Finance* 6:487–508.

Joulfaian, David, and James Mackie. 1992. "Sales Taxes, Investment, and the Tax Reform Act of 1986." *National Tax Journal* 45:89–105.

Kaplow, Louis. 1994. "Taxation and Risk-Taking: A General Equilibrium Perspective." *National Tax Journal* 47:789–98.

Katz, Michael L., and Harvey S. Rosen. 1985. "Tax Analysis in an Oligopoly Model." *Public Finance Quarterly* 13:3–19.

Kenyon, Daphne A. 1989. "The Effects of the Tax Reform Act of 1986 on Texas State and Local Governments." In *Rethinking Texas Taxes: Final Report of the Select Committee on Tax Equity*, edited by Billy C. Hamilton. Austin: Reproduction Division of the Texas House of Representatives.

Kieschnick, Michael. 1981. *State Taxation Policy.* Durham, N.C.: Duke University Press.

Killingsworth, Mark R. 1988. *Labor Supply.* Cambridge: Cambridge University Press.

King, Mervyn, and Don Fullerton, eds. 1984. *The Taxation of Income from Capital.* Chicago: University of Chicago Press.

Ladd, Helen F., and Fred C. Doolittle. 1982. "Which Level of Government Should Assist the Poor?" *National Tax Journal* 35:323–36.

Ladd, Helen F., and Dana R. Weist. 1987. "State and Local Tax Systems: Balance Among Taxes vs. Balance Among Policy Goals." In *The Quest for Balance in State-Local Revenue Structures*, edited by Frederick D. Stocker. Cambridge, Mass.: Lincoln Institute of Land Policy.

Lyon, Andrew B., and Robert M. Schwab. 1995. "Consumption Taxes in a Life-Cycle Framework: Are Sin Taxes Regressive?" *Review of Economics and Statistics* 37:389–406.

MaCurdy, Thomas; David Green; and Harry J. Paarsch. 1990. "Assessing Empirical Approaches for Analyzing Taxes and Labor Supply." *Journal of Human Resources* 25:415–90.

Maddala, G. S. 1992. *Introduction to Econometrics.* New York: Macmillan.

McDonald, Stephen L. 1980. "The Incidence of an American Oil Severance Tax under World Pricing by OPEC: A Note." *Natural Resources Journal* 20:547–50.

McDonald, Stephen L. 1989. "A State Personal Income Tax: An Economic Analysis." In *Rethinking Texas Taxes: Final Report of the Select Committee on Tax Equity,* edited by Billy C. Hamilton. Austin: Reproduction Division of the Texas House of Representatives.

McGuire, Therese J. 1989. *Arizona Joint Select Committee on State Revenues and Expenditures, Final Report.* Phoenix: Arizona Joint Select Committee.

———. 1992. "Book Review of 'Who Benefits From State and Local Economic Development Policies' by Timothy J. Bartik." *National Tax Journal* 45:457–59.

McGuire, Therese J., and Michael Wasylenko. 1987. "Employment Growth and State Government Fiscal Behavior: A Report on Economic Development for States from 1973 to 1984." Report prepared for the New Jersey State and Local Expenditure and Revenue Policy Commission.

McLure, Charles E., Jr. 1980. "The State Corporate Income Tax: Lambs in Wolves' Clothing." In *The Economics of Taxation,* edited by Henry J. Aaron and Michael J. Boskin. Washington, D.C.: Brookings Institution.

———. 1981. "The Elusive Incidence of the Corporate Income Tax: The State Case." *Public Finance Quarterly* 9:395–413.

———. 1987. *The Value-Added Tax: Key to Deficit Reduction?* Washington, D.C.: American Enterprise Institute for Public Policy Research.

———. 1992. "Substituting Consumption-Based Direct Taxation for Income Taxes as the International Norm." *National Tax Journal* 45:145–54.

McLure, Charles E., Jr.; Jack Mutti; Victor Thuronyi; and George R. Zodrow. 1990. *The Taxation of Income from Business and Capital in Colombia.* Durham, N.C.: Duke University Press.

McLure, Charles E., Jr., and George R. Zodrow. 1987. "Treasury I and the Tax Reform Act of 1986: The Economics and Politics of Tax Reform." *Journal of Economic Perspectives* 1:37–58.

———. 1990. "Administrative Advantages of the Individual Tax Prepayment Approach to the Direct Taxation of Consumption." In *Heidelberg Congress on Taxing Consumption,* edited by Manfred Rose. Berlin: Springer-Verlag.

———. 1996a. "A Hybrid Approach to the Direct Taxation of Consumption." In *Frontiers of Tax Reform,* edited by Michael Boskin. Stanford, Calif.: Hoover Institution Press.

———. 1996b. "A Hybrid Consumption-Based Direct Tax Proposed for Bolivia." *International Tax and Public Finance* 3:97–112.

Mehay, Stephen L., and Loren M. Solnick. 1990. "Defense Spending and State Economic Growth." *Journal of Regional Science* 30:477–88:

Menchik, Paul L., and Martin David. 1982. "The Incidence of a Lifetime Consumption Tax." *National Tax Journal* 35:189–203.

Merjanian, Ara. 1989. "Texas Oil and Gas Severance Taxes." In *Rethinking Texas Taxes: Final Report of the Select Committee on Tax Equity*, edited by Billy C. Hamilton. Austin: Reproduction Division of the Texas House of Representatives.

Metcalf, Gilbert E. 1994. "The Lifetime Incidence of State and Local Taxes: Measuring Changes During the 1980s." In *Tax Progressivity and Income Inequality*, edited by Joel Slemrod. Cambridge: Cambridge University Press.

———. 1996. "The Role of a Value-Added Tax in Fundamental Tax Reform." In *Frontiers of Tax Reform*, edited by Michael J. Boskin. Stanford, Calif.: Hoover Institution Press.

Mieszkowski, Peter. 1977. "The Cash Flow Version of an Expenditure Tax." U.S. Treasury Department Office of Tax Analysis Paper No. 26.

———. 1980. "The Advisability and Feasibility of an Expenditure Tax System." In *The Economics of Taxation*, edited by Henry J. Aaron and Michael J. Boskin. Washington, D.C.: Brookings Institution.

Mieszkowski, Peter, and George R. Zodrow. 1985. "The Incidence of a Partial State Corporate Income Tax." *National Tax Journal* 38:489–96.

Mieszkowski, Peter, and George R. Zodrow. 1989. "Taxation and the Tiebout Model: The Differential Effects of Head Taxes, Taxes on Land Rents, and Property Taxes." *Journal of Economic Literature* 28:1098–1146.

Mikesell, John L. 1996. "Is the Retail Sales Tax Really Inferior to the Value Added Tax?" Manuscript, Indiana University, Bloomington, Ind.

Misiolek, Walter S., and D. Grady Perdue. 1987. "The Portfolio Approach to State and Local Tax Structures." *National Tax Journal* 40:111–14.

Moore, Stephen. 1994. "Texas Too Tax-and-Spend." *Houston Chronicle* (June 12).

———. 1996. "The Economic and Civil Liberties Case for a National Sales Tax." In *Frontiers of Tax Reform*, edited by Michael J. Boskin. Stanford, Calif.: Hoover Institution Press.

Morgan, William E. 1967. *Taxes and the Location of Industry*. Boulder: University of Colorado Press.

Mueller, Dennis C. 1989. *Public Choice II*. Cambridge: Cambridge University Press.

Munnell, Alicia H. 1990. "How Does Public Infrastructure Affect Regional Economic Performance?" *New England Economic Review* (Sept./Oct.):11–33.

Musgrave, Richard A. 1959. *The Theory of Public Finance: A Study in Political Economy*. New York: McGraw-Hill.

Musgrave, Richard A., and Peggy B. Musgrave. 1976. *Public Finance in Theory and Practice*. New York: McGraw-Hill.

Nerlove, Marc; Assaf Razin; Efraim Sadka; and Robert K. von Weizsacker. 1993. "Comprehensive Income Taxation, Investments in Human and Physical Capital, and Productivity." *Journal of Public Economics* 50:397–406.

Netzer, Dick. 1992. "Differences in Reliance on User Charges by American State and Local Governments." *Public Finance Quarterly* 20:499–511.

Newman, Robert J. 1983. "Industry Migration and Growth in the South." *The Review of Economics and Statistics* 65:76–86.

Oakland, W. 1983. "Income Redistribution in a Federal System." In *Local Provision of*

Public Services: The Tiebout Model After Twenty-Five Years, edited by George R. Zodrow. New York: Academic Press.

Oakland, William H. 1992. "How Should Businesses Be Taxed?" In *State Taxation of Business,* edited by Thomas F. Pogue. London: Praeger.

Oates, Wallace E. 1968. "The Theory of Public Finance in a Federal System." *Canadian Journal of Economics* 1:37–54.

———. 1991. "Fiscal Federalism: An Overview." In *Public Finance with Several Levels of Government,* edited by Remy Prud'homme. The Hague: Foundation Journal Public Finance.

Ondrich, Jan, and Michael Wasylenko. 1993. *Foreign Direct Investment in the United States.* Kalamazoo, Mich.: W. E. Upjohn Institute.

Papke, Leslie E. 1987. "Subnational Taxation and Capital Mobility: Estimates of Tax Price Elasticities." *National Tax Journal* 40:191–204.

———. 1990. "Taxes and Other Determinants of Gross State Product in Manufacturing: A First Look." In *Proceedings of the Eighty-Second Annual Conference 1989,* edited by Frederick D. Stocker. Columbus, Ohio: National Tax Association–Tax Institute of America.

———. 1991a. "Interstate Business Tax Differentials and New Firm Location Evidence from Panel Data." *Journal of Public Economics* 45:47–68.

———. 1991b. "The Responsiveness of Industrial Activity to Interstate Tax Differentials: A Comparison of Elasticities." In *Industry Location and Public Policy,* edited by Henry Herzog and Alan Schlottmann. Knoxville: University of Tennessee Press.

Pauly, Mark V. 1973. "Income Redistribution as a Local Public Good." *Journal of Public Economics* 2:35–58.

Pechman, Joseph A. 1985. *Who Paid the Taxes, 1966–85.* Washington, D.C.: Brookings Institution.

———, ed. 1980. *What Should Be Taxed: Income or Expenditure.* Washington, D.C.: Brookings Institution.

Perdue, D. Grady, and Norman L. Weed. 1991. "Tax Revenues, Economic Development and Portfolio Analysis: A Texas Application." *Public Administration Quarterly* 15:341–77.

Peterson, Paul E., and Mark C. Rom. 1990. *Welfare Magnets: A New Case for a National Standard.* Washington, D.C.: Brookings Institution.

Phares, Donald. 1980. *Who Pays State and Local Taxes?* Cambridge, Mass.: Oelgeschlager, Gunn and Hain.

Plaut, Thomas R., and Joseph E. Pluta. 1983. "Business Climate, Taxes and Expenditures, and State Industrial Growth in the United States." *Southern Economic Journal* 50:99–119.

Pollock, Stephen H. 1991. "Mechanisms for Exporting the State Sales Tax Burden in the Absence of Federal Deductibility." *National Tax Journal* 44 (September): 297–310.

Poterba, James M. 1987. "Tax Policy and Corporate Saving." Brookings Papers on Economic Activity, no. 2:455–503.

———. 1989. "Lifetime Incidence and the Distributional Burden of Excise Taxes." *American Economic Review, Papers and Proceedings* 79:325–30.

———. 1991. "Is the Gasoline Tax Regressive?" In *Tax Policy and the Economy,* edited by David Bradford. Cambridge: MIT Press.

Premus, Robert. 1982. "Location of High Technology Firms and Regional Economic Development." Report to the Subcommittee on Monetary and Fiscal Policy of the Joint Economic Committee, U.S. Congress.

Quan, Nguyen T., and John H. Beck. 1987. "Public Education Expenditures and State Economic Growth: Northeast and Sunbelt Regions." *Southern Economics Journal* 54:361–76.

Ring, Raymond R., Jr. 1989. "The Proportion of Consumers' and Producers' Goods in the General Sales Tax." *National Tax Journal* 42:167–79.

Robison, Clay. 1991. "Bullock Says Income Tax Plan Would Raise $12 Billion by '95." *Houston Chronicle* (March 29).

———. 1993. "Texans May Get Chance to Vote on Income Tax." *Houston Chronicle* (April 21).

Romer, Thomas, and Howard Rosenthal. 1979. "Bureaucrats versus Voters: On the Political Economy of Resource Allocation by Direct Democracy." *Quarterly Journal of Economics* 93:563–87.

Rosen, Harvey S. 1995. *Public Finance.* Homewood, Ill.: Irwin.

Sarkar, Shounak, and George R. Zodrow. 1993. "Transitional Issues in Moving to a Direct Consumption Tax." *National Tax Journal* 46:359–76.

Schmenner, Roger W. 1982. *Making Business Location Decision.* Englewood Cliffs, N.J.: Prentice-Hall.

Schmenner, Roger W.; Joel C. Huber; and Randall L. Cook. 1987. "Geographic Differences and the Location of New Manufacturing Facilities." *Journal of Urban Economics* 21:83–104.

Schwab, Robert M. 1990. "The Relationship Between Income and Expenditures." In *Report of the Maryland Commission on State Taxes,* Philip M. Dearborn and Jay Ladin. Annapolis: Maryland Commission on State Taxes.

Shannon, John. 1987. "State Revenue Diversification—The Search for Balance." In *The Quest for Balance in State-Local Revenue Structures,* edited by Frederick D. Stocker. Cambridge, Mass.: Lincoln Institute of Land Policy.

Skinner, Jonathan, and Daniel Feenberg. 1990. "The Impact of the 1986 Tax Reform on Personal Saving." In *Do Taxes Matter? The Impact of the Tax Reform Act of 1986,* edited by Joel Slemrod. Cambridge: MIT Press.

Slemrod, Joel. 1986. "The Optimal Progressivity of the Minnesota Tax System." *Minnesota Tax Study Commission.* Vol. 2. St. Paul: Butterworths.

———. 1988. "Effect of Taxation with International Capital Mobility." In *Uneasy Compromise: Problems of a Hybrid Income-Consumption Tax,* edited by Henry J. Aaron, Harvey Galper, and Joseph A. Pechman. Washington, D.C.: Brookings Institution.

Summers, Lawrence H. 1981. "Capital Taxation and Capital Accumulation in a Life Cycle Growth Model." *American Economic Review* 71:533–44.

Tannenwald, Robert. 1990. *Research of the Massachusetts Special Commission on Tax Reform.* Boston: Massachusetts Special Commission on Tax Reform.

———. 1993. "Massachusetts' Tax Competitiveness." Working Paper prepared for Massachusetts Special Commission on Business Tax Policy.

Texas Comptroller of Public Accounts. 1974a–1995a. *State of Texas Annual Cash Report.* Vol. 1. Austin: Comptroller of Public Accounts.

———. 1989b. *The Texas Input-Output Model, 1986 Update: 40-Sector Version.* Austin: Texas Annual Property Tax Report 1991.

———. 1992b. *Sales Tax Bulletin April 1992*. Austin: Comptroller of Public Accounts.

———. 1993b. *1994–95 Biennial Revenue Estimate*. Austin: Comptroller of Public Accounts.

———. 1993c. *Sales and Franchise Tax Exemptions*. Austin: Comptroller of Public Accounts.

———. 1994b. *Sources of Revenue Growth: A History of State Taxes in Texas, 1972–1995*. Austin: Comptroller of Public Accounts.

———. 1995b. *1996–97 Biennial Revenue Estimate*. Austin: Comptroller of Public Accounts.

———. 1995c. *Special Financial Report*. Austin: Comptroller of Public Accounts.

Texas Legislative Budget Board. 1995. *Fiscal Size Up, 1996–97*. Austin: Legislative Budget Board.

Thaler, Richard H. 1990. "Saving, Fungibility, and Mental Accounts." *Journal of Economic Perspectives* 4:193–205.

Thrash, Joe. 1989a. "Alternatives for Local Government Finance." In *Rethinking Texas Taxes: Final Report of the Select Committee on Tax Equity*, edited by Billy C. Hamilton. Austin: Reproduction Division of the Texas House of Representatives.

———. 1989b. "Recent Directions in Texas Sales Tax Policy." In *Rethinking Texas Taxes: Final Report of the Select Committee on Tax Equity*, edited by Billy C. Hamilton. Austin: Reproduction Division of the Texas House of Representatives.

Thrash, Joe, and J. Lloyd Kennedy. 1989. "The State Business Income Tax." In *Rethinking Texas Taxes: Final Report of the Select Committee on Tax Equity*, edited by Billy C. Hamilton. Austin: Reproduction Division of the Texas House of Representatives.

Tiebout, Charles M. 1956. "A Pure Theory of Local Expenditures." *Journal of Political Economy* 64:416–24.

Triest, Robert K. 1990. "The Effect of Income Taxation on Labor Supply in the United States." *Journal of Human Resources* 25:491–516.

———. 1993. "The Efficiency Cost of Increased Progressivity." National Bureau of Economic Research Working Paper No. 4535.

Trostel, Philip A. 1993. "The Effect of Taxation on Human Capital." *Journal of Political Economy* 101:327–50.

"Unlimited Savings Allowance (USA) Tax System." 1995. Tax Notes. Vol. 66, no. 11 (March 10): 1485–1575.

U.S. Advisory Commission on Intergovernmental Relations. 1982. *Tax Capacity of the Fifty States: Methodology and Estimates*. Washington, D.C.: ACIR.

———. 1987. *Local Revenue Diversification: User Charges*. Washington, D.C.: ACIR.

———. 1988. *The Tax Reform Act of 1986—Its Effect on Both Federal and State Personal Income Tax Liabilities*. Washington, D.C.: ACIR.

———. 1990. *Representative Expenditures: Addressing the Neglected Dimension of Fiscal Capacity*. Washington, D.C.: ACIR.

———. 1991. *Changing Public Attitudes on Governments and Taxes 1991*. Washington, D.C.: ACIR.

———. 1992a. *Significant Features of Fiscal Federalism: 1992*. Vol. 1. Washington, D.C.: ACIR.

———. 1992b. *Significant Features of Fiscal Federalism: 1992*. Vol. 2. Washington, D.C.: ACIR.

————. 1994. *Significant Features of Fiscal Federalism: 1994.* Vol. 2. Washington, D.C.: ACIR.

————. 1995. *Significant Features of Fiscal Federalism: 1995.* Vol. 1. Washington, D.C.: ACIR.

U.S. Bureau of the Census. 1993. *City Government Finances: 1990–91.* Washington, D.C.: GPO.

————. 1994a. *Government Finances: 1991–92* (Preliminary Report). Washington, D.C.: GPO.

————. 1994b. *State Government Tax Collections: 1992.* Washington, D.C.: GPO.

U.S. Congressional Budget Office. 1990. *Federal Taxation of Tobacco, Alcoholic Beverages, and Motor Fuels.* Washington, D.C.: GPO.

————. 1993. *The Growth of Federal User Charges.* Washington, D.C.: GPO.

U.S. Department of the Treasury. 1977. *Blueprints for Basic Tax Reform.* Washington, D.C.: GPO. Also available as Bradford, D.F., and the U.S. Treasury Tax Policy Staff. *Blueprints for Basic Tax Reform.* Arlington: Tax Analysts, 1984.

U.S. House of Representatives. 1993. *Omnibus Budget Reconciliation Act of 1993.* Washington, D.C.: GPO.

U.S. Internal Revenue Service. 1995a. *Statistics of Income: 1992 Individual Income Tax Returns.* Washington, D.C.: GPO.

————. 1995b. *Statistics of Income Bulletin, Winter 1994–1995.* Washington, D.C.: GPO.

U.S. Joint Committee on Taxation. 1993. *Methodology and Issues in Measuring Changes in the Distribution of Tax Burdens.* Washington, D.C.: GPO.

Vedder, Richard. 1982. "Rich States, Poor States: How High Taxes Inhibit Growth." *Journal of Contemporary Studies* 5:19–32.

Viard, Alan D. 1993. "The Productivity Slowdown and the Savings Shortfall: A Challenge to the Permanent Income Hypothesis." *Economic Inquiry* 31:549–63.

Wasylenko, Michael J. 1988. "Economic Development in Nebraska." Comprehensive Tax Study Staff Paper No. 1, Metropolitan Studies Program, The Maxwell School, Syracuse University, Syracuse, N.Y.

————. 1991. "Empirical Evidence on Interregional Business Location Decisions and the Role of Fiscal Incentives in Economic Development." In *Industry Location and Public Policy,* edited by Henry Herzog and Alan Schlottmann. Knoxville: University of Tennessee Press.

Wasylenko, Michael J., and Robert Carroll. 1989. "Employment Growth and State Government Fiscal Behavior: A Report on Economic Development for States from 1973 to 1987." Preliminary report prepared for the Arizona Joint Select Committee and State Revenues and Expenditures.

Wasylenko, Michael J., and Therese McGuire. 1985. "Jobs and Taxes: The Effect of Business Climate on States' Employment Growth Rates." *National Tax Journal* 4:497–512.

Wasylenko, Michael, and John Yinger. 1988. *Final Report, Nebraska Comprehensive Study.* Syracuse, N.Y.: Maxwell School, Syracuse University.

Weidenbaum, Murray. 1996. "The Nunn-Domenici USA Tax: Analysis and Comparisons." In *Frontiers of Tax Reform,* edited by Michael Boskin. Stanford, Calif.: Hoover Institution Press.

Whalley, John. 1988. "Lessons from General Equilibrium Models." In *Uneasy Compromise: Problems of a Hybrid Income-Consumption Tax,* edited by Henry J. Aaron,

Harvey Galper and Joseph A. Pechman. Washington, D.C.: Brookings Institution.

White, Fred. 1983. "Trade-Off in Growth and Stability in State Taxes." *National Tax Journal* 36:103–14.

Wieferman, John. 1989. "The Value Added Tax." In *Rethinking Texas Taxes: Final Report of the Select Committee on Tax Equity,* edited by Billy C. Hamilton. Austin: Reproduction Division of the Texas House of Representatives.

Wildasin, David E. 1986. *Urban Public Finance.* London: Harwood Academic.

———. 1992. "Relaxation of Barriers to Factor Mobility and Income Redistribution." *Public Finance* 47 (supplement):216–30.

———. 1993. "State Income Taxation with Mobile Labor." *Journal of Policy Analysis and Management* 12:51–75.

Wildasin, David E., and John Douglas Wilson. 1991. "Theoretical Issues in Local Public Economics: An Overview." *Regional Science and Urban Economics* 21:317–31.

Zodrow, George R. 1991. "On the 'Traditional' and 'New' Views of Dividend Taxation." *National Tax Journal* 44:497–509.

———. 1995. "Taxation, Uncertainty and the Choice of a Consumption Tax Base." *Journal of Public Economics* 58:257–65.

———. forthcoming. "Reflections on the Consumption Tax Option." In *Taxation Towards 2000,* edited by John G. Head. Australian Tax Research Foundation.

———, ed. 1983. *Local Provision of Public Services: The Tiebout Model After Twenty-Five Years.* New York: Academic Press.

Zodrow, George R., and Charles E. McLure. 1991. "Alternative Methods of Taxing Consumption in Developing Countries." *Tax Law Review* 46:407–87.

Zodrow, George R., and Peter Mieszkowski. 1986. "Pigou, Tiebout, Property Taxation and the Underprovision of Local Public Goods." *Journal of Urban Economics* 19:356–70.

INDEX

David, Martin, 169, 170
Davies, James B., 47, 170
Dearborn, Philip M., 177
Deich, Michael, 33
Diamond, Peter A., 165
Diewert, W. Erwin, 39
direct taxation, 4, 25, 29, 72
Doolittle, Fred C., 53
Downing, Paul B., 85, 86, 172–73, 181
Driffill, John E., 47
Due, John F., 102, 161, 166, 168, 180
Dye, Richard F., 65, 66, 171

Ebel, Robert, 163, 177, 180
efficiency: asset choice, 41, 74, 115;
    business location and investment, 13,
    29–38; business taxes and, 5–6, 73–75;
    capital supply and location, 25–29;
    consumption choice, 43–44;
    corporate/noncorporate choice, 40,
    74, 115; debt/equity choice, 42, 74, 115;
    defined, 12; distribution of corporate
    earnings, 42; empirical studies of,
    30–40, 42, 46–47; excess burden and,
    12, 24–25, 40, 47, 72–73; government
    services, 48–50, 75, 82, 116; human
    capital accumulation decision, 46;
    individual location choice, 43, 52–53,
    75–76 (see also labor mobility);
    individual taxes and, 6, 75; input
    choice, 39; intersectoral distortions,
    41, 74; labor/leisure choice, 45–46,
    75; marginal effective tax rate and,
    34–35, 37; marginal tax rate and, 24;
    risk-taking, 39–40; savings choice,
    44–45, 75
enforcement costs, 9, 16, 69, 79, 121
equity: ability-to-pay principle, 7, 15,
    51–52, 54–56, 77 (see also progressive
    state income tax; state sales tax:
    regressivity of; tax incidence); benefit
    principle, 7, 15, 51–52, 54, 80, 119;
    empirical studies of, 117; horizontal,
    15; perceptions of, 64, 81–82; vertical,
    15. See also tax incidence
excise taxes. See selective sales and excise
    taxes

exportability. See tax exporting
externalities, 14, 72, 76

Fairchild, Loretta, 168
federal corporate income tax. See
    corporate income tax, federal
federal personal income tax. See personal
    income tax, federal
Feenberg, Daniel, 44
Feldstein, Martin, 52, 53, 76, 167
Fox, William F., 171, 177
Francis, James, 176
Friedman, Milton, 55
Fritz, Randy, 58, 114, 117–18, 169, 179
Fullerton, Don, 61, 62, 166, 167, 170, 171

Galper, Harvey, 89, 161
general equilibrium model, 38, 75, 116, 131
general sales tax. See state sales tax
Gentry, William M., 66, 121, 174–75
Gillette, Robert, 167
Gillis, Malcom, 180
Gokhale, Jagadeesh, 63
Gold, Stephen D., 172
Goodspeed, Timothy J., 54, 169
Gordon, Roger H., 42, 165, 167, 176
government spending. See efficiency:
    government services; representative
    expenditures; Texas public
    expenditures
Gravelle, Jane G., 40, 167
Green, David, 46
Greenhut, Melvin L., 177
Gyourko, Joseph, 166

Haliassos, Michael, 40
Hall, Robert E., 44, 57, 161, 173
Hamilton, Billy C., 120, 166, 176–77, 179
Hamilton, Bruce W., 87, 173
Hamilton, Jonathan H., 47
Harmon, Oskar, 66–67, 121
Hausman, Jerry A., 45, 168
Hellerstein, Walter, 177
Helms, L. Jay, 36, 38
Henderson, Yolanda K., 163, 167
Hines, James R., Jr., 35
Hobby, Bill, 176–77

personal income tax, state:
administrative costs of, 9, 79, 121;
benefit tax aspects of, 86; compliance
with, 26–27; efficiency aspects of, 6,
43–47, 75; equity properties of, 8,
62–63, 77–78, 123; federal deductibility
of, 4, 19–20, 122 (*see also* personal
income tax, federal: state income tax
deductions in); personal deductions
and exemptions (*see* personal income
tax, state: equity properties of);
political opposition to, 100;
progressivity of (*see* progressive state
income tax); revenue growth and, 49,
64–65; states without, 109; Texas
debate, 112–24; user charges and, 9,
78, 123, 130; visibility of, 6, 14, 48, 116.
See also progressive state income tax
Peterson, Paul E., 53, 169
Phares, Donald, 114, 117, 179
Plaut, Thomas R., 34, 36
Pluta, Joseph E., 34, 36
Pollock, Stephen H., 19, 20, 23, 113, 163,
164
Poterba, James M., 59, 60, 168, 170
Premus, Robert, 30, 37, 165
progressive state income tax: equity
aspects of, 7, 77, 116; federal
deductibility of, 4, 20–21, 71–72, 122;
labor mobility and, 24, 43, 53–54,
75–76; labor supply and, 46;
measurement of, 7, 60, 77; revenue
growth and, 6, 49, 64–66, 79; revenue
stability and, 68
property tax: benefit tax aspects of,
86–87; visibility of, 14, 48. *See also*
Texas local property tax
public good: defined, 51, 83; income
distribution as, 53; optimal provision
of, 83–85; price of, 4, 21, 71
Puri, Sandeep, 178

Quan, Nguyen T., 36

Rabushka, Alvin, 161, 173
Razin, Assaf, 47
regressivity. *See* state sales tax:

regressivity of; Texas state tax system:
regressivity of
representative expenditures, 142–44, 149,
155, 157–58
residence-based tax: defined, 164*n* 18;
types of, 84–85
revenue adequacy, 15, 64, 66–67
revenue stability, 9, 16, 64–67, 78, 119–20
Ring, Raymond R., Jr., 101, 161, 177
Rogers, Diane Lim, 61–62, 170–71
Rom, Mark C., 53, 169
Romer, Thomas, 173
Rosen, Harvey S., 47, 164, 168–69, 172–73,
175, 179
Rosenthal, Howard, 173

Sadka, Efraim, 47
Sale, Hillary, 178
sales tax. *See* state sales tax; Texas state
sales tax
Sarkar, Shounak, 175
Schmenner, Roger W., 31, 33
Schwab, Robert M., 57, 60
selective sales and excise taxes:
regressivity of, 59, 60; tax exporting
and, 4, 5, 21, 23, 72; tourism and, 5,
78. *See also* Texas selective sales and
excise taxes
Shannon, John, 163
Simplified Alternative Tax (SAT):
consumption base of, 89–91;
deductibility of, 91; disadvantages of,
94–97; efficiency aspects of, 91–93;
equity aspects of, 93–94; exportability
of, 91; progressivity of, 87, 89, 91,
93–94; revenue stability of, 94;
structure of, 87–89; as tax reform
option, 10, 131–32
sin taxes, 14
Skinner, Jonathan, 44
Slemrod, Joel, 163, 165, 169
Solnick, Loren M., 36
source-based taxes: capital mobility and,
25–29; defined, 164*n* 18; public goods
and, 84–85
Speyrer, Janet Furman, 180
stability. *See* revenue stability

state sales tax: benefit tax aspects of, 86; on business purchases, 5, 23, 40, 41, 73; cascading and, 41, 73, 75; on consumer purchases, 14, 71; elderly consumption and, 8, 63, 78; exemptions in, 8, 63, 75, 77; mail order sales and, 44; regressivity of, 7, 8, 55–60, 62, 77 (*see also* tax incidence); states without, 109; tourism and, 5, 8, 21, 78; visibility of, 6, 14, 48. *See also* Texas state sales tax

Stiglitz, Joseph E., 167

Summers, Lawrence H., 44

Tannenwald, Robert, 30–31, 37, 111–12, 177–78

tax exporting: through deductibility, 4, 19–20, 54, 71, 112, 122; defined, 11; methods of, 12; national perspective on, 18; through price changes, 4–5, 12, 21–23, 72, 114, 131; tourism and, 5, 21

tax incidence: annual measures of, 7, 54–57, 61–62, 77, 117–18; empirical studies of, 59–61, 117–18; lifetime measure of, 7, 55–57, 59–62, 77, 118, 122; price changes and, 25, 114, 117

tax rebate, 127

Tax Reform Act of 1986, 12, 19–20, 41, 58, 60

Terza, Joseph V., 166

Texas Comptroller of Public Accounts, 101, 103, 105, 177–79

Texas corporate franchise tax: described, 100, 102–103, 106, 112; income base of, 103, 115–16, 121, 128; reforms in, 128; wealth base of, 103, 115, 120, 122, 128

Texas local property tax: described, 105; reduction in, 124, 144; reliance on, 110–11

Texas oil and gas production taxes: described, 104–106; exporting potential of, 114

Texas public expenditures: change in, 158–59; comparison with other states, 135–39, 144–59; described, 134–35, 139, 144

Texas selective sales and excise taxes:

described, 104–106; reliance on, 109–10

Texas state sales tax: business exemptions in, 101; of business purchases, 101, 111–12, 115, 121, 132; consumer exemptions in, 102, 119, 121, 123, 125; of consumer purchases, 102, 113, 123, 126–27; described, 101–102; efficiency aspects of, 115–16; elderly consumption and, 119, 123; nondeductibility cost of, 113–14, 131; rebates in, 126; reforms in, 125–27, 130; regressivity of, 117–19, 122; reliance on, 105–10; revenue stability and adequacy of, 119–21; tourism and, 119, 123

Texas state tax system: administrative costs of, 121, 126–27; business competitiveness of, 111–12; comparison with other states, 108–12; compliance costs of, 121, 126; components of, 101–104; enforcement costs of, 121; recent trends in, 105–108; regressivity of, 117–19; revenue stability of, 119–20

Thaler, Richard H., 170

Thrash, Joe, 171, 180–81

Thuronyi, Victor, 161, 163, 173, 176

Tiebout, Charles M., 173

Triest, Robert K., 46, 168

Trostel, Philip A., 168

underground economy, 9, 16, 58, 69

U.S. Advisory Commission on Intergovernmental Relations, 64, 82, 135, 142, 144, 149, 157–58, 181–82

user charges: benefit tax aspects of, 7, 53, 80; on businesses, 72–73, 76; efficiency aspects of, 24, 82; equity aspects of, 80–81; nondeductibility of, 81; price changes and, 4; public goods and, 84–85; reliance on, 128–30; revenue potential of, 9, 10, 85–86, 132

Vaillant, Marian, 52–53, 76

value-added tax, 61, 87, 88, 127

Varian, Hal R., 165